PRONUNCIATION OF CHINESE MEDICINE TERMS IN MANDARIN AND CANTONESE

HAROLD ASBURY

outskirts
press™

Acknowledgements:

I would like to thank my Hung Ga Kung Fu teacher Sifu Yee Chi Wai, who started me on the path of Chinese medicine. I thank my Xing Yi Quan and Ba Gua Zhang teacher Sifu Tom Bisio who encouraged and developed my studies in Chinese medicine including Tui Na and Zheng Gu techniques. Without either of these gentlemen, I doubt I would have pursued knowledge in Chinese medicine at all. Thanks to Kenny K. Huang, my Chinese language teacher at Hunter College that put up with me being a so-so student, but helped me learn some of the National language speech and written forms. Similarly, I thank Craig Mitchell, whose classes in Touro College's Graduate Program in Chinese medicine in my first year helped me gain some knowledge of simplified characters, medical terminology, and a bit of Classical Chinese sentence structure and vocabulary. Marnae Ergil also was of great help to me similarly in nurturing my desire to learn more about medical Chinese. Thanks also to another of my Touro instructors, Josh Paynter also was often a help to me, not only because of his interests in Chinese language and Taoist thought, but also his encouragement. It goes without saying that my wife Mo-Kit Wong has always been there for me, and has had to put up with many an hour of me studying during my schooling and afterward. Lastly, I thank Dr. Guidun Bai of PCOM NY for answering the occasional question despite his busy schedule.

Introduction:

My Hung Ga Kung Fu (洪家功夫) teacher Sifu Yee Chi-Wai (余志偉) was the first person to teach me anything about Chinese Herbal medicine. He was from a family that originally came from Taishan (Toisan) in Guangdong (廣東台山)province in China, where he has since relocated. He himself grew up in Hong Kong and came to North America in 1968. By 1974, he was living in New York City. While in New York City, he studied with an elderly herbalist and my teacher was able to learn Dit Da traumatology (跌打) from that herbalist. The old herbalist was sick and needed help doing everything. In return for that, my teacher learned from him. I by no means know everything that my teacher learned in that realm, particularly his manual medicine, as he didn't spend all that much time teaching that material during my 22 years with him. I learned my manual medicine from Sifu Tom Bisio, from whom I also learned Xing Yi Quan and Ba Gua Zhang, two of the three best known "internal" martial arts. I was given a notebook of my Hung Ga teacher's to copy containing many formulae he learned, some of which were clearly meant to treat internal medicine disorders like gallstones and hemiplegia, though such disorders were outside his personal focus. This copy was to come in handy later, when my he lost the original book while moving, and I was able to give a copy back, so he still had the original information, perhaps not all of which was stored in his head. Many young people in America who happen to be of Chinese ancestry and who for the most part have grown up here can speak Cantonese, like he did. Unlike him, many of them cannot read Chinese well or at all, and find that even if they learn Chinese medicine here in the United States-that the technical jargon is typically presented in the national language (Mandarin) pronunciation rather than the Cantonese they already speak. This is fine for the majority of students, since the United States has gotten to the point where many newer immigrants speak that way, and the National language (Mandarin) is beginning to push out Toisan and Cantonese as the dominant form of spoken Chinese language in the United States. Many people don't mind this trend, and just the herb and point names as taught because many of their patients don't care as long as the practitioner they use is treating them effectively. Still, there might be a few people who speak Cantonese who might like to be able to pronounce the basic herb names, formula names, and acupuncture points in Cantonese, just because they don't speak Mandarin otherwise. They'll always be able to use the standard pronunciations they learned in school when needed, but might want to use Cantonese pronunciations of these technical terms among others who can, or must, speak that way. I had that problem when taking formulas to a Cantonese speaking Chinese Herbal Medicine shop near where I lived in Brooklyn, New York. They needed to ask me to replace an herb or two, and it was cumbersome, as they didn't know the Mandarin pronunciations of the herbs, and I still didn't know the Cantonese pronunciations or how to write them from memory. My knowledge of spoken

Chinese of either dialect is not very advanced, but I have learned some on both sides of this and wanted out of curiosity to accumulate the Cantonese pronunciations of at least the basic material because my Hung Ga teacher taught them that way, and my wife's family speaks that way. Any mistakes made in this work are my own, though I have worked to avoid as many mistakes as possible. I invite people to correct me when necessary so I can repair it in future versions.

   With the acupuncture points, the alphanumeric point number will appear first along with a standard point name translation. This is followed by simplified Chinese Characters for the point followed by the traditional characters. If there is one entry, then there are no simplified versions. This is then followed by Mandarin pronunciation in pinyin and lastly Cantonese pronunciation in Jyutping romanization. Medicinals and formulas are handled in a similar manner. English name for things first, Chinese characters in both simplified and traditional forms, followed by mandarin pronunciation with tones, and lastly Cantonese pronunciation with tones. Where my old teacher used alternate names for medicinals, I have noted it. In the Mandarin pronunciation, the first tone is high-level, the second is the rising tone, the third is low tone, and the fourth is falling tone. There is a "fifth", or neutral tone used in Mandarin which is seen in Romanized writings by leaving out a tone number, typically at the end of a two syllable word. Cantonese is usually treated as having anywhere from six to nine tones, depending on whether words ending in consonants are given separate tones. In this work, the tones are as follows: first tone is high level or high falling, second tone is high rising, the third tone is middle level, the fourth tone is low falling, the fifth tone is low rising, and the sixth tone is low level. I have followed a similar pattern when reporting the individual herb names, and formula names and ingredients. It should be remembered that this work is only about pronunciation, and isn't useful for learning how to use the acupuncture points, individual medicinals, and formulas.

Table of Contents:

Acupuncture Point Names 8
Individual Herbs 21
Formulas 35
Basic Pattern Names 149
Herb Index by Pharmaceutical Name 158
Herb Index by Pinyin (Mandarin) Name...................................... 170
Herb Index by Jyutping (Cantonese) Name 182
Formula Index by English Name.. 194
Formula Index by Pinyin (Mandarin) Name 205
Formula Index by Jyutping (Cantonese) Name 215

Jyutping Pronunciation

One of the considerations with regard to the use of this Romanization was the fact that tone numbers are used instead of diacritical marks, like the mark over the u to the right (ú). Such marks are awkward to insert when using computer input. It's true that tones laid out with numbers are awkward in that the person has to remember which number goes with which tone, but the slowness of entry made the decision for me. Jyutping (pronounced Yuht-ping) is a Romanization method created in 1993 by the Linguistic Society of Hong Kong. Since it uses such tone numbers and many online sources use it, I have decided to use it as well, though I was used to Yale Romanization. Yale's method is a little more easy to learn initially, but awkward to employ when inputting information on a computer because of the use of diacritical marks over the letters. One downside of all Romanization methods including jyutping, is that it uses letters in a different way than westerners are used to. For example, it uses j as an initial sound in words that to a westerner would be seen as a "y" sound. Thus "Jam" is not jam like jelly, but sounds more like "yum". All Romanization methods are challenging to westerners for another reason. There are sounds both in Mandarin and Cantonese that don't exist in English, so you have to learn how to make those sounds if you are an English speaker. The assumption is that readers of this small dictionary are familiar with Cantonese sounds, otherwise, there would be little reason to learn the Cantonese way to pronounce things. Schools in the United States teach Mandarin pronunciations for things. Mandarin is the official language in the People's Republic of China, and that country insists people learn it, even if they live in areas where the other dialects are spoken still. This means that over time, these other dialects are likely to be used less and less as time passes. Still, cultural elements cling to these languages, and eliminating the languages has a way of undermining the unique cultural identities of these areas. That difference of not only language, but cultural identity is probably seen as an impediment to a unified national identity in China. I'm mainly going to outline parts of Jyutping Romanization that are problematic for westerners.

Initials:
Initials are letters or clusters of letters that start words.
Ng- this sounds like the ng sound that is in "leaking all" The hard thing for English speakers is that for us, no words begin this way.
N-is like the English letter n except that many native Cantonese speakers replace it with what sounds like "L" for some words. Nin (年) may very well be pronounced something like "lean" by many speakers.

J-if you see this at the beginning of a word, it's meant to sound like the English letter "y". The word for ginseng in cantonese "jan4 sam1" (人參) sounds like Yahn sum. The word for two (ji6) (二) sounds like "yee".

C- only appears at the beginning of words and is pronounced somewhere between the "ch" and a "ts" sound. The word for car in Cantonese would be written like (ce1)(車), meaning "vehicle", and sounds like cheh/tseh which almost rhymes with "yeah".

Z- The sound of a word that begins with this "z" is meant to sound like the English "J" although there is a slight lean toward dz pronounded like the ds sound in the middle of " in a cod's eye". A word with this might be zung1(中) "center" which sounds like joong/dzoong. Other initials are more like their English counterparts.

Letters in the middle of words:
u- like "oo" in soon. Thus, lung4 (龍) would sound like "loong".
a-sounds like the vowel u in "fun" or "sun".
aa- like the sound "ah" in English. The number three "saam" (三) would rhyme with palm or bomb.
i-sounds a little like "ee" in tree. A word using this that means heaven "Tin" (天) sounds like "teen".

Letters that come at the end of words:
i-same as above
u-if the u is after jy, this is a sound that doesn't exist in English at all. The sound is made with your mouth in the lips as if you were going to say "oo" but the inside of your mouth saying "ee". The word for "fish" (jyu4) (魚) which begins with the 'j' that sounds like "y" in English, and uses this difficult ending for English speakers. The assumption is that if you are reading the current work, that you can pronounce Cantonese, but may not read Chinese Characters fluently. (if you could read totally fluently with Cantonese pronunciation, this lexicon would not be needed)
aa-as a final this is used as above. "Flower" (faa1) (花) uses the 'a' like in father.
eoi-another sound that doesn't exist in English. Somewhat similar to the 'oy' in "soy", but the e part is more like "uh"
au-like the 'ow' sound in cow.
eot-another sound alien to English. This word is vaguely like "soot" in English. The word "seot6" is part of "Mou5 Seot6" (武術), which means martial arts.
oek- another sound alien to English. This is slightly similar to the 'erk' sound in "jerk". The word for "foot" goek3 (腳) is almost like "gerk".

Acupuncture Point Names

Lung Channel: Hand Tai Yin Lung Channel

手太阴肺经 / 手太陰肺經： Shou3 tai4 yin1 fei4 jing1/Sau2 taai3 jam1 fai3 ging1

LU-1(Central Treasury): 中府：Zhong1 Fu3/Zung1 fu2
LU-2 (Cloud Gate): 云门 / 雲門: Yun2 men2/Wan4 mun4
LU-3 (Celestial Storehouse): 天府：Tian1 fu3/Tin1 fu2
LU-4 (Guarding White): 侠白 / 俠白: Xia2 bai2/Haap6 baak6
LU-5 (Cubit Marsh): 尺泽 / 尺澤:Chi3 ze2/Cek3 zaak6
LU-6 (Collection Hole): 孔最: Kong3 zui4/Hung2 zeoi3
LU-7 (Broken Sequence): 列缺: Lie4 que1/Lit6 kyut3
LU-8 (Channel Ditch): 经渠 / 經渠: Jing1 qü2/Ging1 keoi4
LU-9 (Great Abyss): 太渊 / 太淵: Tai4 yuan1/Taai3 jyun1
LU-10 (Fish Border): 鱼际 / 魚際: Yü2 ji4/Jyu4 zai3
LU-11 (Lesser Shang): 少商: Shao4 Shang1/Siu2 soeng1

Large Intestine Channel: Hand yang Ming Large Intestine Channel

手阳明大肠经 / 手陽明大腸經：

Shou3 yang2 ming2 da4 chang2 jing1/Sau2 joeng4 ming4 daai6 coeng4 ging1

LI-1 (Shang Yang): 商阳 / 商陽: Shang1 yang2/Soeng1 joeng4
LI-2 (Second Space): 二间 / 二間: Er4 jian1/Ji6 gaan3
LI-3 (Third Space): 三间 / 三間: San1 Jian1/Saam1 gaan3
LI-4 (Union Valley): 合谷: He2 gu3/Hap6 guk1
LI-5 (Yang Ravine): 阳谿 / 陽谿: Yang2 xi1/Joeng4 kai1
LI-6 (Veering Passage): 偏历 / 偏歷: Pian1 li4/Pin1 Lik6
LI-7(Warm Flow): 温溜 / 溫溜: Wen1 Liu1/Wan1 lau6
LI-8 (Lower Ridge): 下廉: Xia4 lian2/Haa6 lim4
LI-9 (Upper Ridge): 上廉: Shang4 lian2/Soeng5 lim4
LI-10 (Arm Three Li): 手三里: Shou3 san1 li3/Sau2 saam1 lei5
LI-11 (Pool at the Bend): 曲池: Qü1 chi2/Kuk1 ci4
LI-12 (Elbow Bone Hole): 肘髎: Zhou3 liao2/Zau2 liu4
LI-13 (Arm Five Li): 手五里: Shou3 wu3 li3/Sau2 ng5 lei5
LI-14 (Upper Arm): 臂臑: Bi4 nao4/Bei3 nou6
LI-15 (Shoulder Bone): 肩髃: Jian1 yü2/Gin1 jyu4
LI-16 (Great Bone): 巨骨: Jü4 gu3/Geoi6 gwat1
LI-17 (Celestial Tripod): 天鼎: Tian1 ding3/Tin1 ding2
LI-18 (Protuberance Assistant): 扶突 Fu2 tu2/Fu4 dat6
LI-19 (Grain Bone Hole): 口禾髎: Kou3 he2 liao2/Hau2 wo4 liu4
LI-20 (Welcome Fragrance): 迎香: Ying2 xiang1/Jing4 hoeng1

Stomach Channel: Foot Yang Ming Stomach Channel

足阳明胃经 / 足陽明胃經：

Zu2 yang2 ming2 wei4 jing1/Zuk1joeng4 ming4 wai6 ging1

ST-1 (Tear Container): 承泣: Cheng2 qi4/Sing4 jap1

ST-2 (Four Whites): 四白: Si4 bai2/Sei3 baak6

ST-3 (Great Bone Hole): 巨髎: Jü4 liao2/Geoi6 liu4

ST-4 (Earth Granary): 地仓 / 地倉: Di4 cang1/Dei6 cong1

ST-5 (Great Reception): 大迎: Da4 ying2/Daai6 jing4

ST-6 (Jaw Bone): 颊车 / 頰車: Jia2 che1/Gaap3 ce1

ST-7 (Below the Joint): 下关 / 下關: Xia4 guan1/Haa6 gwaan1

ST-8 (Head Corner): 头维 / 頭維: Tou2 wei2/Tau4 wai4

ST-9 (Man's Prognosis): 人迎: Ren2 ying2/Jan4 jing4

ST-10 (Water Prominence): 水突: Shui3 tu2/Seoi2 dat6

ST-11 (Qi Abode): 气舍 / 氣舍: Qi4 She4/Hei3 se3

ST-12 (Empty Basin): 缺盆: Que1 pen2/Kyut3 pun4

ST-13 (Qi Door): 气户 / 氣戶: Qi4 hu4/Hei3 wu6

ST-14 (Storeroom): 库房 / 庫房: Ku4 fang2/Fu3 fong4

ST-15 (Roof): 屋翳: Wu1 yi4/Uk1 ai3 or Nguk1 ji1

ST-16 (Breast Window): 膺窗: Ying1 chuang1/Jing1 coeng1

ST-17 (Breast Center): 乳中: Ru3 zhong1/Jyu5 zung1

ST-18 (Breast Root): 乳根: Ru3 gen1/Jyu5 gan1

ST-19 (Not Contained): 不容: Bu4 rong2/Bat1 jung4

ST-20 (Assuming Fullness): 承满 / 承滿: Cheng2 man3/Sing4 mun5

ST-21 (Beam Gate): 梁门 / 梁門: Liang2 men2/Loeng4 mun4

ST-22 (Pass Gate): 关门 / 關門: Guan1 men2/Gwaan1 mun4

ST-23 (Supreme Unity): 太乙: Tai4 yi3/Taai3 jyut3

ST-24 (Slippery Flesh Gate): 滑肉门 / 滑肉門: Hua2 rou4 men2/Waat6 juk6 mun4

ST-25 (Celestial Pivot): 天枢 / 天樞: Tian1 shu1/Tin1 syu1

ST-26 (Outer Mound): 外陵: Wai4 ling2/Ngoi6 ling4

ST-27 (Great Gigantic): 大巨: Da4 jü4/Daai6 geoi6

ST-28 (Waterway): 水道: Shui3 dao4/Seoi2 dou6

ST-29 (Return): 归来 / 歸來: Gui1 lai2/Gwai1 loi4

ST-30 (Qi Thoroughfare): 气冲 / 氣衝: Qi4 chong1/Hei3 cung1

ST-31 (Thigh Gate): 髀关 / 髀關: Bi4 guan1/Bei2 gwaan1

ST-32 (Crouching Rabbit): 伏兔: Fu2 tu4/Fuk6 tou3

ST-33 (Yin Market): 阴市 / 陰市: Yin1 shi4/Jam1 si5

ST-34 (Beam Hill): 梁丘: Liang2 qiu1/Loeng4 jau1

ST-35 (Calf's Nose): 犊鼻 / 犢鼻: Du2 bi2/Duk6 bei6

ST-36 (Leg Three Li): 足三里: Zu2 san1 li3/Zuk1 saam1 lei5

ST-37 (Upper Great Hollow):上巨虚 / 上巨虛: Shang4 jü4 xü1/Soeng5 geoi6 heoi1

ST-38 (Ribbon Opening): 条口 / 條口: Tiao2 kou3/Tiu4 hau2

ST-39 (Lower Great Hollow): 下巨虚 / 下巨虛: Xia4 jü4 xü1/Haa6 geoi6 heoi1

ST-40 (Bountiful Bulge): 丰隆 / 豐隆: Feng1 long2/Fung1 lung4

ST-41 (Ravine Divide): 解谿: Jie3 xi1/Gaai2 kai1

ST-42 (Surging Yang): 冲阳 / 衝陽: Chong1 yang2/Cung1 joeng4

ST-43 (Sunken Valley): 陷谷: Xian4 gu3/Haam6 guk1

ST-44 (Inner Courtyard): 内庭: Nei4 ting2/Noi6 ting4

ST-45 (Severe Mouth): 厉兑 / 厲兌: Li4 dui4/Lai6 deoi3

Spleen Channel: Foot Tai Yin Spleen Channel
足太阴脾经 / 足太陰脾經
Zu2 tai4 yin1 pi2 jing1/Zuk1 taai3 jam1 pei4 ging1

SP-1 (Hidden White): 隐白 / 隱白: Yin3 bai2/Jan2 baak6

SP-2 (Great Metropolis): 大都: Da4 du1/Daai6 dou1

SP-3 (Supreme White): 太白: Tai4 bai2/Taai3 baak6

SP-4 (Yellow Emperor): 公孙 / 公孫: Gong1 sun1/Gung1 syun1

SP-5 (Shang Hill): 商丘: Shang1 qiu1/Soeng1 jau1

SP-6 (Three Yin Intersection): 三阴交 / 三陰交: San1 yin1 jiao1/Saam1 jam1 gaau1

SP-7 (Leaking Valley): 漏谷: Lou4 gu3/Lau6 guk1

SP-8 (Earth's Crux): 地机 / 地機: Di4 ji1/Dei6 gei1

SP-9 (Yin Mound Spring): 阴陵泉 / 陰陵泉: Yin1 ling2 quan2/Jam1 ling4 cyun4

SP-10 (Sea of Blood): 血海: Xue4 hai3/Hyut3 hoi2

SP-11 (Winnower Gate): 箕门 / 箕門: Ji1 men2/Gei1 mun4

SP-12 (Surging Gate): 冲门 / 衝門: Chong1 men2/Cung1 mun4

SP-13 (Bowel Abode): 府舍: Fu3 she4/Fu2 se3

SP-14 (Abdomen Bind): 腹结 / 腹結: Fu4 jie2/Fuk1 git3

SP-15 (Great Horizontal): 大横 / 大橫: Da4 heng2/Daai6 waang4

SP-16 (Abdominal Lament): 腹哀: Fu4 ai1/Fuk1 oi1

SP-17 (Food Hole): 食窦 / 食竇: Shi2 dou4/Sik6 dau6

SP-18 (Celestial Ravine): 天谿: Tian1 xi1/Tin1 kai1

SP-19 (Chest Village): 胸乡 / 胸鄉: Xiong1 xiang1/Hung1 hoeng1

SP-20 (All-Round Flourishing): 周荣 / 周榮: Zhou1 rong2/Zau1 wing4

SP-21 (Great Embracement): 大包: Da4 bao1/Daai6 baau1

Heart Channel: Hand Shao Yin Heart Channel
手少阴心经 / 手少陰心經
Shou3 shao4 yin1 xin1 jing1/Sau2 siu2 jam1 sam1 ging1

HT-1 (Highest Spring): 极泉 / 極泉: Ji2 quan2/ Gik6 cyun4
HT-2 (Cyan Spirit): 青灵 / 青靈: Qing1 ling2/Cing1 ling4
HT-3 (Lesser Sea): 少海: Shao4 hai3/Siu3 hoi2
HT-4 (Spirit Pathway): 灵道 / 靈道: Ling2 dao4/Ling4 dou6
HT-5 (Connecting Li): 通里: Tong1 li3/Tung1 lei5
HT-6 (Yin Cleft): 阴郄 / 陰郄: Yin1 xi1/Jam1 gwik1
HT-7 (Spirit Gate): 神门 / 神門: Shen2 men2/San4 mun4
HT-8 (Lesser Mansion): 少府: Shao4 fu3/Siu3 fu2
HT-9 (Lesser Surge): 少冲 / 少衝: Shao4 chong1/Siu3 cung1

Small Intestine Channel: Hand Tai Yang Small Intestine Channel
手太阳小肠经 / 手太陽小腸經
Shou3 tai4 yang2 xiao3 chang2 jing1/Sau2 taai3 joeng4 siu2 coeng4 ging1

SI-1 (Lesser Marsh) 少泽 / 少澤: Shao4 ze2/Siu3 zaak6
SI-2 (Front Valley) 前谷: Qian2 gu3/Cin4 guk1
SI-3 (Back Ravine) 后谿 / 後谿: Hou4 xi1/Hau6 kai1
SI-4 (Wrist Bone): 腕骨: Wan4 gu3/Wun2 gwat1
SI-5 (Yang Valley): 阳谷 / 陽谷: Yang2 gu3/Joeng4 guk1
SI-6 (Nurse the Aged): 养老 / 養老: Yang3 lao3/Joeng5 lou5
SI-7 (Branch to the Correct): 支正: Zhi1 zheng4/Zi1 zing3
SI-8 (Small Sea): 小海: Xiao3 hai3/Siu2 hoi2
SI-9 (True Shoulder): 肩贞 / 肩貞: Jian1 zhen1/Gin1 zing1
SI-10 (Upper Arm Shu): 臑俞 Nao4 shu4/Nou6 jyu4
SI-11 (Celestial Gathering): 天宗: Tian1 zong1/Tin1 zung1
SI-12 (Grasping the Wind): 秉风 / 秉風: Bing3 feng1/Bing2 fung1
SI-13 (Crooked Wall): 曲垣: Qü1 yuan2/Kuk1wun4
SI-14 (Outer Shoulder Shu): 肩外俞: Jian1 wai4 shu4/Gin1 ngoi6 jyu4
SI-15 (Central Shoulder Transport): 肩中俞: Jian1 zhong1 shu4/Gin1 zung1 jyu4
SI-16 (Celestial Window): 天窗: Tian1 chuang1/Tin1 coeng1
SI-17 (Celestial Countenance): 天容: Tian1 rong2/Tin1 jung4
SI-18 (Cheek Bone-Hole): 颧髎 / 顴髎: Quan2 liao2/Kyun4 liu4
SI-19 (Auditory Palace): 听宫 / 聽宮: Ting1 gong1/Teng1gung1

Bladder Channel: Foot Tai Yang Bladder Channel

足太阳膀胱经 / 足太陽膀胱經

Zu2 tai4 yang2 pang2 guang1 jing1/Zuk1 taai3 joeng4 pong4 gwong1 ging1

UB-1 (Bright Eyes) 睛明: Jing1 ming2/Zing1 ming4

UB-2 (Bamboo Gathering): 赞竹 / 攢竹: Zan3 zhu2/Zaan2 zuk1

UB-3 (Eyebrow Ascension): 眉冲 / 眉衝: Mei2 chong1/Mei4 cung1

UB-4 (Deviating Turn): 曲差: Qü1 cha1/Kuk1 caa1

UB-5 (Fifth Place): 五处 / 五處: Wu3 chu4/Ng5 syu2

UB-6 (Light Guard): 承光: Cheng2 guang1/Sing4 gwong1

UB-7 (Celestial Connection): 通天: Tong1 tian1/Tung1 tin1

UB-8 (Declining Connection): 络却 / 絡卻: Luo4 que4/Lok3 koek3

UB-9 (Jade Pillow): 玉枕: Yu4 zhen3/Juk6 zam2

UB-10 (Celestial Pillar): 天柱: Tian1 zhu4/Tin1 cyu5

UB-11 (Great Shuttle): 大杼: Da4 zhu4/Daai6 cyu5

UB-12 (Wind Gate): 风门 / 風門: Feng1 men2/Fung1 mun4

UB-13 (Lung Shu): 肺俞: Fei4 shu4/Fai3 jyu4

UB-14 (Reverting Yin Shu): 厥阴俞 / 厥陰俞: Jue2 yin1 shu4/Kyut3 jam1 jyu4

UB-15 (Heart Shu): 心俞: Xin1 shu4/Sam1 jyu4

UB-16 (Governing Transport): 督俞: Du1 shu4/Duk1 jyu4

UB-17 (Diaphragm Shu): 膈俞: Ge2 shu4/Gaak3 jyu4

UB-18 (Liver Shu): 肝俞: Gan1 shu4/Gon1 jyu4

UB-19 (Gallbladder Shu): 胆俞 / 膽俞: Dan3 shu4/Daam2 jyu4

UB-20 (Spleen Shu): 脾俞: Pi2 shu4/Pei4 jyu4

UB-21 (Stomach Shu): 胃俞: Wei4 shu4/Wai6 jyu4

UB-22 (Triple Burner Shu): 三焦俞: San1jiao1 shu4/Saam1 ziu1 jyu4

UB-23 (Kidney Shu): 肾俞 / 腎俞: Shen4 shu4/San6 jyu4

UB-24 (Sea of Qi Transport): 气海俞 / 氣海俞: Qi4 hai3 shu4/Hei3 hoi2 jyu4

UB-25 (Large Intestine Shu): 大肠俞 / 大腸俞: Da4 chang2 shu4/Daai6 coeng4 jyu4

UB-26 (Origin Pass Shu): 关元俞 / 關元俞: Guan1 yuan2 shu4/Gwaan1 jyun4 jyu4

UB-27 (Small Intestine Shu): 小肠俞 / 小腸俞: Xiao3 chang2 shu4/Siu2 coeng4 jyu4

UB-28 (Bladder Shu): 膀胱俞: Pang2 guang1 shu4/Pong4 gwong1 jyu4

UB-29 (Central Backbone Shu): 中膂俞: Zhong1 lü3 shu4/Zung1 leoi5 jyu4

UB-30 (White Ring Shu): 白环俞 / 白環俞: Bai2 huan2 shu4/Baak6 waan4 jyu4

UB-31 (Upper Bone Hole): 上髎: Shang4 liao2/Soeng5 liu4

UB-32 (Second Bone Hole): 次髎: Ci4 liao2/Ci3 liu4

UB-33 (Central Bone Hole): 中髎: Zhong1 liao2/Zung1 liu4

UB-34 (Lower Bone Hole): 下髎: Xia4 liao2/Haa6 liu4

UB-35 (Meeting of Yang): 会阳 / 會陽: Hui4 yang2/Wui5 joeng4

UB-36 (Support): 承扶: Cheng2 fu2/Sing4 fu4

UB-37 (Gate of Abundance): 殷门 / 殷門: Yin1 men2/Jin1 mun4

UB-38 (Superficial Cleft): 浮郄: Fu2 xi1/Fau4 gwik1

UB-39 (Bend Yang): 委阳 / 委陽: Wei3 yang2/Wai2 joeng4

UB-40 (Bend Middle): 委中: Wei3 zhong1/Wai2 zung1

UB-41 (Attached Branch): 附分: Fu4 fen1/Fu6 fan1

UB-42 (Po Door): 魄户 / 魄戶: Po4 hu4/Paak3 wu6

UB-43 (Gao Huang Shu): 膏肓俞: Gao1 huang1 shu4/Gou1 fong1 jyu4

UB-44 (Spirit Hall): 神堂: Shen2 tang2/San4 tong4

UB-45 (Yi Xi): 譩譆: Yi1 xi3/Ji1 hei1

UB-46 (Diaphragm Pass): 膈关 / 膈關: Ge2 guan1/Gaak3 gwaan1

UB-47 (Hun Gate): 魂门 / 魂門: Hun2 men2/Wan4 mun4

UB-48 (Yang Headrope): 阳纲 / 陽綱: Yang2 gang1/Joeng4 gong1

UB-49 (Reflection Abode): 意舍: Yi4 she4/Ji3 se3

UB-50 (Stomach Granary): 胃仓 / 胃倉: Wei4 cang1/Wai6 cong1

UB-51 (Huang Gate): 肓门 / 肓門: Huang1 men2/Fong1 mun4

UB-52 (Will Chamber): 志室: Zhi4 shi4/Zi3 sat1

UB-53 (Bladder Huang): 胞肓: Bao1 huang1/Baau1 fong1

UB-54 (Sequential Limit): 秩边 / 秩邊: Zhi4 bian1/Dit6 bin1

UB-55 (Yang Union): 合阳 / 合陽: He2 yang2/Hap6 joeng4

UB-56 (Sinew Support): 承筋: Cheng2 jin1/Sing4 gan1

UB-57 (Mountain Support): 承山: Cheng2 shan1/Sing4 saan1

UB-58 (Taking Flight): 飞扬 / 飛揚: Fei1 yang2/Fei1 joeng4

UB-59 (Instep Yang): 跗阳 / 跗陽: Fu1 yang2/Fu1 joeng4

UB-60 (Kun Lun Mountains): 昆仑 / 崑崙: Kun1 lun2/Kwan1 leon4

UB-61 (Subservient Visitor): 僕参 / 僕參: Pu2 can1/Buk6 caam1

UB-62 (Extending Vessel): 申脉 / 申脈: Shen1 mai4/San1 mak6

UB-63 (Metal Gate): 金门 / 金門: Jin1 men2/Gam1 mun4

UB-64 (Capital Bone): 京骨: Jing1 gu3/Ging1 gwat1

UB-65 (Bundle Bone): 束骨: Shu4 gu3/Cuk1 gwat1

UB-66 ([Leg] Valley Passage): 足通谷: Zu2 tong1 gu3/Zuk1 tung1 guk1

UB-67 (Reaching Yin): 至阴 / 至陰: Zhi4 yin1/Zi3 jam1

Kidney Channel: Foot Shao Yin Kidney Channel

足少阴肾经 / 足少陰腎經

Zu2 shao4 yin1 shen4 jing1/Zuk1 siu3 jam1 san6 ging1

KI-1 (Gushing Spring): 湧泉: Yong3 quan2/Jung2 cyun4

KI-2 (Blazing Valley): 然谷: Ran2 gu3/Jin4 guk1

KI-3 (Great Ravine): 太谿: Tai4 xi1/Taai3 kai1

KI-4 (Large Goblet): 大钟 / 大鐘: Da4 zhong1/Daai6 zung1

KI-5 (Water Spring): 水泉: Shui3 quan2/Seoi2 cyun4

KI-6 (Shining Sea): 照海: Zhao4 hai3/Ziu3 hoi2

KI-7 (Recover Flow): 复溜 / 復溜: Fu4 liu1/Fuk1 lau6

KI-8 (Intersection Reach): 交信: Jiao1 xin4/Gaau1 Seon3

KI-9 (Guest House): 筑宾 / 築賓: Zhu2 bin1/Zuk1 ban1

KI-10 (Yin Valley): 阴谷 / 陰谷: Yin1 gu3/Jam1 guk1

KI-11 (Pubic Bone): 横骨: Heng2 gu3/Waang4 gwat1

KI-12 (Great Manifestation): 大赫: Da4 he4/Daai6 haak1

KI-13 (Qi Point): 气穴 / 氣穴: Qi4 xue2/Hei3 jyut6

KI-14 (Fourfold Fullness): 四满 / 四滿: Si4 man3/Sei3 mun5

KI-15 (Central Flow): 中注: Zhong1 zhu4/Zung1 zyu3

KI-16 (Huang Transport): 肓俞: Huang1 shu4/Fong1 jyu4

KI-17 (Shang Bend): 商曲: Shang1 qü1/Soeng1 kuk1

KI-18 (Stone Pass): 石关 / 石關: Shi2 guan1/Sek6 gwaan1

KI-19 (Yin Metropolis): 阴都 / 陰都: Yin1 du1/Jam1 dou1

KI-20 (Abdomen Open Valley): 腹通谷: Fu4 tong1 gu3/Fuk1 tung1 guk1

KI-21 (Dark Gate): 幽门 / 幽門: You1 men2/Jau1 mun4

KI-22 (Corridor Walk): 步廊: Bu4 lang2/Bou6 long4

KI-23 (Spirit Seal): 神封: Shen2 feng1/San4 fung1

KI-24 (Spirit Ruins): 灵墟 / 靈墟: Ling2 xu1/Ling4 heoi1

KI-25 (Spirit Storehouse): 神藏: Shen2 cang2/San4 cong4

KI-26 (Lively Center): 彧中: Yü4 zhong1/Juk1 zung1

KI-27 (Transport Mansion): 俞府: Shu4 fu3/Jyu4 fu2

Pericardium Channel: Hand Jue Yin Pericardium Channel

手厥阴心包经 / 手厥陰心包經

Shou3 jue2 yin1 xin1 bao1 jing1/Sau2 kyut3 jam1sam1baau1 ging1

PC-1 (Celestial Pool): 天池: Tian1 chi2/Tin1 ci4
PC-2 (Celestial Spring): 天泉: Tian1 quan2/Tin1 cyun4
PC-3 (Marsh at the Bend): 曲泽 / 曲澤: Qü1 ze2/Kuk1 zaak6
PC-4 (Cleft Gate): 郄门 / 郄門: Xi1 men2/Gwik1 mun4
PC-5 (Intermediary Courier): 间使 / 間使: Jian1 shi3/Gaan3 si2
PC-6 (Inner Pass): 内关 / 內關: Nei4 Guan1/Noi6 gwaan1
PC-7 (Great Mound): 大陵: Da4 ling2/Daai6 ling4
PC-8 (Palace of Toil): 劳宫 / 勞宮: Lao2 gong1/Lou4 gung1
PC-9 (Central Hub): 中冲 / 中衝: Zhong1 chong1/Zung1 cung1

Triple Burner Channel: Hand Shao Yang Triple Burner Channel

手少阳三焦经 / 手少陽三焦經

Shou3 shao4 yang2 san1 jiao1 jing1/Sau2 siu3 joeng4 saam1 ziu1 ging1
TB-1 (Passage Hub): 关冲 / 關衝: Guan1 chong1/Gwaan1 cung1
TB-2 (Humor Gate): 液门 / 液門: Ye4 men2/Jik6 mun4
TB-3 (Central Islet): 中渚: Zhong1 zhu3/Zung1 zyu2
TB-4 (Yang Pool): 阳池 / 陽池: Yang2 chi2/Joeng4 ci4
TB-5 (Outer Pass): 外关 / 外關: Wai4 guan1/Ngoi6 gwaan1
TB-6 (Branch Ditch): 支沟 / 支溝: Zhi1 gou1/Zi1 kau1
TB-7 (Convergence and Gathering): 会宗 / 會宗: Hui4 zong1/Wui5 zung1
TB-8 (Three Yang Connection): 三阳络 / 三陽絡: San1 yang2 luo4/Saam1 joeng4 lok3
TB-9 (Four Rivers): 四渎 / 四瀆: Si4 du3/Sei3 duk6
TB-10 (Celestial Well): 天井: Tian1 jing3/Tin1 zeng2
TB-11 (Clear Cold Abyss): 清冷渊 / 清冷淵: Qing1 leng3 yuan1/Cing1 laang5 jyun1
TB-12 (Dispersing Riverbed): 消泺 / 消濼: Xiao1 luo4/Siu1 lok6
TB-13 (Upper Arm Convergence): 臑会 / 臑會: Nao4 hui4/Nou6 wui5
TB-14 (Shoulder Bone-hole): 肩髎: Jian1 liao2/Gin1 liu4
TB-15 (Celestial Bone-hole): 天髎： Tian1 liao2/Tin1 liu4
TB-16 (Celestial Window): 天牖: Tian1 you3/Tin1 jau5
TB-17 (Wind Screen): 翳风 / 翳風: Yi4 feng1/Ji1 fung1
TB-18 (Tugging Vessel): 瘈脉 / 瘈脈: Chi4 mai4/Kai3 mak6
TB-19 (Skull Rest): 颅息／顱息: Lu2 xi1/Lou4 sik1
TB-20 (Angle Vertex): 角孙／角孫: Jiao3 sun1/Gok3 syun1
TB-21 (Ear Gate): 耳门 / 耳門: Er3 men2/Ji5 mun4

Gallbladder Channel: Leg Shao Yang Gallbladder Channel
足少阳胆经／足少陽膽經
Zu2 shao4 yang2 dan3 jing1/Zuk1 siu2 joeng4 daam2 ging1

GB-1 (Pupil Bone-Hole): 瞳子髎: Tong2 zi3 liao2/Tung4 zi2 liu4
GB-2 (Auditory Convergence): 听会／聽會: Ting1 hui4/Ting3 wui2
GB-3 (Upper Gate): 上关／上關: Shang4 guan1/Soeng5 gwaan1
GB-4 (Forehead Fullness): 颔厌／頷厭: Han4 yan4/Ham5 jim3
GB-5 (Suspended Skull): 悬颅／懸顱: Xuan2 lu2/Jyun4 lou4
GB-6 (Suspended Tuft): 悬厘／懸厘: Xuan2 li2/Jyun4 lei4
GB-7 (Temporal Hairline Curve): 曲鬓／曲鬢: Qü1 bin4/Kuk1 ban3
GB-8 (Valley Lead): 率谷: Shuai4 gu3/Seot1 guk1
GB-9 (Celestial Hub): 天冲／天衝: Tian1 chong4/Tin1 cung1
GB-10 (Floating White): 浮白: Fu2 bai2/Fau4 baak6
GB-11 (Head Portal Yin): 头窍阴／頭竅陰: Tou2 qiao4 yin1/Tau4 hiu3 jam1
GB-12 (Completion Bone): 完骨: Wan2 gu3/Jyun4 gwat1
GB-13 (Root Spirit): 本神: Ben3 shen2/Bun2 san4
GB-14 (Yang White): 阳白／陽白: Yang2 bai2/Joeng4 baak6
GB-15 (Head Overlooking Tears): 头临泣／頭臨泣: Tou2 lin2 qi4/Tau4 lam4 jap1
GB-16 (Eye Window): 目窗: Mu4 chuang1/Muk6 coeng1
GB-17 (Upright Construction): 正营／正營: Zheng4 ying2/Zing3 jing4
GB-18 (Spirit Support): 承灵／承靈: Cheng2 ling2/Sing4 ling4
GB-19 (Brain Hollow): 脑空／腦空: Nao3 kung1/Nou5 hung1
GB-20 (Wind Pool): 风池／風池: Feng1 chi2/Fung1 ci4
GB-21 (Shoulder Well): 肩井: Jian1 jing3/Gin1 zeng2
GB-22 (Armpit Abyss): 渊腋／淵腋: Yuan1 ye4/Jyun1 jik6
GB-23 (Sinew Seat): 辄筋／輒筋: Zhe2 jin1/Zip3 gan1
GB-24 (Sun and Moon): 日月: Ri4 yue4/Jat6 jyut6
GB-25 (Capital Gate): 京门／京門: Jing1 men2/Ging1 mun4
GB-26 (Girdling Vessel): 带脉／帶脈: Dai4 mai4/Daai3 mak6
GB-27 (Fifth Pivot): 五枢／五樞: Wu3 shu1/Ng5 syu1
GB-28 (Linking Path): 维道／維道: Wei2 dao4/Wai4 dou6
GB-29 (Squatting Bone-hole): 居髎: Jü1 liao2/Geoi1 liu4
GB-30 (Jumping Round): 环跳／環跳: Huan2 tiao4/Waan4 tiu3
GB-31 (Wind Market): 风市／風市: Feng1 shi4/Fung1 si5
GB-32 (Central River): 中渎／中瀆: Zhong1 du2/Zung1 duk6
GB-33 (Knee Yang Joint): 膝阳关／膝陽關: Xi1 yang2 guan1/Sat1 joeng4 gwaan1
GB-34 (Yang Mound Spring): 阳陵泉／陽陵泉: Yang2 ling2 quan2/Joeng4 ling4 cyun4
GB-35 (Yang Intersection): 阳交／陽交: Yang2 jiao1/Joeng4 gaau1

GB-36 (Outer Hill): 外丘: Wai4 qiu1/Ngoi6 jau1

GB-37 (Bright Light): 光明: Guang1 ming2/Gwong1 ming4

GB-38 (Yang Assistance): 阳辅 / 陽輔: Yang2 fu3/Joeng4 fu6

GB-39 (Suspended Bell): 悬钟 / 懸鐘: Xuan2 zhong1/Jyun4 zung1

GB-39 (Severed Bone): 绝骨 / 絕骨: Jue2 gu3/Zyut6 gwat1

GB-40 (Hill Ruins): 丘墟: Qiu1 xü1/Jau1 heoi1

GB-41 (Foot Overlooking Tears): 足临泣 / 足臨泣: Zu2 lin2 qi4/Zuk1 lam4 jap1

GB-42 (Earth Fivefold Convergence): 地五会 / 地五會: Di4 wu3 hui4/Dei6 Ng5 wui5

GB-43 (Pinched Ravine): 侠溪 / 俠谿: Xia2 xi1/Haap6 kai1

GB-44 (Foot Portal Yin): 足窍阴 / 足竅陰: Zu2 qiao4 yin1/Zuk1 hiu3 jam1

Liver Channel: Leg Jue Yin Liver Channel
足厥阴肝经 / 足厥陰肝經
Zu2 jue2 yin1 gan1 jing1/Zuk1 kyut3 jam1 gon1 ging1

LV-1 (Large Pile): 大敦: Da4 dun1/Daai6 deon1

LV-2 (Moving Between): 行间 / 行間: Xing2 jian1/Hang4 gaan3

LV-3 (Supreme Surge): 太冲 / 太衝: Tai4 chong1/Taai3 cung1

LV-4 (Mound Center): 中封: Zhong1 feng1/Zung1 fung1

LV-5 (Woodworm Canal): 蠡沟 / 蠡溝: Li3 gou1/Lai5 kau1

LV-6 (Central Metropolis): 中渎 / 中瀆: Zhong1 du2/Zung1 duk6

LV-7 (Knee Joint): 膝关 / 膝關: Xi1 guan1/Sat1 gwaan1

LV-8 (Spring at the Bend): 曲泉: Qü1 quan2/Kuk1 cyun4

LV-9 (Yin Bladder): 阴包 / 陰包: Yin1 bao1/Jam1 baau1

LV-10 (Foot Five Li): 足五里: Zu2 wu3 li3/Zuk1 ng5 lei5

LV-11 (Yin Corner): 阴廉 / 陰廉: Yin1 lian2/Jam1 lim4

LV-12 (Urgent Pulse): 急脉 / 急脈: Ji2 mai4/Gap1 mak6

LV-13 (Camphorwood Gate): 章门 / 章門: Zhang1 men2/Zoeng1 mun4

LV-14 (Cycle Gate): 期门 / 期門: Qi1 men2/Kei4 mun4

Conception Vessel: 任脉 / 任脈: Ren4 mai4/Jam6 mak6

CV-1 (Meeting of Yin): 会阴 / 會陰: Hui4 yin1/Wui6 jam1

CV-2 (Curved Bone): 曲骨: Qü1 gu3/Kuk1 gwat1

CV-3 (Central Pole): 中极 / 中極: Zhong1 ji2/Zung1 gik6

CV-4 (Origin Pass): 关元 / 關元: Guan1 yuan2/Gwaan1 jyun4

CV-5 (Stone Gate): 石门 / 石門: Shi2 men2/Sek6 mun4

CV-6 (Sea of Qi): 气海 / 氣海: Qi4 hai3/Hei3 hoi2

CV-7 (Yin Intersection): 阴交 / 陰交: Yin1 jiao1/Jam1 gaau1

CV-8 (Spirit Tower Gate): 神阙 / 神闕: Shen2 que4/San4 kyut3

CV-9 (Water Divide): 水分 / 水份: Shui3 fen4/Seoi2 fan6

CV-10 (Lower Stomach Duct): 下脘: Xia4 wan3/Haa6 gun2

CV-11 (Strengthen the Interior): 建里: Jian4 li3/Gin3 lei5

CV-12 (Central Stomach Duct): 中脘: Zhong1 wan3/Zung1 gun2

CV-13 (Upper Stomach Duct): 上 脘: Shang4 wan3/Seong5 gun2

CV-14 (Great Tower Gate): 巨阙 / 巨闕: Jü4 que4/Geoi6 kyut3

CV-15 (Turtledove Tail): 鸠尾 / 鳩尾: Jiu1 wei3/Gau1 mei5

CV-16 (Center Palace): 中庭: Zhong1 ting2/Zung1 ting4

CV-17 (Chest Center): 膻中: Shan1 zhong1/Zin1 zung1

CV-18 (Jade Hall): 玉堂: Yü4 tang2/Juk6 tong4

CV-19 (Purple Palace): 紫宫 / 紫宮: Zi3 gong1/Zi2 gung1

CV-20 (Florid Canopy): 华盖 / 華蓋: Hua2 gai4/Waa4 goi3

CV-21 (Jade Pivot): 璇玑 / 璇璣: Xuan2 ji1/Syun4 gei1

CV-22 (Celestial Chimney): 天突: Tian1 tu2/Tin1 dat6

CV-23 (Ridge Spring): 廉泉: Lian2 quan2/Lim4 cyun4

CV-24 (Sauce Receptacle): 承浆 / 承漿: Cheng2 jiang1/Sing4 zoeng1

Governing Vessel: 督脉 / 督脈: Du1 mai4/Duk1 mak6

GV-1 (Long Strong): 长强 / 長強: Chang2 qiang2/Coeng4 koeng4

GV-2 (Lumbar Shu): 腰俞: Yao1 shu4/Jiu1 jyu4

GV-3 (Lumbar Yang Pass): 腰阳关 / 腰陽關: Yao1 yang2 guan1/Jiu1 joeng4 gwaan1

GV-4 (Life Gate): 命门 / 命門: Ming4 men2/Ming6 mun4

GV-5 (Suspended Pivot): 悬枢 / 懸樞: Xuan2 shu1/Jyun4 syu1

GV-6 (Spinal Center): 脊中: Ji3 zhong1/Zek 3 zung1

GV-7 (Middle Pivot): 中枢 / 中樞: Zhong1 shu1/Zung1 syu1

GV-8 (Sinew Contraction): 筋缩 / 筋縮: Jin1 suo1/Gan1 suk1

GV-9 (Extremity of Yang): 至阳 / 至陽: Zhi4 yang2/Zi3 joeng4

GV-10 (Spirit Tower): 灵台 / 靈臺: Ling2 tai2/Ling4 toi4

GV-11 (Spirit Path): 神道: Shen2 dao4/San4 dou6

GV-12 (Body Pillar): 神柱: Shen1 zhu4/San1 cyu5

GV-13 (Kiln Path): 陶道: Tao2 dao4/Tou4 dou6

GV-14 (Great Hammer): 大椎: Da4 zhui1/Daai6 ceoi4

GV-15 (Mutes Gate): 哑门 / 啞門: Ya3 men2/Aa2 mun4

GV-16 (Wind Mansion): 风府 / 風府: Feng1 fu3/Fung1 fu2

GV-17 (Brain Door): 脑户 / 腦戶: Nao3 hu4/Nou5 wu6

GV-18 (Unyielding Space): 强间 / 強間: Qiang2 jian1/Koeng5 gaan3

GV-19 (Behind the Vertex): 后顶 / 後頂: Hou4 ding3/Hau6 ding2

GV-20 (Hundred Meetings): 百会/百會: Bai3 hui4/Baak6 wui5

GV-21 (Before the Vertex): 前顶 / 前頂: Qian2 ding3/Cin4 ding2
GV-22 (Fontanel Meeting): 囟会 / 囟會: Xin4 hui4/Seon3 wui5
GV-23 (Upper Star): 上星: Shang4 xing1/Soeng5 sing1
GV-24 (Spirit Court): 神庭: Shen2 ting2/San4 ting4
GV-25 (White Bone-hole): 素髎: Su4 liao2/Sou3 liu4
GV-26 (Human Center): 人中: Ren2 zhong1/Jan4 zung1
GV-27 (Extremity of the Mouth): 兑端 / 兌端: Dui4 duan1/Deoi3 dyun1
GV-28 (Gum Intersection): 龈交 / 齦交: Yin2 jiao1/Ngan4 gaau1

Extra Points:

M-UE-29: (Two Whites):二白：Er4 Bai2/Ji6 baak6

M-UE-46: (Elbow Tip):肘尖：Zhou3 jian1/Jaau2 zim1

M-BW-16: (Root of Glomus): 痞根: Pi3 Gen1/Pei2 Gan1

M-BW-24: (Lumbar Eye): 腰眼: Yao1 yan3/Jiu1 ngaan5

*(Hair Line): 发在 / 髮在: Fa4 zai4/Faat3 zoi6

*(Trigeminal): 三叉 / 三扠: San1 cha1/Saam1 caa1

M-HN-9 (Tai Yang) 太阳 / 太陽: Tai4 yang2/Taai3 joeng4

M-HN-3 (Hall of Impression): 印堂: Yin4 tang2/Jan3 tong4

M-HN-6 (Fish Lumbus): 鱼腰 / 魚腰: Yü2 yao1/Jyu4 jiu1

*(Nose Eyes) 鼻眼: Bi2 yan3/Bei6 ngaan5

M-HN-18 (Beside Sauce Receptacle)：夹承浆 / 夾承醬: Jia1 cheng2 jiang1/Gaap3 sing4 zoeng1

EX-HN-11 (Sea Spring): 海泉: Hai3 quan2/Hoi2 cyun4

M-HN-20 a and b (Golden Liquid/Jade Humor) 金津 / 玉液: Jin1 jin1/Gam1 zeon1 and Yü4 ye4/Juk6 jik6

M-UE-9 (Four Seams): 四缝 / 四縫: Si4 feng4/Sei3 fung6

EX-UE-4 (Central Eminence): 中魁: Zhong1 Kui2/Zung1 fui1

M-UE-22 (Eight Evils): 八邪: Ba1 xie2/Baat3 ce4

M-UE-1to5 (Ten Drain-off): 十宣: Shi2 xuan1/Sap6 syun1

M-UE-15 (Greater Bone Hollow):大骨空: Da4 gu3 kong1/Daai6 gwat1 hung1

M-UE-17 (Lesser Bone Hollow): 小骨空: Xiao3 gu3 kong1/Siu2 gwat1 hung1

*(Five Tigers): 五虎: Wu3 hu3/Ng5 fu2

*(Tip of the Crease): 纹头 / 紋頭: Wen2 tou2/Man4 tau2

M-LE-8 (Eight Winds): 八风 / 八風: Ba1 Feng1/Baat3 fung1

M-HN-30 (Hundred Taxations): 百劳 / 百勞: Bai3 lao2/Baak3 lou4

M-HN-10 (Tip of the Ear): 耳尖: Er3 jian1/Ji5 zim1

M-HN-1 (Alert Spirit Quartet): 四神聪/四神聰: Si4 shen2 cong1/Sei3 san4 cong1

M-LE-16 (Inner Eye of the Knee): 内膝眼: Nei4 xi1 yan3/Noi6 sat1 ngaan5

*(Wings of the Knee): 膝翼: Xi1 yi4/Sat1 yik6

EX-LE-2 (Crane's Summit): 鹤顶 / 鶴頂: He4 ding3/Hok6 ding2

*(Below the Mountain): 山下: Shan1 xia4/Saan1 haa5

*(Middle of the Circle): 环中 / 環中: Huan2 zhong1/Waan4 zung1

*(Turtle Head): 龟头 / 龜頭: Gui1 tou2/Gwai1 tau4

*(Bag Bottom): 囊地: Nang2 di4/Nong4 dei6.

M-BW-35 (Hua Tuo's Paravertebral Points): 华佗夹脊 / 華佗夾脊: Hua2 tuo2 jia1 ji3/Waa4 to4 gaap3 zek3

EX-LE-11 (Solitary Yin): 独阴 / 獨陰: Du2 yin1/Duk6 jam1

*The extra points without accompanying numbers were drawn from **The Book of Acupuncture Points** by Tin Yau So ©1984 Paradigm Publications, Brookline MA

INDIVIDUAL HERBS (390):
Warm Acrid Exterior-Releasing Medicinals

(Ephedrae Herba): 麻黄: Ma2 huang2/Maa4 wong4

(Cinnamomi Ramulus): 桂枝: Gui4 zhi1/Gwai3 zi1

(Schizonepetae Herba): 荆芥 / 荊芥: Jing1 jie4/Ging1 gaai3

(Saposhnikoviae Radix): 防风 / 防風: Fang2 feng1/Fong4 fung1

(Notopterygii Rhizoma seu Radix): 羌活: Qiang1 huo2/Goeng1 wut6

(Angelicae Dahuricae Radix): 白芷: Bai2 zhi3/Baak6 zi2

(Perillae Folium): 紫苏叶 / 紫蘇葉: Zi3 su1 ye4/Zi2 sou1 jip6

(Ligustici Rhizoma): 藁本: Gao3 ben3/Gou2 bun2

(Asari Radix et Rhizoma): 细辛 / 細辛: Xi4 xin1/Sai3 san1

(Zingiberis Rhizoma Recens): 生姜 / 生薑: Sheng1 jiang1/Saang1 goeng1
(Allii Fistulosi Bulbus): 葱白 / 蔥白: Cong1 bai2/Cung1 baak6
(Moslae Herba): 香薷: Xiang1 ru2/Hoeng1 jyu4
(Xanthii Fructus): 苍耳子 / 蒼耳子: Cang1 er3 zi3/Cong1 ji5 zi2
(Magnoliae Flos): 辛夷花: Xin1yi2 hua1/San1 ji4 faa1

Cool Acrid Exterior-Resolving Medicinals

(Menthae Herba): 薄荷: Bo4 he2/Bok6 ho4

(Mori Folium): 桑叶 / 桑葉: Sang1 ye4/Song1 jip6

(Chrysanthemi Flos): 菊花: Jü2 hua1/Guk1 faa1

(Puerariae Radix): 葛根: Ge2 gen1/Got3 gan1

(Bupleuri Radix): 柴胡: Chai2 hu2/Caai4 wu4

(Arctii Fructus): 牛蒡子: Niu2 bang4 zi3/Ngau4 bong2 zi2

(Cicadae Periostracum): 蝉蜕 / 蟬蛻: Chan2 tui4/Sim4 teoi3

(Viticis Fructus): 蔓荆子: Man4 jing1 zi3/Maan4 ging1 zi2

(Sojae Semen Preparatum): 淡豆豉: Dan4 dou4 chi3/Daam6 dau6 si6

(Sojae Semen Germinatum): 大豆卷 / 大豆捲: Da4 dou4 juan3/Daai6 dau6 gyun2

(Spirodelae Herba): 浮萍: Fu2 ping2/Fau4 ping4

(Equiseti Hiemalis Herba): 木贼 / 木賊: Mu4 zei2/Muk6 caak6

(Cimicifugae Rhizoma): 升麻: Sheng1 ma2/Sing1 maa4

Heat-Clearing Fire Draining Medicinals:
(Gypsum Fibrosum): 石膏: Shi2 gao1/Sek6 gou1

(Anemarrhenae Rhizoma): 知母:Zhi1 mu3/Zi1 mou5

(Gardeniae Fructus): 栀子 / 梔子: Zhi1 zi3/Zi1 zi2

(Lophatheri Herba): 淡竹叶 / 淡竹葉: Dan4 zhu2 ye4/Daam6 zuk1 jip6

(Citrulli Fructus): 西瓜: Xi1 gua1/Sai1 gwaa1

(Prunellae Spica): 夏枯草: Xia4 ku1 cao3/Haa6 fu1 cou2

(Glauberitum): 寒水石: Han2 shui3 shi2/Hon4 seoi2 sek6

(Nelumbinis Plumula): 莲子心 / 蓮子心: Lian2 zi3 xin1/Lin4 zi2 sam1

(Phragmitis Rhizoma): 芦根 / 蘆根: Lu2 gen1/Lou4 gan1

(Trichosanthis Radix): 天花粉: Tian1 hua1 fen3/Tin1 faa1 fan2

(Cassiae Semen): 决明子 / 決明子: Jue2 ming2 zi3/Kyut3 ming4 zi2

(Celosiae Semen): 青箱子: Qing1 xiang1 zi3/Cing1 soeng1 zi2

(Buddlejae Flos): 密蒙花: Mi4 meng2 hua1/Mat6 mung4 faa1

Heat-Clearing, Dampness-drying Medicinals
(Scutellariae Radix): 黄芩: Huang2 qin2/Wong4 kam4

(Coptidis Rhizoma): 黄连 / 黃連: Huang2 Lian2/Wong4 lin4

my teacher always referred to this medicinal in its Sichuan version: 川连 / 川連 Chuan1 lian2/Cyun1 lin4.

(Phellodendri Cortex): 黄柏: Huang2 bai3/Wong4 paak3

(Gentianae Radix): 龙胆草 / 龍膽草: Long2 dan3 cao3/Lung4 daam2 cou2

(Sophorae Flavescentis Radix): 苦参 / 苦參: Ku3 shen1/Fu2 sam1

(Fraxini Cortex): 秦皮: Qin2 pi2/Ceon4 pei4

Heat-Clearing, Blood-Cooling Medicinals

(Rhinocerotis Cornu): 犀角: Xi1 jiao3/Sai1 Gok3 this medicinal comes from an endangered species, and has been typically substituted with

(Bubali Cornu): 水牛角: Shui3 niu2 jiao3/Seoi2 ngau4 gok3

(Rehmanniae Radix): 生地黄: Sheng1 di4 huang2/Sang1 dei6 wong4

(Scrophulariae Radix): 玄参 / 玄參: Xuan2 shen1/Jyun4 sam1

(Moutan Cortex): 牡丹皮: Mu3 dan1 pi2/Maau5 daan1 pei4

(Paeoniae Radix Rubra): 赤芍: Chi4 shao2/Cek3 zeok3

(Arnebiae/Lithospermi Radix): 紫草: Zi3 cao3/Zi2 cou2

(Radicis Lycii Chinensis Cortex): 地骨皮: Di4 gu3 pi2/Dei6 gwat1 pei4

(Stellariae Radix): 银柴胡 / 銀柴胡: Yin2 chai2 hu2/Ngan4 caai4 wu4

Heat-Clearing, Toxin-Resolving Medicinals

(Lonicerae Flos): 金银花 / 金銀花: Jin1 yin2 hua1/Gam1 ngan4 faa1

(Lonicerae Caulis): 忍冬藤: Ren3 dong1 teng2/Jan2 dung1 tang4

(Forsythiae Fructus): 连翘 / 連翹: Lian2 qiao2/Lin4 kiu4

(Isatidis Folium): 大青叶 / 大青葉: Da4 qing1 ye4/Daai6 cing1 jip6

(Isatidis Radix): 板蓝根 / 板藍根: Ban3 lan2 gen1/Baan2 laam4 gan1

(Indigo Naturalis): 青黛: Qing1 dai4/Cing1 doi6

(Pulsatillae Radix): 白头翁 / 白頭翁: Bai2 tou2 weng1/Baak6 tau4 jung1

(Taraxaci Herba): 蒲公英: Pu2 gong1 ying1/Pou4 gung1 jing1

(Violae Herba): 紫花地丁: Zi3 hua1di4 ding1/Zi2 faa1 dei6 ding1

(Chrysanthemi Indici Flos): 野菊花: Ye3 jü2 hua1/Je5 guk1 faa1

(Houttuyniae Herba): 鱼腥草 / 魚腥草: Yü2 xing1 cao3/Jyu4 seng1 cou2

(Patriniae Herba): 败酱草 / 敗醬草: Bai4 jiang4 cao3/Baai6 zoeng3 cou2

(Hedyotis Diffusae Herba): 白花蛇舌草: Bai2 hua1 she2 she2 cao3/Baak6 faa1 se4 sit3 cou2

(Bruceae Fructus): 鸦胆子 / 鴉膽子: Ya1 dan3 zi3/Aa1 daam2 zi2

(Portulacae Herba): 马齿苋 / 馬齒莧: Ma3 chi3 xian4/Maa5 ci2 jin6

(Dictamni Cortex): 白鲜皮 / 白鮮皮: Bai2 xian1 pi2/Baak6 sin1 pei4

(Smilacis Glabrae Rhizoma): 土茯苓: Tu3 fu2 ling2/Tou2 fuk6 ling4

(Sargentodoxae Caulis): 红藤 / 紅藤: Hong2 teng2/Hung4 tang4

(Lasiosphaera/Calvatia): 马勃 / 馬勃: Ma3 bo2/Maa5 but6

(Scutellariae Barbatae Herba): 半枝莲 / 半枝蓮: Ban4 zhi1 lian2/Bun3 zi1 lin4

(Sophorae Tonkinensis Radix): 山豆根: Shan1 dou4 gen1/Saan1 dau6 gan1

(Belamcandae Rhizoma): 射干: She4 gan1/Se6 gon1

(Ampelopsis Radix): 白蔹 / 白蘞: Bai2 lian3/Baak6 lim4

(Rhapontici Radix): 漏芦 / 漏盧: Lou4 lu2/Lau6 lou4

(Cyrtomii Rhizoma): 贯众 / 貫眾: Guan4 zhong4/Gun3 zung3

Summerheat-Resolving, Heat-Clearing Medicinals
(Nelumbinis Folium): 荷叶 / 荷葉: He2 ye4/Ho4 jip6

(Phaseoli Radiati Semen): 绿豆 / 綠豆: Lü4 dou4/Luk 6 dau2

(Lablab Semen Album): 白扁豆: Bai2 bian3 dou4/Baak6 bin2 dau6

Vacuity Heat Clearing and Receding Medicinals
(Artemisiae Annuae Herba): 青蒿: Qing1 hao1/Cing1 hou1

(Lycii Cortex): 地骨皮: Di4 gu3 pi2/Dei6 gwat1 pei4

(Cynanchi Atrati Radix): 白薇: Bai2 wei1/Baak6 mei4

(Stellariae Radix): 银柴胡 / 銀柴胡: Yin2 chai2 hu2/Ngan4 caai4 wu4

(Picrorhizae Rhizoma): 胡黄连 / 胡黃連: Hu2 huang2 lian2/Wu4 wong4 lin4

Phlegm-Transforming, Cough Stopping, Panting-Leveling Medicinals
Transform Cold Phlegm
(Pinelliae Rhizoma Preparatum): 制半夏: Zhi4 ban4 xia4/Zai3 bun3 haa6

(Inulae Flos): 旋覆花: Xuan2 fu4 hua1/Syun4 fuk1 faa1

(Sinalpis Albae Semen): 白芥子: Bai2 jie4 zi3/Baak6 gaai3 zi2

(Arisaematis Rhizoma): 天南星 / 天南星: Tian1 nan2 xing1/Tin1 naam4 sing1

(Typhonii Rhizoma Preparatum): 制白附子 / 製白附子: Zhi4 bai2 fu4 zi3/Zai3 baak6 fu6 zi2

(Gleditsiae Fructus): 皂荚 / 皂莢: Zao4 jia2/Zou6 gaap3

(Gleditsiae Spina): 皂角刺: Zao4 jiao3 ci4/Zou6 gok3 ci3

(Platycodi Radix): 桔梗: Jie2 geng3/Gat1 gang2

(Cynanchi Stauntonii Rhizoma): 白前: Bai2 qian2/Baak6 cin4

Hot Phlegm Clearing and Transforming Medicinals

(Trichosanthis Fructus): 瓜蒌 / 瓜蔞: Gua1 lou2/Gwaa1 lau4

(Trichosanthis Pericarpium): 栝楼皮 / 瓜蒌皮 / 栝蔞皮 / 瓜蔞皮
Gua1 lou2 pi2/Gwaa1 lau4 pei4

(Trichosanthis Semen): 栝楼仁 / 瓜蒌仁 / 栝蔞仁 / 瓜蔞
Gua1 lou2 ren2/Gwaa1 lau4 jan4

(Bambusae Caulis in Taeniam): 竹茹: Zhu2 ru2/Zuk1 jyu4

(Bambusae Succus): 竹沥 / 竹瀝: Zhu2 li4/Zuk1 lik6

(Eckloniae Thallus): 昆布: Kun1 bu4/Kwan1 bou3

(Sargassii Herba): 海藻: Hai3 zao3/Hoi2 zou2

(Sterculiae Lychnophorae Semen): 胖大海: Pang4 da4 hai3/Bun6 daai6 hoi2

(Changii Radix): 明党参 / 明黨參: Ming2 dang3 shen1/Ming4 dong2 Sam1

(Fritillariae Cirrhosae Bulbus): 川贝母 / 川貝母: Chuan1 bei4 mu3/Cyun1 bui3 mou5

(Fritillariae Thunbergii Bulbus): 浙贝母 / 浙貝母: Zhe4 bei4 mu3/Zit3 bui3 mou5

(Peucedani Radix): 前胡: Qian2 hu2/Cin4 wu4

Cough-Stopping, Panting-Leveling Medicinals

(Armeniacae Semen): 杏仁: Xing4 ren2/Hang6 jan4

(Perillae Fructus): 紫苏子 / 紫蘇紫: Zi3 su1 zi3/Zi2 sou1 zi2

(Asteris Radix): 紫菀: Zi3 wan3/Zi2 jyun2

(Farfarae Flos): 款冬花: Kuan3 dong1 hua1/Fun2 dung1 faa1

(Eriobotryae Folium): 枇杷叶 / 枇杷葉: Pi2 pa2 ye4/Pei4 paa4 jip6

(Stemonae Radix): 百部: Bai3 bu4/Baak3 bou6

(Mori Cortex): 桑白皮: Sang1 bai2 pi2/Song1 baak6 pei4

(Lepidii/Descurainiae Semen): 葶苈子 / 葶藶子: Ting2 li4 zi3/Ting4 lik6 zi2

(Momordicae Fructus): 罗汉果/羅漢果: Luo2 han4 guo3/Lo4 hon3 gwo2

(Veratri Nigri Radix et Rhizoma) 藜芦 / 藜蘆: Li2 lu2/Lai4 lou4

Draining and Precipitating Medicinals

(Rhei Radix et Rhizoma): 大黄: Da4 huang2/Daai6 wong4

(Natrii Sulfas): 硭硝: Mang2 xiao1/Mong4 siu1

(Sennae Folium): 番泻叶 / 番瀉葉: Fan1 xie4 ye4/Faan1 se3 jip6

(Aloe): 芦荟 / 蘆薈: Lu2 hui4/Lou4 wui6

Moistening and Precipitating Medicinals

(Cannabis Semen): 火麻仁: Huo3 ma2 ren2/Fo2 maa4 jan4

(Pruni Semen): 郁李仁 / 鬱李仁: Yü4 li3 ren2/Jyu4 lei5 jan4

Drastic Precipitating and Expelling Water Medicinals
(Kansui Radix): 甘遂: Gan1 sui4/Gam1 seoi6
(Knoxiae/Euphorbiae Radix): 大戟: Da4 ji3/Daai6 gik1
(Genkwa Flos): 芫花: Yuan2 hua1/Jyun4 faa1

(Pharbitidis Semen): 牵牛子 / 牽牛子: Qian1 niu2 zi3/Hin1 ngau4 zi2

(Crotonis Fructus): 巴豆: Ba1 dou4/Baa1 dau2

(Phytolaccae Radix): 商陆 / 商陸: Shang1 lu4/Soeng1 luk6

Dampness-Dispelling Medicinals
a.Wind-Damp Dispelling Medicinals
(Angelicae Pubescentis Radix): 独活 / 獨活: Du2 huo2/Duk6 wut6
(Stephaniae Tetrandrae Radix): 汉防己 / 漢防己: Han4 fang2 ji3/Hon3 fong4 gei2
(Clematidis Radix): 威灵仙 / 威靈仙: Wei1 ling2 xian1/Wai1 ling4 sin1
(Erythrinae Cortex): 海桐皮: Hai3 tong2 pi2/Hoi2 tung4 pei4
(Chaenomelis Fructus): 木瓜: Mu4 gua1/Muk6 gwaa1
(Bombycis Faeces): 蚕砂 / 蠶砂: Can2 sha1/Caam4 saa1
(Mori Ramulus): 桑枝: Sang1 zhi1/Song1 zi1
(Acanthopanacis Cortex): 五加皮: Wu3 jia1 pi2/Ng5 gaa1 pei4
(Taxilli Herba): 桑寄生: Sang1 ji4 sheng1/Song1 gei3 sang1
(Dioscoreae Nipponicae Rhizoma): 穿山龙 / 穿山龍: Chuan1 shan1 long2/Cyun1 saan1 lung4
(Zanthoxyli Radix): 两面针 / 兩面針: Liang3 mian4 zhen1/Loeng5 min6 zam1
(Piperis Kadsurae Caulis): 海风藤 / 海風藤: Hai3 feng1 teng2/Hoi2 fung1 tang4
(Homalomenae Rhizoma): 千年建: Qian1 nian2 jian4/Cin1nin4 gin3
(Gentianae Macrophyllae Radix): 秦艽: Qin2 jiao1/Ceon4 gau2
(Siegesbeckiae Herba): 豨莶草 / 豨薟草: Xi1 xian1 cao3/Hei1 cim1 cou2
(Clerodendri Folium): 臭梧桐: Chou4 wu2 tong2/Cau3 ng4 tung4
(Trachelospermi Caulis): 络石藤 / 絡石藤: Luo4 shi2 teng2/Lok3 sek6 tang4
(Tinosporae Sinensis Caulis): 宽筋藤 / 寬筋藤: Kuan1 jin1 teng2/Fun1 gan1 tang4
(Agkistrodon): 蕲蛇 / 蘄蛇: Qi2 she2/Kei4 se4

(Bungarus Parvus): 白花蛇: Bai2 hua1 she2/Baak6 faa1 se4 [these two are similar and are often substituted for one another—from **Chinese Medical Herbology and Pharmacology** by John K. Chen and Tina T. Chen ©2004 Art of Medicine Press, City of Industry, CA

(Pini Nodi Lignum): 松节 / 松節: Song1 jie2/Cung4 zit3

b.Penetrating, Aromatic, Dampness-Transforming Medicinals
(Atractylodis Rhizoma): 苍术 / 蒼術: Cang1 zhu2/Cong1 seot6
(Magnoliae Officinalis Cortex): 厚朴: Hou4 po4/Hau5 pok3
(Pogostemonis Herba): 藿香: Huo4 xiang1/Fok3 hoeng1
(Eupatorii Herba): 佩兰 / 佩蘭: Pei4 lan2/Pui3 laan4
(Amomi Fructus): 砂仁: Sha1 ren2/Saa1 jan4
(Amomi Fructus Rotundus): 白豆蔻: Bai2 dou4 kou4/Baak6 dau6 kau3
(Alpiniae Katsumadai Semen): 草豆蔻: Cao3 dou4 kou4/Cou2 dau6 kau3
(Tsaoko Fructus): 草果: Cao3 guo3/Cou2 gwo2

c. Water-Disinhibiting, Dampness-Percolating Medicinals
(Poria): 茯苓: Fu2 ling2/Fuk6 ling4
(Polyporus): 猪苓 / 豬苓: Zhu1 ling2/Zyu1 ling4
(Alismatis Rhizoma): 泽泻 / 澤瀉: Ze2 xie4/Zaak6 se3
(Plantaginis Semen): 车前子 / 車前子: Che1 qian2 zi3/Ce1 cin4 zi2
(Akebiae Caulis): 木通: Mu4 tong3/Muk6 tung1
(Lysimachiae Herba): 金钱草 / 金錢草: Jin1 qian2 cao3/Gam1 cin4 cou2
(Talcum): 滑石: Hua2 shi2/Waat6 sek6
(Coicis Semen): 薏苡仁: Yi4 yi3 ren2/Ji3 ji5 jan4
(Benincasae Semen): 冬瓜人: Dong1 gua1 ren2/Dung1 gwaa1 jan4

also known as 冬瓜子: Dong1 gua1 zi3/Dung1 gwaa1 zi2

(Benincasae Exocarpium): 冬瓜皮: Dong1 gua1 pi2/Dung1 gwaa1 pei4

(Lygodii Spora): 海金沙: Hai3 jin1 sha1/Hoi2 gam1 saa1
(Tetrapanacis Medulla): 通草: Tong1 cao3/Tung1 cou2
(Junci Medulla): 灯心草 / 燈心草: Deng1 xin1 cao3/Dang1 sam1 cou2
(Dianthi Herba): 瞿麦 / 蘧麥: Qü2 mai4/Keoi4 mak6
(Kochiae Fructus): 地肤子 / 地膚子: Di4 fu1 zi3/Dei6 fu1 zi2
(Polygoni Avicularis Herba): 萹蓄: Bian3 xü4/Bin2 cuk1
(Malvae Semen): 冬葵子: Dong1 kui2 zi3/Dung1 kwai4 zi2
(Dioscoreae Hypoglaucae Rhizoma): 萆薢: Bi4 xie4/Bei1 gaai1
(Phaseoli Semen): 赤小豆: Chi4 xiao3 dou4/Cek3 siu2 dau2

(Artemisiae Scopariae Herba): 茵陈蒿 / 茵陳蒿: Yin1 chen2 hao1/Jan1 can4 hou1

(Lobeliae Chinensis Herba): 半边莲 / 半邊蓮: Ban4 bian1 lian2/Bun3 bin1 lin4

(Maydis Stigma): 玉米须 / 玉米鬚: Yü4 mi3 xü1/Juk6 mai5 seoi1

Interior-Warming Medicinals
(Aconiti Radix Lateralis Preparata): 制附子 / 製附子: Zhi4 fu4 zi3/Zai3 fu6 zi2

(Aconiti Radix Preparata): 制川乌 / 製川烏: Zhi4 chuan1 wu1/Zai3 cyun1 wu1

(Aconiti Kusnezoffi Radix Preparata): 制草乌 / 製草烏: Zhi4 cao3 wu1/Zai3 cou2 wu1

(Zingiberis Rhizoma): 干姜 / 乾薑: Gan1 jiang1/Gon1 Goeng1

(Cinnamomi Cortex): 肉桂: Rou4 gui4/Juk6 gwai3

(Evodiae Fructus): 吴茱萸 / 吳茱萸: Wu2 zhu1 yü2/Ng4 zyu1 jyu4

(Zantholxyli Pericarpium): 川椒: Chuan1 jiao1/Cyun1 ziu1

(Zanthoxyli Pericarpium): 花椒: Hua1 jiao1/Faa1 ziu1

(Alpiniae Officinarum Rhizoma): 高良姜 / 高良薑: Gao1 liang2 jiang1/Gou1 loeng4 goeng1

(Caryophylli Flos): 丁香: Ding1 xiang1/Ding1 hoeng1

(Foeniculi Fructus): 小茴香: Xiao3 hui2 xiang1/Siu2 wui4 hoeng1

(Piperis Longi Fructus): 荜芨 / 蓽芨: Bi4 ba2/Bat1 baat6

(Piperis Fructus): 胡椒: Hu2 jiao1/Wu4 ziu1

Qi-Rectifying Medicinals
(Citri Reticulatae Pericarpium): 陈皮 / 陳皮: Chen2 pi2/Can4 pei4

(Citri Reticulatae Pericarpium Viride): 青皮: Qing1 pi2/Cing1 pei4

(Citri Reticulatae Exocarpium Rubrum): 橘红 / 橘紅: Jü2 hong2/Gwat1 hung4

(Aurantii Fructus Immaturus): 枳实 / 枳實: Zhi3 shi2/Zi2 sat6

(Aurantii Fructus): 枳壳 / 枳殼: Zhi3 ke2/Zi2 hok3

(Citri Sarcodactylis Fructus): 佛手: Fo2 shou3/Fat6 sau2

(Aucklandiae Radix): 木香: Mu4 xiang1/Muk6 hoeng1

(Cyperi Rhizoma): 香附: Xiang1 fu4/Hoeng1 fu6

(Allii Macrostemonis Bulbus): 薤白: Xie4 bai2/Haai6 baak6

(Linderae Radix): 乌药 / 烏藥: Wu1 yao4/Wu1 joek6

(Arecae Pericarpium): 大腹皮: Da4 fu4 pi2/Daai6 fuk1 pei4

(Aquilariae Lignum Resinatum): 沉香: Chen2 xiang1/Cam4 hoeng1

(Santali Albi Lignum): 檀香: Tan2 xiang1/Taan4 hoeng1

(Citri Reticulatae Semen): 橘核: Jü2 he2/Gwat1 wat6

(Toosendan Fructus): 川楝子: Chuan1 lian4 zi3/Cyun1 lin6 zi2

(Litchi Semen): 荔枝核: Li4 zhi1 he2/Lai6 zi1 wat6

(Kaki Calyx): 柿蒂: Shi4 di4/Ci2 dai3

(Strychni Semen): 马钱子 / 馬錢子: Ma3 qian2 zi3/Maa5 cin4 zi2

Dispersing and Abducting Medicinals

(Crataegi Fructus): 山楂: Shan1 zha1/Saan1 zaa1

(Corneum Gigeriae Galli Endothelium): 鸡内金 / 雞内金: Ji1 nei4 jin1/Gai1 noi6 gam1

(Hordei Fructus Germinatus): 麦芽 / 麥芽: Mai4 ya2/Mak6 ngaa4

(Setariae Fructus Germinatus): 谷芽 / 穀芽: Gu3 ya2/Guk1 ngaa4

(Setariae Fructus Germinatus): 粟芽: Su4 ya2/Suk1 ngaa4

(Raphani Semen): 莱菔子 / 萊菔子: Lai2 fu2 zi3/Loi4 fuk6 zi2

(Massa Medica Fermentata): 神曲/神麴: Shen2 qü1/San4 kuk1

Worm-Expelling Medicinals

(Quisqualis Fructus): 使君子: Shi3 jun1 zi3/Si2 gwan1 zi2

(Meliae Cortex): 苦楝皮 / 苦楝皮: Ku3 lian4 pi2/Fu2 lin6 pei4

(Arecae Semen): 槟榔 / 檳榔: Bing1 lang2/Ban1 long4

(Cucurbitae Moschatae Semen): 南瓜子: Nan2 gua1 zi3/Naam4 gwaa1 zi2

(Allii Sativi Bulbus): 大蒜: Da4 suan4/Daai6 syun3

(Dichroae Radix): 常山: Chang2 shan1/Soeng4 saan1

Stop Bleeding Medicinals

(Cirsii Herba): 小蓟 / 小薊: Xiao3 ji4/Siu2 gai3

(Sanguisorbae Radix): 地榆: Di4 yü2/Dei6 jyu4

(Bletillae Striatae Rhizoma): 白及: Bai2 ji2/Baak6 kap6

(Imperatae Rhizoma): 白茅根: Bai2 mao2 gen1/Baak6 maau4 gan1

(Notoginseng Radix): 三七: San1 qi1/Saam1 cat1

(Typhae Pollen): 蒲黄: Pu2 huang2/Pou4 wong4

(Cirsii Japonici Herba Seu Radix):大蓟 / 大薊: Da4 ji4/Daai6 gai3

(Sophorae Fructus): 槐角: Huai2 jiao3/Waai4 gok3

(Artemisiae Argyii Folium): 艾叶 / 艾葉: Ai4 ye4/Ngaai6 jip6

(Agrimoniae Herba): 仙鹤草 / 仙鶴草: Xian1 he4 cao3/Sin1 hok6 cou2

(Sophorae Flos): 槐花米: Huai2 hua1 mi3/Waai4 faa1 mai5

(Rubiae Radix): 茜草根: Qian4 cao3 gen1/Sin3 cou2 gan1

(Platycladi Cacumen): 侧柏叶 / 側百葉: Ce4 bai3 ye4/Zak1 paak3 jip6

(Crinis Carbonisatus): 血余炭 / 血餘炭: Xue4 yü2 tan4/Hyut3 jyu4 taan3

(Trachycarpi Petiolus): 棕榈皮 / 棕櫚皮: Zong1 lü2 pi2/Zung1 leoi4 pei4

(Nelumbinis Rhizomatis Nodus): 藕节 / 藕節: Ou3 jie2/Ngau5 zit3

(Nelumbinis Receptaculum): 莲房 / 蓮房: Lian2 fang2/Lin4 fong4

(Terra Flava Usta): 伏龙肝 / 伏龍肝: Fu2 long2 gan1/Fuk6 lung4 gon1

(Terra Flava Usta): 灶心土: Zao4 xin1 tu3/Zou3 sam1 tou2

Blood-Quickening, Stasis-Dispelling Medicinals

(Chuanxiong Rhizoma): 川芎: Chuan1 xiong1/Cyun1 gung1

(Salviae Miltiorrhizae Radix): 丹参 / 丹參: Dan1 shen1/Daan1 sam1

(Spatholobi Caulis): 鸡血藤 / 雞血藤: Ji1 xue4 teng2/Gai1 hyut3 tang4

(Leonuri Herba): 益母草: Yi4 mu3 cao3/Jik1 mou5 cou2

(Corydalis Rhizoma): 延胡索: Yan2 hu2 suo3/Jin4 wu4 sok3

(Curcumae Radix): 郁金 / 鬱金: Yü4 jin1/Juk1 gam1

(Curcumae Longae Rhizoma): 姜黄 / 薑黃: Jiang1 huang2/Goeng1 wong4

(Rosae Chinensis Flos): 月季花: Yue4 ji4 hua1/Jyut6 gwai3 faa1

(Polygoni Cuspidati Rhizoma): 虎杖: Hu3 zhang4/Fu2 zoeng6

(Paeoniae Radix Rubra): 赤芍: Chi4 shao2/Cek3 zoek3

(Carthami Flos): 红花 / 紅花: Hong2 hua1/Hung4 faa1

(Persicae Semen): 桃仁: Tao2 ren2/Tou4 jan4

(Achyranthis Bidentatae Radix): 怀牛膝 / 懷牛膝: Huai2 niu2 xi1/Waai4 ngau4 sat1 My teacher always wrote this "cow seven" or 牛七: Niu2 qi1/Ngau4 cat1

(Cyathulae Radix): 川牛膝: Chuan1 niu2 xi1/Cyun1 ngau4 sat1 My teacher always wrote this "cow seven" or 牛七: Niu2 qi1/Ngau4 cat1

(Manitis Pentadactylis Squama): 穿山甲: Chuan1 shan1 jia3/Cyun1 saan1 gaap3

(Lycopi Herba): 泽兰 / 澤蘭: Ze2 lan2/Zaak6 laan4

(Curcumae Rhizoma): 莪术 / 莪術: E2 zhu2/Ngo4 seot6

(Sparganii Rhizoma): 三棱: San1 leng2/Saam1 ling4

(Olibanum): 乳香: Ru3 xiang1/Jyu5 hoeng1

(Myrrha): 没药 / 沒藥: Mo4 yao4/Mut6 joek6

(Vaccariae Semen): 王不留行: Wang2 bu4 liu2 xing2/Wong4 bat1 lau4 hang4

(Liquidambaris Fructus): 路路通: Lu4 lu4 tong1/Lou6 lou6 tung1

(Artemisiae Anomalae Herba): 刘寄奴 / 劉寄奴: Liu2 ji4 nu2/Lau4 gei3 nou4

(Daemonoropis Resina): 血竭: Xue4 jie2/Hyut3 kit3

(Sappan Lignum): 苏木 / 蘇木: Su1 mu4/Sou1 muk6

(Trogopteri Faeces): 五灵脂 / 五靈脂: Wu3 ling2 zhi1/Ng5 ling4 zi1

(Dalbergiae Odoriferae Lignum): 降香: Jiang4 xiang1/Gong3 hoeng1

(Arcae Concha): 瓦楞子: Wa3 leng2 zi3/Ngaa5 ling4 zi2

(Ilicis Pubescentis Radix): 毛冬青: Mao2 dong1 qing1/Mou4 dung1 cing1

(Verbenae Herba): 马鞭草 / 馬鞭草: Ma3 bian1 cao3/Maa5 bin1cou2

(Eupolyphaga/Steleophaga): 土鳖虫 / 土鱉蟲: Tu3 bie1 chong2/Tou2 bit3 cung4

(Pyritum): 自然铜 / 自然銅: Zi4 ran2 tong2/Zi6 jin4 tung4

Spirit-Quieting Medicinals:

(Mastodi Ossis Fossilia): 龙骨 / 龍骨: Long2 gu3/Lung4 gwat1

(Mastodi Dentis Fossilia): 龙齿 / 龍齒: Long2 chi3/Lung4 ci2

(Ostreae Concha): 牡蛎 / 牡蠣: Mu3 li4/Maau5 lai6

(Magnetitum): 磁石: Ci2 shi2/Ci4 sek6
(Margaritiferae Concha Usta): 珍珠母: Zhen1 zhu1 mu3/Zan1 zyu1 mou5
(Cinnabaris): 朱砂: Zhu1 sha1/Zyu1 saa1
(Zizyphi Spinosae Semen): 酸枣仁 / 酸棗仁: Suan1 Zao3 ren2/Syun1 zou2 jan4
(Platycladi Semen): 柏子仁: Bai3 zi3 ren2/Paak3 zi2 jan4
(Polygalae Radix): 远志 / 遠志: Yuan3 zhi4/Jyun5 zi3
(Ganoderma Lucidum): 灵芝 / 靈芝: Ling2 zhi1/Ling4 zi1
(Albiziae Cortex): 合欢皮 / 合歡皮: He2 huan1 pi2/Hap6 fun1 pei4
(Albiziae Flos): 合欢花 / 合歡花: He2 huan1 hua1/Hap6 fun1 faa1
(Polygoni Multiflori Caulis): 夜交藤: Ye4 jiao1 teng1/Je6 gaau1 tang4
(Bovis Calculus): 牛黄: Niu2 huang2/Ngau4 wong4

Liver-Leveling, Wind-Extinguishing Medicinals
(Saigae Tataricae Cornu): 羚羊角: Ling2 yang2 jiao3/Ling4 joeng4 gok3
(Haematitum): 代赭石: Dai4 zhe3 shi2/Doi6 ze2 sek6
(Haliotidis Concha): 石决明 / 石決明: Shi2 jue2 ming2/Sek6 kyut3 ming4
(Uncariae Ramulus Cum Uncis): 钩藤 / 鉤藤: Gou1 teng2/Ngau1 tang4
(Gastrodiae Rhizoma): 天麻: Tian1 ma2/Tin1 maa4
(Scorpio): 全蝎: Quan2 xie1/Cyun4 hit3
(Pheretima): 地龙 / 地龍: Di4 long2/Dei6 lung4
(Bombyx Batryticatus): 僵蚕 / 僵蠶: Jiang1 can2/Goeng1 caam4
also commonly called 白僵蚕 / 白僵蠶: Bai2 jiang1 can2/Baak6 goeng1 caam4
(Tribuli Fructus): 白蒺藜: Bai2 ji2 li2/Baak6 zat6 lai4
this is also commonly called 刺蒺藜: Ci4 ji2 li2/Ci3 zat6 lai4
(Scolopendra): 蜈蚣: Wu2 gong1/Ng4 gung1

Orifice-Opening Medicinals:
(Moschus): 麝香: She4 xiang1/Se6 hoeng1
(Borneolum): 冰片: Bing1 pian4/Bing1 pin3
(Acori Tatarinowii Rhizoma): 石菖蒲: Shi2 chang1 pu2/Sek6 coeng1 pou4
(Styrax): 苏合香 / 蘇合香: Su1 he2 xiang1/Sou1 hap6 hoeng1
(Benzoinum): 安息香: An1 xi1 xiang1/On1 Sik1 hoeng1

Supplementing and Boosting Medicinals
a.Qi Supplementing Medicinals
(Ginseng Radix): 人参 / 人參: Ren2 shen1/Jan4 sam1
(Codonopsis Radix): 党参 / 黨參: Dang3 shen1/Dong2 sam1/防黨Fong4 dong2
(Pseudostellariae Radix): 太子参 / 太子參: Tai4 zi3 shen1/Taai3 zi2 sam1
(Astragali Radix): 黄芪 / 黃耆: Huang2 qi2/Wong4 kei4
my teacher referred to this medicinal as 北芪: Bak1 kei4.
(Atractylodis Macrocephalae Rhizoma): 白术 / 白術: Bai2 zhu2/Baak6 seot6

(Dioscoreae Rhizoma): 山药／山藥: Shan1 yao4/Saan1 joek

(Glycyrrhizae Radix): 甘草: Gan1 Cao3/Gam1 cou2

(Jujubae Fructus): 大枣／大棗: Da4 zao3/Daai6 zou2

(Polygonati Rhizoma): 黄精: Huang2 jing1/Wong4 zing1

(Maltosum): 饴糖／飴糖: Yi2 tang2/Ji4 tong4

b. Yang-Supplementing Medicinals

(Cervi Cornu Pantotrichum): 鹿茸: Lu4 rong3/Luk6 jung4

(Gecko): 蛤蚧: Ge2 jie4/Gap3 gaai3

(Cordyceps): 冬虫夏草／冬蟲夏草: Dong1 chong2 xia4 cao3/Dung1 cung4 haa6 cou2

(Cistanches Herba): 肉苁蓉／肉蓯蓉: Rou4 cong1 rong2/Juk6 cung1 jung4

(Epimedii Herba): 淫羊藿: Yin2 yang2 huo4/Jam4 joeng4 fok3

also commonly called: 仙灵脾／仙靈脾: Xian1 ling2 pi2/Sin1 ling4 pei4

(Curculiginis Rhizoma): 仙茅: Xian1 mao2/Sin1 maau4

(Eucommiae Cortex): 杜仲: Du4 zhong4/Dou6 zung6

(Psoraleae Fructus): 补骨脂／補骨脂: Bu3 gu3 zhi1/Bou2 gwat1 zi1

(Alpiniae Oxyphyllae Fructus): 益知仁: Yi4 zhi4 ren2/Jik1 zi3 jan4

(Cuscutae Semen): 菟丝子／菟絲子: Tu4 si1 zi3/Tou3 si1 zi2

(Morindae Officinalis Radix): 巴戟天: Ba1 ji3 tian1/Baa1 gik1 tin1

(Trigonellae Semen): 葫芦巴／葫蘆巴: Hu2 lu2 ba1/Wu4 lou4 baa1

(Juglandis Regiae Semen): 核桃仁: He2 tao2 ren2/Hat6 tou4 jan4

(Cynomorii Herba): 锁阳／鎖陽: Suo3 yang2/So2 joeng4

(Cibotii Rhizoma): 狗脊: Gou3 ji3/Gau2 zek3

(Dipsaci Radix): 续断／續斷: Xü4 duan4/Zuk6 dyun6

(Drynariae Rhizoma): 骨碎补／骨碎補: Gu3 sui4 bu3/Gwat1 seoi3 bou2

(Astragali Complanati Semen): 沙苑子: Sha1 yuan4 zi3/Saa1 jyun2 zi2

(Callorhini Testes et Penis): 海狗肾／海狗腎: Hai3 gou3 shen4/Hoi2 gau2 san6

(Hippocampus): 海马／海馬: Hai3 ma3/Hoi2 maa5

(Hominis Placenta): 紫河车／紫河車: Zi3 he2 che1/Zi2 ho4 ce1

c. Blood-Supplementing Medicinals

(Angelicae Sinensis Radix): 当归／當歸: Dang1 gui1/Dong1 gwai1

(Rehmanniae Radix Preparata): 熟地黄: Shu2 di4 huang2/Suk6 dei6 wong4

(Polygoni Multiflori Radix): 何首乌／何首烏: He2 shou3 wu3/Ho4 sau4 wu1

(Paeoniae Radix Alba): 白芍: Bai2 shao2/Baak6 zoek3

(Asini Corii Colla): 阿胶／阿膠: E1 jiao1/Aa3 gaau1

(Lycii Fructus): 枸杞子: Gou3 qi3 zi3/Gau2 gei2 zi2 [my teacher called this 杞子: Gei2 zi2

(Mori Fructus): 桑椹: Sang1 shen4/Song1 sam6

(Longan Arillus): 龙眼肉／龍眼肉: Long2 yan3 rou4/Lung4 ngaan5 juk6

d. Yin-Supplementing Medicinals

(Glehniae/Adenophorae Radix): 沙参 / 沙參: Sha1shen1/Saa1 sam1

Two versions are seen commonly: 北沙参 / 北沙參: Bei3 sha1 shen1/Bak1 saa1 sam1

and also: 南沙参 / 南沙參: Nan2 sha1 shen1/Naam4 saa1 sam1

(Panacis Quinquefolii Radix): 西洋参 / 西洋參: Xi1 yang2 shen1/Sai1 joeng4 sam1

(Ophiopogonis Radix): 麦门冬 / 麥門冬: Mai4 men2 dong1/Mak6 mun4 dung1

(Asparagi Radix): 天门冬 / 天門冬: Tian1 men2 dong1/Tin1 mun4 dung1

(Dendrobii Herba): 石斛: Shi2 hu2/Sek6 huk6

(Lilii Bulbus): 百合: Bai3 he2/Baak3 hap6

(Tryonycis Carapax): 鳖甲 / 鱉甲: Bie1 jia3/Bit3 gaap3

(Testudinis Plastrum): 龟板 / 龜板: Gui1 ban3/Gwai1 baan2

(Polygonati Odorati Rhizoma): 玉竹: Yü4 zhu2/Juk6 zuk1

(Ecliptae Herba): 旱莲草 / 旱蓮草: Han4 lian2 cao3/Hon5 lin4 cou2

also commonly known as: 墨旱莲 / 墨旱蓮: Mo4 han4 lian2/Mak6 hon5 lin4

(Ligustri Lucidi Fructus): 女贞子 / 女貞子: Nü3 zhen1 zi3/Neoi5 zing1 zi2

(Sesami Semen Nigrum): 黑芝麻: Hei1 zhi1 ma2/Hak1 zi1 maa4

Restraining and Astringing Medicinals

(Tritici Fructus Levis): 浮小麦 / 浮小麥: Fu2 xiao3 mai4/Fau4 siu2 mak6

(Schisandrae Fructus): 五味子: Wu3 wei4 zi3/Ng5 mei6 zi2

(Mume Fructus): 乌梅 / 烏梅: Wu1 mei2/Wu1 mui4

(Nelumbinis Semen): 莲子 / 蓮子: Lian2 zi3/Lin4 zi2

(Corni Fructus): 山茱萸: Shan1 zhu1 yü2/Saan1 zyu1 jyu4

(Alpiniae Oxyphyllae Fructus): 益智仁: Yi4 zhi4 ren2/Jik1 zi3 jan4

(Sepiae Endoconcha): 乌贼骨 / 烏賊骨: Wu1 zei2 gu3/Wu1 caak6 gwat1 [this is also called 海螵蛸: Hai3 piao1 xiao1/Hoi2 piu1 siu1

(Halloysitum Rubrum): 赤石脂: Chi4 shi2 zhi1/Cek3 sek6 zi1

(Chebulae Fructus): 诃子 / 訶子: He1 zi3/Ho1 zi2

(Myristicae Semen): 肉豆蔻: Rou4 dou4 kou4/Juk6 dau6 kau3

(Granati Pericarpium): 石榴皮: Shi2 liu2 pi2/Sek6 lau4 pei4

(Ailanthi Cortex): 椿皮: Chun1 pi2/Ceon1 pei4

(Nelumbinis Stamen): 莲须 / 蓮鬚: Lian2 xü1/Lin4 sou1

(Papaveris Pericarpium): 罂粟壳 / 罌粟殼: Ying1 su4 ke2/Aang1 suk1 hok3

(Euryales Semen): 芡实 / 芡實: Qian4 shi2/Him3 Sat6

(Rosae Laevigatae Fructus): 金樱子 / 金櫻子: Jin1ying1zi3/Gam1 jing1 zi2

(Rubi Fructus): 覆盆子: Fu4 pen2 zi3/Fuk1 pun4 zi2

(Galla Chinensis): 五倍子: Wu3 bei4 zi3/Ng5 pui5 zi2

(Ginkgo Semen): 白果: Bai2 guo3/Baak6 gwo2

(Ephedrae Radix): 麻黄根: Ma2 huang2 gen1/Maa4 wong4 gan1

(Oryzae Glutinosae Radix): 糯稻根: Nuo4 dao4 gen1/No6 dou6 gan1

(Mantidis Ootheca): 桑螵蛸: Sang1 piao1 xiao1/Song1 piu1 siu1

Topical Application Medicinals:

(Alumen): 白帆 / 白礬: Bai2 fan2/Baak6 faan4

(Calamina): 炉甘石 / 爐甘石: Lu2 gan1 shi2/Lou4 gam1 sek6

(Sulfur): 硫磺: Liu2 huang2/Lau4 wong4

(Cnidii Fructus): 蛇床子: She2 chuang2 zi3/Se4 cong4 zi2

(Catechu): 儿茶 / 兒茶: Er2 cha2/Ji4 caa4

(Camphora): 樟脑 / 樟腦: Zhang1 nao3/Zoeng1 nou5

(Mylabris): 斑蝥: Ban1 mao2/Baan1 maau4

(Bufonis Venenum): 蟾酥: Chan2 su1/Sim4 sou1

(Vespae Nidus): 蜂房 / 蜂房: Feng1 fang2/Fung1 fong4

Formulas (349)
Acrid, Warm Exterior-Resolving Formulas

(Scallion and Prepared Soybean Decoction)
葱豉汤 / 蔥豉湯: Cong1 chi3 tang1/Cung1 si6 tong1
(Allii Fistulosi Bulbus): 葱白 / 蔥白: Cong1 bai2/Cung1 baak6
(Sojae Semen Preparatum) 淡豆豉: Dan2 dou2 chi3/Daam6 dau6 si6

(Ephedra Decoction)
麻黄汤 / 麻黃湯: Ma2 huang2 tang1/Maa4 wong4 tong1
(Ephedrae Herba): 麻黄: Ma2 huang2/Maa4 wong4
(Cinnamomi Ramulus): 桂枝: Gui4 zhi1/Gwai3 zi1
(Armeniacae Semen): 杏仁: Xing4 ren2/Hang6 jan4
(Glycyrrhizae Radix Preparata): 炙甘草: Zhi4 gan1 cao3/Zek3 gam1 cou2

(Three Unbinding Decoction)
三拗汤 / 三拗湯: San1 ao4 tang1/Saam1 aau3 tong1
(Ephedrae Herba): 麻黄: Ma2 huang2/Maa4 wong4
(Armeniacae Semen): 杏仁: Xing4 ren2/Hang6 jan6
(Glycyrrhizae Radix): 炙甘草: Zhi4 gan1 cao3/Zek3 gam1 cou2
(Zingiberis Rhizoma Recens): 生姜 / 生薑: Sheng1 Jiang1/Sang1 goeng1

(Mosla Powder)
香薷散: Xiang1 ru2 san3/Hoeng1 jyu4 saan3
(Moslae Herba): 香薷: Xiang1 ru3/Hoeng1 jyu4
(Dry-fried Lablab Semen Album): 炒扁豆: Chao3 bian3 dou4/Caau2 bin2 dau6
(Ginger Magnoliae Officinalis Cortex): 姜厚朴 / 薑厚朴: Jiang1 hou4 po4/Goeng1 hau5 pok3

(Schizonepeta and Saposhnikovia Powder to Overcome Pathogenic Influences)
荆防败毒散 / 荊防敗毒散: Jing1 fang2 bai4 du2 san3/Ging1 fong4 baai6 duk6 saan3
(Schizonepetae Herba): 荆芥 / 荊芥: Jing1 jie4/Ging1 gaai3
(Saposhikoviae Radix): 防风 / 防風: Fang2 feng1/Fong4 fung1
(Bupleuri Radix): 柴胡: Chai2 hu2/Caai4 wu4
(Peucedani Radix): 前胡: Qian2 hu2/Cin4 wu4
(Chuanxiong Rhizoma): 川芎: Chuan1 xiong1/Cyun1 gung1
(Aurantii Fructus): 枳壳 / 枳殼: Zhi3 ke2/Zi2 hok3
(Notopterygii Rhizoma seu Radix): 羌活: Qiang1 huo2/Goeng1 wut6
(Angelicae Pubescentis Radix): 独活 / 獨活: Du2 huo2/Duk6 wut6
(Poria): 茯苓: Fu2 ling2/Fuk6 ling4
(Platycodi Radix): 桔梗: Jie2 geng3/Gat1 gang2
(Zingiberis Rhizoma Recens): 生姜 / 生薑: Sheng1 jiang1/Sang1 goeng1
(Glycyrrhizae Radix): 甘草: Gan1 cao3/Gam1 cou2

(Magnolia Flower Powder)
辛夷散: Xin1 yi2 san3/San1 ji4 saan3
(Magnoliae Flos): 辛夷花: Xin1 yi2 hua1/San1 ji4 faa1
(Chuanxiong Rhizoma): 川芎: Chuan1 xiong1/Cyun1 gung1
(Akebiae Caulis): 木通: Mu4 tong1/Muk6 tung1
(Asari Herba): 细辛 / 細辛: Xi4 xin1/Sai3 san1
(Saposhnikoviae Radix): 防风 / 防風: Fang2 feng1/Fong4 fung1
(Notopterygii Rhizoma seu Radix): 羌活: Qiang1 huo2/Goeng1 wut6
(Ligustici Rhizoma): 藁本: Gao3 ben3/Gou2 bun2
(Cimicifugae Rhizoma): 升麻: Sheng1 ma2/Sing1 maa4
(Angelicae Dahuricae Radix): 白芷: Bai2 zhi3/Baak6 zi2
(Glycyrrhizae Radix Praeparata): 炙甘草: Zhi4 gan1 cao3/Zek3 gam1 cou2

(Canopy Powder)
华盖散 / 華蓋散: Hua2 gai2 san3/Waa4 goi3 saan3
(Ephedrae Herba): 麻黄: Ma2 huang2/Maa4 wong4
(Armeniacae Semen): 杏仁: Xing4 ren2/Hang6 jan6
(Glycyrrhizae Radix): 炙甘草: Zhi4 gan1 cao3/Zek3 gam1 cou2
(Mori Cortex): 桑白皮: Sang1 bai2 pi2/Song1 Baak6 pei4
(Perillae Fructus): 紫苏子 / 紫蘇子: Zi3 Su1 Zi3/Zi2 sou1 zi2
(Poria Rubra): 赤茯苓: Chi4 fu2 ling2/Cek3 fuk6 ling4
(Citri Reticulatae Pericarpium): 陈皮 / 陳皮: Chen2 pi2/Can4 pei4

(Ephedra with Atractylodis added Decoction)
麻黄加术汤 / 麻黄加術湯: Ma2 huang2 jia1 zhu2 tang1/Maa4 wong4 gaa1 seot6 tong1
(Ephedrae Herba): 麻黄: Ma2 huang2/Maa4 wong4
(Cinnamomi Ramulus): 桂枝: Gui4 zhi1/Gwai3 zi1
(Armeniacae Semen): 杏仁: Xing4 ren2/Hang6 jan4
(Glycyrrhizae Radix Preparata): 炙甘草: Zhi4 gan1 cao3/Zek3 gam1 cou2
(Atractylodis Macrocephalae Rhizoma): 白术 / 白術: Bai2 zhu2/Baak6 seot6

(Minor Bluegreen Dragon Decoction)
小青龙汤 / 小青龍湯: Xiao3 qing1 long2 tang1/Siu2 cing1 lung4 tong1
(Ephedra Herba): 麻黄: Ma2 huang2/Maa4 wong4
(Cinnamomi Ramulus):桂枝: Gui4 zhi1/Gwai3 zi1
(Zingiberis Rhizoma): 干姜 / 乾薑: Gan1 jiang1/Gon1 goeng1
(Asari Radix et Rhizoma): 细辛 / 細辛: Xi4 xin1/Sai3 san1
(Schisandrae Fructus): 五味子: Wu3 wei4 zi3/Ng5 mei6 zi2
(Paeoniae Radix Alba): 白芍: Bai2 shao2/Baak6 zoek3
(Pinelliae Rhizoma Preparatum): 制半夏 / 製半夏: Zhi4 ban4 xia4/Zai3 bun3 haa6
(Glycyrrhizae Radix Preparata): 炙甘草: Zhi4 gan1 cao3/Zek Gam1 cou2

(Major Bluegreen Dragon Decoction)
大青龙汤 / 大青龍湯: Da4 qing1 long2 tang1/Daai6 cing1 lung4 tong1
(Ephedrae Herba): 麻黄: Ma2 huang2/Maa4 wong4
(Armeniacae Semen): 杏仁: Xing4 ren2/Hang6 jan4
(Cinnamomi Ramulus): 桂枝: Gui4 zhi1/Gwai3 zi1
(Glycyrrhizae Radix Preparata): 炙甘草: Zhi4 gan1 cao3/Zek3 gam1 cou2
(Gypsum Fibrosum): 石膏: Shi2 gao1/Sek6 gou1
(Zingiberis Rhizoma Recens): 生姜 / 生薑: Sheng1 jiang1/Sang1 goeng1
(Jujubae Fructus): 大枣 / 大棗: Da4 zao3/Daai6 zou2

(Kudzu Decoction)
葛根汤 / 葛根湯: Ge2 gen1tang1/Got3 gan1 tong1
(Puerariae Radix): 葛根: Ge2 gen1/Got3 gan1
(Ephedrae herba): 麻黄: Ma2 huang2/Maa4 wong4
(Cinnamomi Ramulus): 桂枝: Gui4 zhi1/Gwai3 zi1
(Paeoniae Radix Alba): 白芍: Bai2 shao2/Baak6 zoek3
(Zingiberis Rhizoma Recens): 生姜 / 生薑: Sheng1 jiang1/Sang1 goeng1
(Jujubae Fructus): 大枣 / 大棗: Da4 zao3/Daai6 zou2
(Glycyrrhizae Radix Preparata): 炙甘草: Zhi4 gan1 cao3/Zek3 gam1 cou2

(Cinnamon Twig Decoction)
桂枝汤 / 桂枝湯: Gui4 zhi1 tang1/Gwai3 zi1 tong1
(Cinnamomi Ramulus): 桂枝: Gui4 zhi1/Gwai3 zi1
(Paeoniae Radix Alba): 白芍: Bai2 shao2/Baak6 zoek3
(Glycyrrhizae Radix Preparata): 炙甘草: Zhi4 gan1 cao3/Zek3 gam1 cou2
(Zingiberis Rhizoma Recens): 生姜 / 生薑: Sheng1 jiang1/Sang1 goeng1
(Jujubae Fructus): 大枣 / 大棗: Da4 zao3/Daai6 zou2

(Cinnamon Twig Decoction plus Kudzu Root)
桂枝加葛根汤 / 桂枝加葛根湯: Gui4 zhi1 jia1 ge2 gen1 tang1/Gwai3 zi1 gaa1 got3 gan1 tong1
(Cinnamomi Ramulus): 桂枝: Gui4 zhi1/Gwai3 zi1
(Paeoniae Radix Alba): 白芍: Bai2 shao2/Baak6 zoek3
(Puerariae Radix): 葛根: Ge2 gen1/Got3 gan1
(Glycyrrhizae Radix Preparata): 炙甘草: Zhi4 gan1 cao3/Zek3 gam1 cou2
(Zingiberis Rhizoma Recens): 生姜 / 生薑: Sheng1 jiang1/Sang1 goeng1
(Jujubae Fructus): 大枣 / 大棗: Da4 zao3/Daai6 zou2

(Cinnamon Twig Decoction Plus Magnolia Bark and Apricot Kernel)
桂枝加厚朴杏仁汤 / 桂枝加厚朴杏仁湯: Gui4 zhi1 jia1 hou4 po4 xing4 ren2 tang1/Gwai3 zi1 gaa1 hau5 pok3 hang6 jan4 tong1
(Cinnamomi Ramulus): 桂枝: Gui4 zhi1/Gwai3 zi1
(Paeoniae Radix Alba): 白芍: Bai2 shao2/Baak6 zoek3
(Glycyrrhizae Radix Preparata): 炙甘草: Zhi4 gan1 cao3/Zek3 gam1 cou2
(Zingiberis Rhizoma Recens): 生姜 / 生薑: Sheng1 jiang1/Sang1 goeng1
(Jujubae Fructus): 大枣 / 大棗: Da4 zao3/Daai6 zou2
(Magnoliae Officinalis Cortex): 厚朴: Hou4 po4/Hau5 pok3
(Armeniacae Semen): 杏仁: Xing4 ren2/Hang6 jan4

(Cinnamon, Peony and Anemarrhena Decoction)

桂枝芍药知母汤 / 桂枝芍藥知母湯: Gui4 zhi1 shao2 yao4 zhi1 mu3 tang1/Gwai3 zi1 zoek3 joek6 zi1 mou5 tong1

(Ephedrae Herba): 麻黄: Ma2 huang2/Maa4 wong4

(Atractylodis Macrocephalae Rhizoma): 白术 / 白術: Bai2 zhu2/Baak6 seot6

(Anemarrhenae Rhizoma): 知母: Zhi1 mu3/Zi1 mou5

(Aconiti Radix Lateralis Praeparata): 炮附子: Pao2 fu4 zi3/Paau4 fu6 zi2

(Zingiberis Rhizoma Recens): 生姜 / 生薑: Sheng1 jiang1/Sang1 goeng1

(Cinnamomi Ramulus): 桂枝: Gui4 zhi1/Gwai3 zi1

(Paeoniae Radix Alba): 白芍: Bai2 shao2/Baak6 zoek3

(Saposhnikoviae Radix): 防风 / 防風: Fang2 feng1/Fong4 fung1

(Glycyrrhizae Radix Preparata): 炙甘草: Zhi4 gan1 cao3/Zek3 gam1 cou2

(Jujubae Fructus): 大枣 / 大棗: Da4 zao3/Daai6 zou2

(Five-Accumulation Powder)

五积散 / 五積散: Wu3 ji1 san3/Ng5 zik1 saan3

(Ephedrae Herba): 麻黄: Ma2 huang2/Maa4 wong4

(Angelica Dahuricae Radix): 白芷: Bai2 zhi3/Baak6 zi2

(Zingiberis Rhizome): 干姜 / 乾薑: Gan1 jiang1/Gon1 goeng1

(Cinnamomi Cortex): 肉桂: Rou4 gui4/Juk6 gwai3

(Atractylodis Rhizoma): 苍术 / 蒼術: Cang1 zhu2/Cong1 seot6

(Magnoliae Officinalis Cortex): 厚朴: Hou4 po4/Hau5 pok3

(Citri Reticulatae Pericarpium): 陈皮 / 陳皮: Chen2 pi2/Can4 pei4

(Pinelliae Rhizoma Preparatum): 制半夏 / 製半夏: Zhi4 ban4 xia4/Zai3 bun3 haa6

(Poria): 茯苓: Fu2 ling2/Fuk6 ling4

(Platycodi Radix): 桔梗: Jie2 geng3/Gat1 gang2

(Aurantii Fructus): 枳壳 / 枳殼: Zhi3 ke2/Zi2 hok3

(Angelicae Sinensis Radix): 当归 / 當歸: Dang1 gui1/Dong1 gwai1

(Paeoniae Radix Alba): 白芍: Bai2 shao2/Baak6 zoek3

(Chuanxiong Rhizoma): 川芎: Chuan1 xiong1/Cyun1 gung1

(Glycyrrhizae Radix): 甘草: Gan1 cao3/Gam1 cou2

(Ephedra and Notopterygium Decoction)
麻黄羌活汤 / 麻黃羌活湯: Ma2 huang2 qiang1 huo2 tang1/Maa4 wong4 goeng1 wut6 tong1
(Ephedrae Herba): 麻黃: Ma2 huang2/Maa4 wong4
(Atractylodis Macrocephalae Rhizoma): 白术 / 白術: Bai2 zhu2/Baak6 seot6
(Anemarrhenae Rhizoma): 知母: Zhi1 mu3/Zi1 mou5
(Aconiti Radix Lateralis Praeparata): 炮附子: Pao2 fu4 zi3/Paao4 fu6 zi2
(Zingiberis Rhizoma Recens): 生姜 / 生薑: Sheng1 jiang1/Sang1 goeng1
(Cinnamomi Ramulus): 桂枝: Gui4 zhi1/Gwai3 zi1
(Paeoniae Radix Alba): 白芍: Bai2 shao2/Baak6 zoek
(Saposhnikoviae Radix): 防风 / 防風: Fang2 feng1/Fong4 fung1
(Glycyrrhizae Radix Preparata): 炙甘草: Zhi4 gan1 cao3/Zek3 gam1 cou2
(Notopterygii Rhizoma Seu Radix): 羌活: Qiang1 huo2/Goeng1 wut6
(Asari Radix et Rhizoma): 细辛 / 細辛: Xi4 xin1/Sai3 san1
(Stephaniae Tetrandrae Radix): 汉防己 / 漢防己: Han4 fang2 ji3/Hon3 fong4 gei2
(Poria): 茯苓: Fu2 ling2/Fuk6 ling4

Acrid, Cool Exterior-Resolving Formulas

(Mulberry Leaf and Chrysanthemum Drink)
桑菊饮 / 桑菊飲: Sang1 Ju2 Yin3/Song1 guk1 jam2
(Mori Folium): 桑叶 / 桑葉: Sang1 ye4/Song1 jip6
(Chrysanthemi Flos): 菊花: Jü2 hua1/Guk1 faa1
(Armeniacae Semen): 杏仁: Xing4 ren2/Hang6 jan4
(Forsythiae Fructus): 连翘 / 連翹: Lian2 qiao2/Lin4 kiu4
(Menthae Haplocalycis Herba): 薄荷: Bo4 he2/Bok6 ho4
(Platycodi Radix): 桔梗: Jie2 geng3/Gat1 gang2
(Glycyrrhizae Radix): 甘草: Gan1 cao3/Gam1 cou2
(Phragmitis Rhizoma): 芦根 / 蘆根: Lu2 gen1/Lou4 gan1

(Honeysuckle and Forsythia Powder)
银翘散 / 銀翹散: Yin2 qiao4 san3/Ngan4 kiu4 saan3
(Forsythiae Fructus): 连翘 / 連翹: Lian2 qiao2/Lin4 kiu4
(Lonicerae Flos): 金银花 / 金銀花: Jin1 yin2 hua1/Gam1 ngan4 faa1
(Menthae Haplocalycis Herba): 薄荷: Bo4 he2/Bok6 ho4
(Platycodi Radix): 桔梗: Jie2 geng3/Gat1 gang2
(Lophatherae Herba): 淡竹叶 / 淡竹葉: Dan4 zhu2 ye4/Daam6 zuk1 jip6
(Glycyrrhizae Radix): 甘草: Gan1 cao3/Gam1 cou2
(Schizonepatae Spica): 荆芥穗: Jing1 jie4 sui4/Ging1 gaai3 seoi6
(Sojae Semen Praeparatum): 淡豆豉: Dan4 dou4 chi3/Daam3 dau6 si6
(Arctii Fructus): 牛蒡子: Niu2 bang4 zi3/Ngau4 bong2 zi2
(Phragmitis Rhizoma Recens): 鲜芦根 / 鮮蘆根: Xian1 lu2 gen1/Sin1 lou4 gan1

(Bupleurum and Kudzu Decoction to Release the Muscle Layer)
柴葛解肌汤 / 柴葛解肌湯: Chai2 ge2 jie3 ji1 tang1/Caai4 got3 gaai2 gei1 tong1
(Bupleuri Radix): 柴胡: Chai2 hu2/Caai4 wu4
(Puerariae Radix): 葛根: Ge2 gen1/Got3 gan1
(Notopterygii Rhizoma seu Radix): 羌活: Qiang1 huo1/Goeng1 wut6
(Angelicae Dahuricae Radix): 白芷: Bai2 zhi3/Baak6 zi2
(Scutellariae Radix): 黄芩: Huang2 qin2/Wong4 kam4
(Gypsum Fibrosum): 石膏: Shi2 gao1/Sek6 gou1
(Platycodi Radix): 桔梗: Jie2 geng3/Gat1 gang2
(Paeoniae Radix Alba): 白芍: Bai2 shao2/Baak6 zoek3
(Glycyrrhizae Radix): 甘草: Gan1 cao3/Gam1 cou2
(Zingiberis Rhizoma Recens): 生姜 / 生薑: Sheng1 jiang1/Sang1 goeng1
(Jujubae Fructus): 大枣 / 大棗: Da4 zao3/Daai6 zou2

(Honeysuckle, Forsythia, and Puffball Powder)
银翘马勃散 / 銀翹馬勃散: Yin2 qiao4 ma3 bo2 san3/Ngan4 kiu4 maa5 but6
saan3
(Lonicerae Flos): 金银花 / 金銀花: Jin1 yin2 hua1/Gam1 ngan4 faa1
(Forsythiae Fructus): 连翘 / 連翹: Lian2 qiao2/Lin4 kiu4
(Arctii Fructus): 牛蒡子: Niu2 bang4 zi3/Ngau4 bong2 zi2
(Belamcandae Rhizoma): 射干: She4 gan1/Se6 gon1
(Lasiosphaera/Calvatia): 马勃 / 馬勃: Ma3 bo2/Maa5 but6

(Cimicifuga and Kudzu Decoction)

升麻葛根汤 / 升麻葛根湯: Sheng1 ma2 ge2 gen1 tang1/Sing1 maa4 got3 gan1 tong1

(Cimicifugae Rhizoma): 升麻: Sheng1 ma2/Sing1 maa4

(Puerariae Radix): 葛根: Ge2 gen1/Got3 gan1

(Glycyrrhizae Radix Preparata): 炙甘草: Zhi4 gan1 cao3/Zek3 gam1 cou2

(Paeoniae Radix Rubra): 赤芍: Chi4 shao2/Cek3 zoek3

(Nine-Herb Decoction with Notopterygium)

九味羌活汤 / 九味羌活湯: Jiu3 wei4 qiang1 huo2 tang1/Gau2 mei6 goeng1 wut6 tong1

(Notoperygii Rhizoma seu Radix): 羌活: Qiang1 huo2/Goeng1 wut6

(Saposhnikoviae Radix): 防风 / 防風: Fang2 feng1/Fong4 fung1

(Atractylodis Rhizoma): 苍术 / 蒼術: Cang1 zhu2/Cong1 seot6

(Asari Radix et Rhizoma): 细辛 / 細辛: Xi4 xin1/Sai3 san1

(Chuanxiong Rhizoma): 川芎: Chuan1 xiong1/Cyun1 gung1

(Angelicae Dahuricae Radix): 白芷: Bai2 shi3/Baak6 zi2

(Scutellariae Radix): 黄芩: Huang2 qin1/Wong4 kam4

(Glycyrrhizae Radix): 甘草: Gan1 cao3/Gam1 cou2

(Rehmanniae Radix): 生地黄: Sheng1 di4 huang2/Sang1 dei6 wong4

(Gypsum Decoction)

石膏汤 / 石膏湯: Shi2 gao1 tang1/Sek6 gou1 tong1

(Gypsum Fibrosum): 石膏: Shi2 gao1/Sek6 gou1

(Ephedrae Herba): 麻黄: Ma2 huang2/Maa4 wong4

(Sojae Semen Preparatum): 淡豆豉: Dan4 dou4 chi3/Daam6 dau6 si6

(Coptidis Rhizoma): 黄连 / 黄連: Huang2 qin2/Wong4 lin4 my teacher always referred to this medicinal in its Sichuan form 川连 / 川連: Chuan1 lian2/Cyun1 lin4

(Scutellariae Radix): 黄芩: Huang2 qin2/Wong4 kam4

(Phellodendri Cortex): 黄柏: Huang2 bai2/Wong4 paak3

(Gardeniae Fructus): 栀子 / 梔子: Zhi1 zi3/Zi1 zi2

(Saposhnikovia Powder that Sagely Unblocks)
防风通圣散 / 防風通聖散: Fang2 feng1 tong1 sheng4 san3/Fong4 fung1 tung1 sing3 saan3
(Saposhnikoviae Radix): 防风 / 防風: Fang2 feng1/Fong4 fung1
(Ephedrae Herba): 麻黄: Ma2 huang2/Maa4 wong4
(Rhei Radix et Rhizoma): 大黄: Da4 huang2/Daai6 wong4
(Natrii Sulfas): 硭硝: Mang2 xiao1/Mong4 siu1
(Schizonepetae Herba): 荆芥 / 荊芥: Jing1 jie4/Ging1 gaai3
(Menthae Haplocalycis Herba): 薄荷: Bo4 he2/Bok6 ho4
(Gardeniae Fructus): 栀子 / 梔子: Zhi1 zi3/Zi1 zi2
(Talcum): 滑石: Hua2 shi2/Waat6 sek6
(Gypsum Fibrosum): 石膏: Shi2 gao1/Sek6 gou1
(Forsythiae Fructus): 连翘 / 連翹: Lian2 qiao2/Lin4 kiu4
(Scutellariae Radix): 黄芩: Huang2 qin2/Wong4 kam4
(Platycodi Radix): 桔梗: Jie2 geng3/Gat1 gang2
(Chuanxiong Rhizoma): 川芎: Chuan1 xiong1/Cyun1 gung1
(Angelicae Sinensis Radix): 当归 / 當歸: Dang1 gui1/Dong1 gwai1
(Paeoniae Radix Alba): 白芍: Bai2 shao2/Baak6 zoek3
Atractylodis Macrocephalae Rhizoma): 白术 / 白術: Bai2 zhu2/Baak6 seot6
Glycyrrhizae Radix): 甘草: Gan1 cao3/Gam1 cou2

(Cyperus and Perilla Leaf Powder)
香苏散 / 香蘇散: Xiang1 su1 san3/Hoeng1 sou1 saan3
(Perillae Folium): 紫苏叶 / 紫蘇葉: Zi3 su1 ye4/Zi2 sou1 jip6
(Cyperi Rhizoma): 香附: Xiang1 fu4/Hoeng1 fu6
(Citri Reticulatae Pericarpium): 陈皮 / 陳皮: Chen2 pi2/Can4 pei4
(Glycyrrhizae Radix Preparata): 炙甘草: Zhi4 gan1 cao2/Zek3 gam1 cou2

(Augmented Cyperus and Perilla Leaf Powder)
加味香苏散 / 加味香蘇散: Jia1 wei4 xiang1 su1 san3/Gaa1 mei6 hoeng1 sou1 saan3
(Perillae Folium): 紫苏叶 / 紫蘇葉: Zi3 su1 ye4/Zi2 sou1 jip6
(Cyperi Rhizoma): 香附: Xiang1 fu4/Hoeng1 fu6
(Citri Reticulatae Pericarpium): 陈皮 / 陳皮: Chen2 pi2/Can4 pei4
(Glycyrrhizae Radix Preparata): 炙甘草: Zhi4 gan1 cao2/Zek3 gam1 cou2
(Schizonepatae Herba): 荆芥 / 荊芥: Jing1 jie4/Ging1 gaai3
(Saposhnikoviae Radix): 防风 / 防風: Fang2 feng1/Fong4 fung1
(Gentianae Macrophyllae Radix): 秦艽: Qin2 jiao1/Ceon4 gau2
(Viticis Fructus): 蔓荆子 / 蔓荊子: Man4 jing1 zi3/Maan4 ging1 zi2
(Chuanxiong Rhizoma): 川芎: Chuan1 xiong1/Cyun1 gung1
(Zingiberis Rhizoma Recens): 生姜 / 生薑: Sheng1 jiang1/Sang1 goeng1

Righteous-Supporting and Exterior-Resolving Formulas

(Ginseng Toxin-Vanquishing Powder)
人参败毒散 / 人參敗毒散: Ren2 shen1 bai4 du2 san3/Jan4 sam1 baai6 duk6 saan3
(Bupleuri Radix): 柴胡: Chai2 hu2/Caai4 wu4
(Peucedani Radix): 前胡: Qian2 hu2/Cin4 wu4
(Chuanxiong Rhizoma): 川芎: Chuan1 xiong1/cyun1 gung1
(Bran-fried Aurantii Fructus): 麸炒枳壳 / 麩炒枳殼: Fu1 chao3 zhi3 ke2/Fu1 caau2 zi2 hok3
(Notopterygii Rhizoma seu Radix): 羌活: Qiang1 huo2/Goeng1 wut6
(Angelicae Pubescentis Radix): 独活 / 獨活: Du2 huo2/Duk6 wut6
(Poria): 茯苓: Fu2 ling2/Fuk6 ling4
(Platycodi Radix): 桔梗: Jie2 geng3/Gat1 gang2
(Ginseng Radix): 人参 / 人參: Ren2 shen1/Jan4 sam1
(Glycyrrhizae Radix): 甘草: Gan1 cao3/Gam1 cou2
(Zingiberis Rhizoma Recens): 生姜 / 生薑: Sheng1 jiang1/Sang1 goeng1
(Menthae Haplocalycis Herba): 薄荷: Bo4 he2/Bok6 ho4

(Ginseng and Perilla Drink)
参苏饮 / 參蘇飲: Shen1 su1 yin3/Sam1 sou1 jam2
(Peucedani Radix): 前胡: Qian2 hu2/Cin4 wu4
(Aurantii Fructus): 麸炒枳壳 / 麩炒枳殼: Fu1 chao3 zhi3 ke2/Fu1 caau2 zi2 hok3
(Poria): 茯苓: Fu2 ling2/Fuk6 ling4
(Pinelliae Rhizoma): 姜半夏 / 薑半夏: Ban4 xia4/Bun3 haa6
(Perillae Folium): 紫苏叶 / 紫蘇葉: Zi3 su1 ye4/Zi2 sou1 jip6
(Puerariae Radix): 葛根: Ge2 gen1/Got3 gan1
(Aucklandiae Radix): 木香: Mu4 xiang1/Muk6 hoeng1
(Platycodi Radix): 桔梗: Jie2 geng3/Gat1 gang2
(Ginseng Radix): 人参 / 人參: Ren2 shen1/Jan4 sam1
(Glycyrrhizae Radix): 炙甘草: Zhi4 gan1 cao3/Zek3 gam1 cou2
(Jujubae Fructus): 大枣 / 大棗: Da4 zao3/Daai6 zou2
(Zingiberis Rhizoma Recens): 生姜 / 生薑: Sheng1 jiang1/Sang1 goeng1

(Ephedra, Asarum, and Aconite Accessory Root Decoction)
麻黄细辛附子汤 / 麻黃細辛附子湯: Ma2 huang2 xi4 xin1 fu4 zi3 tang1/Maa4 wong4 sai3 san1 fu6 zi2 tong1
(Ephedra Herba): 麻黄: Ma2 huang2/Maa4 wong4
(Aconiti Radix Lateralis Preparata): 制附子 / 製附子: Zhi4 Fu4 zi3/Zai3 Fu6 zi2
(Asari Radix et Rhizoma): 细辛 / 細辛: Xi4 xin1/Sai3 san1

(Modified Solomon's Seal Decoction):
加减葳蕤汤 / 加減葳蕤湯: Jia1 jian3 wei1 rui2 tang1/Gaa1 gaam2 wai1 jeoi4 tong1
(Polygonati Odorati Rhizoma) 玉竹: Yü4 zhu2/Juk6 zuk1
(Allii Fistulosi Bulbus): 葱白 / 蔥白: Cong1 bai2/Cung1 baak6
(Platycodi Radix): 桔梗: Jie2 geng3/Gat1 gang2
(Sojae Semen Preparatum): 淡豆豉: Dan4 dou4 chi3/Daam6 dau6 si6
(Menthae Haplocalysis Herba): 薄荷: Bo4 he2/Bok6 ho4
(Cynanchi Atrati Radix): 白薇: Bai2 wei1/Baak6 mei4
(Glycyrrhizae Radix Preparata): 炙甘草: Zhi4 gan1 cao3/Zek3 gam1 cou2
(Jujubae Fructus): 大枣 / 大棗: Da4 zao3/Daai6 zou2

Draining and Precipitating Formulas
Cold Precipitating Formulas

(Major Order the Qi Decoction)
大气汤 / 大承氣湯: Da4 cheng2 qi4 tang1/Daai6 sing4 hei3 tong1
(Rhei Radix Et Rhizoma): 大黄: Da4 huang2/Daai6 wong4
(Prepared Magnoliae Officinalis Cortex): 制厚朴 / 製厚朴: Zhi4 hou4 po4/Zai3 hau5 pok3
(Prepared Aurantii Fructus Immaturus): 制枳实 / 製枳實: Zhi4 zhi3 shi2/Zai3 zi2 sat6
(Natrii Sulfas): 砭硝: Mang2 xiao1/Mong4 siu1

(Minor Order the Qi Decoction)
小气汤 / 小承氣湯: Xiao3 cheng2 qi4 tang1/Siu2 sing4 hei3 tong1
(Wine-washed Rhei Radix Et Rhizoma): 酒洗大黄: Jiu3 xi3 da4 huang2/Zau2 sai2 daai6 wong4
(Prepared Magnoliae Officinalis Cortex): 制厚朴 / 製厚朴: Zhi4 hou4 po4/Zai3 hau5 pok3
(Prepared Aurantii Fructus Immaturus): 制枳实 / 製枳實: Zhi4 zhi3 shi2/Zai3 zi2 sat6

(Increase Fluids and Order the Qi Decoction)

增液承气汤 / 增液承氣湯:

Zeng1 ye4 cheng2 qi4 tang1/Zang1 jik6 sing4 hei3 tong1

(Rhei Radix Et Rhizoma): 大黄: Da4 huang2/Daai6 wong4

(Scrophulariae Radix): 玄参 / 玄參: Xuan2 shen1/Jyun4 sam1

(Rehmanniae Radix): 生地黄: Sheng1 di4 huang2/Saang1 dei6 wong4

(Ophiopogonis Radix): 麦门冬 / 麥門冬: Mai4 men2 dong1/Mak6 mun4 dung1

(Natrii Sulfas): 硭硝: Mang2 xiao1/Mong4 siu1

(Yellow Dragon Decoction)

黄龙汤 / 黃龍湯: Huang2 long2 tang1/Wong4 lung4 tong1

(Rhei Radix Et Rhizoma): 大黄: Da4 huang2/Daai6 wong4

(Natrii Sulfas): 硭硝: Mang2 xiao1/Mong4 siu1

(Aurantii Fructus Immaturus): 枳实 / 枳實: Zhi3 shi2/Zi2 sat6

(Magnoliae Officinalis Cortex): 厚朴: Hou4 po4/Hau5 pok3

(Ginseng Radix): 人参 / 人參: Ren2 shen1/Jan4 sam1

(Angelicae Sinensis Radix): 当归 / 當歸: Dang1 gui1/Dong1 gwai1

(Platycodi Radix): 桔梗: Jie2 geng2/Gat1 gang2

(Zingiberis Rhizoma Recens): 生姜 / 生薑: Sheng1 jiang1/Sang1 goeng1

(Jujubae Fructus): 大枣 / 大棗: Da4 zao3/Daai6 zou2

(Glycyrrhizae Radix): 甘草: Gan1 cao3/Gam1 cou2

(Regulate the Stomach Order the Qi Decoction)

调胃承气汤 / 調胃承氣湯: Tiao2 wei4 cheng2 qi4 tang1/Tiu4 wai6 sing4 hei3 tong1

(Rhei Radix Et Rhizoma): 大黄: Da4 huang2/Daai6 wong4

(Natrii Sulfas): 硭硝: Mang2 xiao1/Mong4 siu1

(Glycyrrhizae Radix Preparata): 炙甘草: Zhi4 gan1 cao3/Zek3 gam1 cou2

(Rhubarb and Moutan Decoction)

大黄牡丹汤 / 大黃牡丹湯: Da4 huang2 mu3 dan1 tang1/Daai6 wong4 maau5 daan1 tong1

(Rhei Radix et Rhizoma): 大黄: Da4 huang2/Daai6 wong4

(Natrii Sulfas): 硭硝: Mang2 xiao1/Mong4 siu1

(Moutan Cortex): 牡丹皮: Mu3 dan1 pi2/Maau5 daan1 pei4

(Persicae Semen): 桃仁: Tao2 ren2/Tou4 jan4

(Benincasae Semen): 冬瓜子: Dong1 gua1 zi3/Dung1 gwaa1 zi2

(Compound Major Order the Qi Decoction)

复方大承气汤 / 複方大承氣湯: Fu4 fang1 da4 cheng2 qi4 tang1/Fuk1 fong1 daai6 sing4 hei3 tong1

(Rhei Radix Et Rhizoma): 大黄: Da4 huang2/Daai6 wong4

(Magnoliae Officinalis Cortex): 厚朴: Hou4 po4/Hau5 pok3

(Aurantii Fructus Immaturus): 枳实 / 枳實: Zhi3 shi2/Zi2 sat6

(Natrii Sulfas): 硭硝: Mang2 xiao1/Mong4 siu1

(Persicae Semen): 桃仁: Tao2 ren2/Tou4 jan4

(Paeoniae Radix Rubra): 赤芍: Chi4 shao2/Cek3 zoek3

(Dry-Fried Raphani Semen): 炒莱菔子 / 炒萊菔子: Chao3 lai2 fu2 zi3/Caau2 loi4 fuk6 zi2

(Three-Substance Decoction with Magnolia Bark)

厚朴散物汤 / 厚朴三物湯: Hou4 po4 san1 wu4 tang1/Hau5 pok3 saam1 mat6 tong1

(Magnoliae Officinalis Cortex): 厚朴: Hou4 po4/Hau5 pok3

(Aurantii Fructus Immaturus): 枳实 / 枳實: Zhi3 shi2/Zi2 sat6

(Rhei Radix et Rhizoma): 大黄: Da4 huang2/Daai6 wong4

(Rhubarb and Licorice Decoction)

大黄甘草汤 / 大黃甘草湯: Da4 huang2 gan1 cao3 tang1/Daai6 wong4 gam1 cou2 tong1

(Rhei Radix Et Rhizoma): 大黄: Da4 huang2/Daai6 wong4

(Glycyrrhizae Radix): 甘草: Gan1 cao3/Gam1 cou2

(Major Decoction [for Pathogens] Stuck in the Chest)
大陷胸汤 / 大陷胸湯: Da4 xian4 xiong1 tang1/Daai6 haam6 hung1 tong1
(Kansui Radix): 甘遂: Gan1 sui4/Gam1 seoi6
(Rhei Radix et Rhizoma): 大黄: Da4 huang2/Daai6 wong4
(Natrii Sulfas): 硭硝: Mang2 xiao1/Mong4 siu1

Warm Precipitating Formulas

(Rhubarb and Aconite Decoction)
大黄附子汤 / 大黄附子湯: Da4 huang2 fu4 zi3 tang1/Daai6 wong4 fu6 zi2 tong1
(Rhei Radix Et Rhizoma): 大黄: Da4 huang2/Daai6 wong4
(Baked Aconiti Radix Lateralis): 炮附子: Pao2 fu4 zi3/Paau4 fu6 zi2
(Asari Herba): 细辛 / 細辛: Xi4 xin1/Sai3 San1

(Warm the Spleen Decoction)
温脾汤 / 溫脾湯: Wen1 pi2 tang1/Wan1 pei4 tong1
(Rhei Radix Et Rhizoma): 大黄: Da4 huang2/Daai6 wong4
(Aconiti Radix Lateralis Preparata): 制附子 / 製附子: Zhi4 fu4 zi3/Zai3 fu6 zi2
(Glycyrrhizae Radix): 甘草: Gan1 cao3/Gam1 cou2
(Zingiberis Rhizoma): 干姜 / 乾薑: Gan1 jiang1/Gon1 goeng1

(Three-Substance Pill Prepared for Emergencies)
三物备急丸: San1 wu4 bei4 ji2 wan2/Saam1 mat6 bei6 gap1 jyun2
(Crotonis Semen): 巴豆: Ba1 dou4/Baa1 dau2
(Zingiberis Rhizoma): 干姜 / 乾薑: Gan1 jiang1/Gon1 goeng1
(Rhei Radix et Rhizoma): 大黄: Da4 huang2/Daai6 wong4

Water-Expelling Formulas

(Ten Dates Decoction)
十枣汤 / 十棗湯: Shi2 zao3 tang1/Sap6 zou2 tong1
(Kansui Radix): 甘遂: Gan1 sui4/Gam1 seoi6
(Euphorbiae Pekinensis Radix): 京大戟: Jing1 da4 ji3/Ging1 daai6 gik1
(Genkwa Flos): 芫花: Yuan2 hua1/Jyun4 faa1

(Stephaniae, Zanthoxylum, Tingli Seed, and Rhubarb Pill)
己椒苈黄丸 / 己椒藶黄丸: Ji3 jiao1 li4 huang2 wan2/Gei2 ziu1 lik6 wong4 jyun2
(Stephaniae Tetrandrae Radix): 汉防己 / 漢防己: Han4 fang2 ji3/Hon3 fong4 gei2
(Zanthoxyli Semen): 椒目: Jiao1 mu4/Ziu1 muk6
(Lepidii/Descurainiae Semen): 葶苈子 / 葶藶子: Ting2 li4 zi3/Ting4 lik6 zi2

(Vessel and Vehicle Pill)
舟车丸 / 舟車丸: Zhou1 che1 wan2/Zau1 ce1 jyun2
(Kansui Radix): 甘遂: Gan1 sui4/Gam1 seoi6
(Vinegar Genkwa Flos): 醋芫花: Cu4 yuan2 hua1/Cou3 jyun4 faa1
(Vinegar Euphorbiae Pekinensis Radix): 醋大戟: Cu4 da4 ji3/Cou3 daai6 gik1
(Pharbitidis Semen): 牵牛子 / 牽牛子: Qian1 niu2 zi3/Hin1 ngau4 zi2
(Citri Reticulatae Viride Pericarpium): 青皮: Qing1 pi2/Cing1 pei4
(Citri Reticulatae Pericarpium): 陈皮 / 陳皮: Chen2 pi2/Can4 pei4
(Arecae Semen): 槟榔 / 檳榔: Bing1 lang2/Ban1 long4
(Aucklandiae Radix): 木香: Mu4 xiang1/Muk6 hoeng1
(Calomelas): 轻粉 / 輕粉: Qing1 fen3/Hing1 fan2
[Qing fen is pretty toxic]
(Rhei Radix et Rhizoma): 大黄: Da4 huang2/Daai6 wong4

Moistening and Precipitating Formulas

(Cannabis Seed Pills)
麻子仁丸: Ma2 zi3 ren2 wan2/Maa4 zi2 jan4 jyun2
(Cannabis Semen): 火麻仁: Huo3 ma2 ren2/Fo2 maa4 jan4
(Paeoniae Radix Alba): 白芍: Bai2 shao2/Baak6 zoek6
(Prepared Aurantii Fructus Immaturus): 制枳实 / 製枳實: Zhi4 zhi3 shi2/Zai3 zi2 sat6
(Rhei Radix et Rhizoma): 大黄: Da4 huang2/Daai6 wong4
(Prepared Magnoliae Officinalis Cortex): 制厚朴 / 製厚朴: Zhi4 hou4 po4/Zai3 hau5 pok3
(Armeniacae Semen): 杏仁: Xing4 ren2/Hang6 jan4

(Moisten the Intestines Pill from Master Shen's Book)
润肠丸 / 潤腸丸: Run4 chang2 wan2/Jeon6 coeng4 jyun2
(Cannabis Semen): 火麻仁: Huo3 ma2 ren2/Fo2 maa4 jan4
(Persicae Semen): 桃仁: Tao2 ren2/Tou4 jan4
(Angelicae Sinensis Radix): 当归 / 當歸: Dang1 gui1/Dong1 gwai1
(Rehmanniae Radix): 生地黄: Sheng1 di4 huang2/Sang1 dei6 wong4
(Aurantii Fructus): 枳壳 / 枳殼: Zhi3 ke2/Zi2 hok3

(Benefit the River Decoction)
济川煎 / 濟川煎: Ji4 Chuan1 jian1/Zai3 cyun1 zin1
(Wine-prepared Cistanches Herba): 酒苁蓉 / 酒蓯蓉: Jiu3 cong1 rong2/Zau2 cung1 jung4
(Angelicae Sinensis Radix): 当归 / 當歸: Dang1 gui1/Dong1 gwai1
(Achyranthis Radix): 牛膝: Niu2 xi1/Ngau4 sat1 My teacher always wrote this "cow seven" or 牛七: Niu2 qi1/Ngau4 cat1
(Alismatis Rhizoma): 泽泻 / 澤瀉: Ze2 xie4/Zaak6 se3
(Aurantii Fructus): 枳壳 / 枳殼: Zhi3 ke2/Zi2 hok3
(Cimicifugae Rhizoma): 升麻: Sheng1 ma2/Sing1 maa4

Harmonizing and Resolving Formulas

(Minor Bupleurum Decoction)
小柴胡汤 / 小柴胡湯: Xiao3 chai2 hu2 tang1/Siu2 caai4 wu4 tong1
(Bupleuri Radix): 柴胡: Chai2 hu2/Caai4 wu4
(Scutellariae Radix): 黄芩: Huang2 qin2/Wong4 kam4
(Ginseng Radix): 人参 / 人參: Ren2 shen1/Jan4 sam1
(Pinelliae Rhizoma Preparatum): 制半夏 / 製半夏: Zhi4 ban4 xia4/Zai3 bun3 haa6
(Glycyrrhizae Radix Prepaerata): 炙甘草: Zhi4 gan1 cao3/Zek3 gam1 cou2
(Zingiberis Rhizoma Recens): 生姜 / 生薑: Sheng1 jiang1/Sang1 goeng1
(Jujubae Fructus): 大枣 / 大棗: Da4 zao3/Daai6 zou2

(Bupleurum and Four-Substance Decoction)
柴胡四物汤 / 柴胡四物湯: Chai2 hu2 si4 wu4 tang1/Caai4 wu4 sei3 mat6 tong1
(Bupleuri Radix): 柴胡: Chai2 hu2/Caai4 wu4
(Scutellariae Radix): 黄芩: Huang2 qin2/Wong4 kam4
(Pinelliae Rhizoma Preparatum): 制半夏 / 製半夏: Zhi4 ban4 xia4/Zai3 bun3 haa6
(Glycyrrhizae Radix Preparata): 炙甘草: Zhi4 gan1 cao3/Zek3 gam1 cou2
(Ginseng Radix): 人参 / 人參: Ren2 shen1/Jan4 sam1
(Paeoniae Radix Alba): 白芍: Bai2 shao2/Baak6 zoek3
(Rehmanniae Radix Preparata): 熟地黄: Shu2 di4 huang2/Suk6 dei6 wong4
(Angelicae Sinensis Radix): 当归 / 當歸: Dang1 gui1/Dong1 gwai1
(Chuanxiong Rhizoma): 川芎: Chuan1 xiong1/Cyun1 gung1

(Bupleurum Plus Dragon Bone and Oyster Shell Decoction)
柴胡加龙骨牡蛎汤 / 柴胡加龍骨牡蠣湯
Chai2 hu2 jia1 long2 gu3 mu3 li4 tang1/Caai4 wu4 gaa1 lung4 gwat1 maau5 lai6 tong1
(Bupleuri Radix): 柴胡: Chai2 hu2/Caai4 wu4
(Scutellariae Radix): 黄芩: Huang2 qin2/Wong4 kam4
(Pinelliae Rhizoma Preparatum): 制半夏 / 製半夏: Zhi4 ban4 xia4/Zai3 bun3 haa6
(Ginseng Radix): 人参 / 人參: Ren2 shen1/Jan4 sam1
(Zingiberis Rhizoma Recens): 生姜 / 生薑: Sheng1 jiang1/Sang1 goeng1
(Cinnamomi Ramulus): 桂枝: Gui4 zhi1/Gwai3 zi1
(Poria): 茯苓: Fu2 ling2/Fuk6 ling4
(Fossilia Ossis Mastodi): 龙骨 / 龍骨: Long2 gu3/Lung4 gwat1
(Ostreae Concha): 牡蛎 / 牡蠣: Mu3 li4/Maau5 lai6
(Rhei Radix et Rhizoma): 大黄: Da4 huang2/Daai6 wong4
(Jujubae Fructus): 大枣 / 大棗: Da4 zao3/Daai6 zou2
(Minium): 铅丹 / 鉛丹: Qian1 dan1/Jyun4 daan1

(Bupleurum Leveling Decoction)
柴平汤 / 柴平湯: Chai2 ping2 tang1/Caai4 ping4 tong1
(Bupleuri Radix): 柴胡: Chai2 hu2/Caai4 wu4
(Scutellariae Radix): 黄芩: Huang2 qin2/Wong4 kam4
(Ginseng Radix): 人参 / 人參: Ren2 shen1/Jan4 sam1
(Pinelliae Rhizoma Preparatum): 制半夏 / 製半夏: Zhi4 ban4 xia4/Zai3 bun3 haa6
(Glycyrrhizae Radix): 甘草: Gan1 cao3/Gam1 cou2
(Atractylodis Rhizoma): 苍术 / 蒼術: Cang1 zhu2/Cong1 seot1
(Magnoliae Officinalis Cortex): 厚朴: Hou4 po4/Hau5 pok3
(Citri Reticulatae Pericarpium): 陈皮 / 陳皮: Chen2 pi2/Can4 pei4

(Bupleurum Fall Decoction/Bupleurum Chest Bind Decoction)
柴陷汤 / 柴陷湯: Chai4 xian4 tang1/Caai4 haam6 tong1
(Scutellariae Radix): 黄芩: Huang2 qin2/Wong4 kam4
(Ginseng Radix): 人参 / 人參: Ren2 shen1/Jan4 sam1
(Pinelliae Rhizoma Preparatum): 制半夏 / 製半夏: Zhi4 ban4 xia4/Zai3 bun3 haa6
(Glycyrrhizae Radix): 甘草: Gan1 cao3/Gam1 cou2
(Zingiberis Rhizoma Recens): 生姜 / 生薑: Sheng1 jiang1/Sang1 goeng1
(Jujubae Fructus): 大枣 / 大棗: Da4 zao3/Daai6 zou2
(Coptidis Rhizoma): 黄连 / 黃連: Huang2 lian2/Wong4 lin4
my teacher used to always refer to the Sichuan version of this and called it
川连 / 川連: Chuan1 lian2/Cyun1 lin4
(Trichosanthis Semen): 瓜蒌仁 / 瓜蔞仁: Gua1 lou2 ren2/Gwaa1 lau4 jan4
(Bupleuri Radix): 柴胡: Chai2 hu2/Caai4 wu4

(Bupleurum and Cinnamon Decoction)
柴胡桂枝汤 / 柴胡桂枝湯: Chai2 hu2 gui4 zhi1 tang1/Caai4 wu4 gwai3 zi1 tong1
(Bupleuri Radix): 柴胡: Chai2 hu2/Caai4 wu4
(Scutellariae Radix): 黄芩: Huang2 qin2/Wong4 kam4
(Ginseng Radix): 人参 / 人參: Ren2 shen1/Jan4 sam1
(Pinelliae Rhizoma Preparatum): 制半夏 / 製半夏: Zhi4 ban4 xia4/Zai3 bun3 haa6
(Glycyrrhizae Radix): 甘草: Gan1 cao3/Gam1 cou2
(Zingiberis Rhizoma Recens): 生姜 / 生薑: Sheng1 jiang1/Sang1 goeng1
(Jujubae Fructus): 大枣 / 大棗: Da4 zao3/Daai6 zou2
(Cinnamomi Ramulus): 桂枝: Gui4 zhi1/Gwai3 zi1
(Paeoniae Radix Alba): 白芍: Bai2 shao2/Baak6 zoek3

(Gentiana Macrophylla Support Marked Emaciation Decoction)
秦艽扶羸汤 / 秦艽扶羸湯: Qin2 jiao1 fu2 lei2 tang1/Ceon4 kau4 fu4 leoi4 tong1
(Bupleuri Radix): 柴胡: Chai2 hu2/Caai4 wu4
(Scutellariae Radix): 黄芩: Huang2 qin2/Wong4 kam4
(Ginseng Radix): 人参 / 人參: Ren2 shen1/Jan4 sam1
(Pinelliae Rhizoma Preparatum): 制半夏 / 製半夏: Zhi4 ban4 xia4/Zai3 bun3 haa6
(Glycyrrhizae Radix): 甘草: Gan1 cao3/Gam1 cou2
(Zingiberis Rhizoma Recens): 生姜 / 生薑: Sheng1 jiang1/Sang1 goeng1
(Jujubae Fructus): 大枣 / 大棗: Da4 zao3/Daai6 zou2
(Gentianae Macrophyllae Radix): 秦艽: Qin2 jiao1/Ceon4 kau4
(Lycii Cortex): 地骨皮: Di4 gu3 pi2/Dei6 gwat1 pei4
(Asteris Radix): 紫菀: Zi3 wan3/Zi2 jyun2
(Trionycis Carapax): 鳖甲 / 鱉甲: Bie1 jia3/Bit3 gaap3
(Angelicae Sinensis Radix): 当归 / 當歸: Dang1 gui1/Dong1 gwai1
(Mume Fructus): 乌梅 / 烏梅: Wu1 mei2/Wu1 mui4

(Bupleurum and Mirabilitum Decoction)
柴胡加硭硝汤 / 柴胡加硭硝湯: Chai2 hu2 jia1 mang2 xiao1 tang1/Caai4 wu4 gaa1 mong4 siu1 tong1
(Bupleuri Radix): 柴胡: Chai2 hu2/Caai4 wu4
(Scutellariae Radix): 黄芩: Huang2 qin2/Wong4 kam4
(Ginseng Radix): 人参 / 人參: Ren2 shen1/Jan4 sam1
(Pinelliae Rhizoma Preparatum): 制半夏 / 製半夏: Zhi4 ban4 xia4/Zai3 bun3 haa6
(Glycyrrhizae Radix Praeparata): 炙甘草: Zhi4 gan1 cao3/Zek3 gam1 cou2
(Zingiberis Rhizoma Recens): 生姜 / 生薑: Sheng1 jiang1/Sang1 goeng1
(Jujubae Fructus): 大枣 / 大棗: Da4 zao3/Daai6 zou2
(Natrii Sulfas): 硭硝: Mang2 xiao1/Mong4 siu1

(Bupleurum, Citrus and Platycodon Decoction)

柴胡枳桔汤 / 柴胡枳桔湯: Chai2 hu2 zhi3 jie2 tang1/Caai4 wu4 zi2 gat1 tong1

(Bupleuri Radix): 柴胡: Chai2 hu2/Caai4 wu4

(Scutellariae Radix): 黄芩: Huang2 qin2/Wong4 kam4

(Ginger-Fried Pinelliae Rhizoma Preparatum): 姜半夏 / 薑半夏: Jiang1 ban4 xia4/Goeng1 bun3 haa6

(Tea picked before early May): 谷雨茶 / 穀雨茶: Gu3 yü3 cha2/Guk1 jyu5 caa4

(Glycyrrhizae Radix): 甘草: Gan1 cao3/Gam1 cou2

(Zingiberis Rhizoma Recens): 生姜 / 生薑: Sheng1 jiang1/Sang1 goeng1

(Aurantii Fructus): 枳壳 / 枳殼: Zhi3 ke2/Zi2 hok3

(Platycododi Radix): 桔梗: Jie2 geng3/Gat1 gang2

(Citri Reticulatae Pericarpium): 陈皮 / 陳皮: Chen2 pi2/Can4 pei4

(Major Bupleurum Decoction)

大柴胡汤 / 大柴胡湯: Da4 chai2 hu2 tang1/Daai6 caai4 wu4 tong1

(Bupleuri Radix): 柴胡: Chai2 hu2/Caai4 wu4

(Scutellariae Radix): 黄芩: Huang2 qin2/Wong4 kam4

(Pinelliae Rhizoma Preparatum): 制半夏 / 製半夏: Zhi4 ban4 xia4/Zai3 bun3 haa6

(Zingiberis Rhizoma Recens): 生姜 / 生薑: Sheng1 jiang1/Sang1 goeng1

(Jujubae Fructus): 大枣 / 大棗: Da4 zao3/Daai6 zou2

(Rhei Radix et Rhizoma): 大黄: Da4 huang2/Daai6 wong4

(Paeoniae Radix Alba): 白芍: Bai2 shao2/Baak6 zoek3

(Prepared Aurantii Fructus Immaturus): 制枳实 / 製枳實: Zhi4 Zhi3 shi2/Zai3 zi2 sat6

(Sweet Wormwood and Scutellaria Decoction to Clear the Gallbladder)

蒿芩清胆汤 / 蒿芩清膽湯: Hao1 qin2 qing1 dan3 tang1/Hou1 kam4 cing1 daam2 tong1

(Artemisiae Annuae Herba): 青蒿: Qing1 hao1/Cing1 hou1

(Scutellariae Radix): 黄芩: Huang2 qin2/Wong4 kam4

(Bambusae Caulis in Taeniam): 竹茹: Zhu2 ru2/Zuk1 jyu4

(Aurantii Fructus): 枳壳 / 枳殼: Zhi3 ke2/Zi2 hok3

(Citri Reticulatae Pericarpium): 陈皮 / 陳皮: Chen2 pi2/Can4 pei4

(Pinelliae Rhizoma Preparatum): 制半夏 / 製半夏: Zhi4 ban4 xia4/Zaie Bun3 haa6

(Poria Rubra): 赤茯苓: Chi4 fu2 ling2/Cek3 fuk6 ling4

(Jasper Powder): 碧玉散: Bi4 yü4 san3/Bik1 juk6 saan3

Regulating and Harmonizing the Liver and Spleen Formulas

(Four Counterflows Powder)
四逆散: Si4 Ni4 San3/Sei3 jik6 saan3
(Glycyrrhizae Radix Preparata): 炙甘草: Zhi4 gan1 cao3/Zek3 gam1 cou2
(Dry-Fried Aurantii Fructus Immaturus): 炒枳实 / 炒枳實: Chao3 zhi3 shi2/Caao2 zi2 sat6
(Bupleuri Radix): 柴胡: Chai2 hu2/Caai4 wu4
(Peioniae Radix Alba): 白芍: Bai2 shao2/Baak6 zoek3

(Rambling Powder)
逍遥散 / 逍遙散: Xiao1 yao2 san3/Siu1 jiu4 saan3
(Bupleuri Radix): 柴胡: Chai2 hu2/Caai4 wu4
(Dry-Fried Angelicae Sinensis Radix): 炒当归 / 炒當歸: Chao3 dang1 gui1/Caau2 dong1 gwai1
(Paeoniae Radix Alba): 白芍: Bai2 shao2/Baak6 zoek3
(Atractylodis Macrocephalae Rhizoma): 白术 / 白術: Bai2 zhu2/Baak6 seot6
(Poria): 茯苓: Fu2 ling2/Fuk6 ling4
(Glycyrrhizae Radix Preparata): 炙甘草: Zhi4 gan1 cao3/Zek3 Gam1 cou2
(Menthae Haplocalycis Herba): 薄荷: Bo4 he2/Bok6 ho4
(Baked Zingiberis Rhizoma Recens): 煨姜 / 煨薑: Wei1 jiang1/Wui1 goeng1

(Moutan and Gardenia Rambling Powder)
丹栀逍遥散 / 丹栀逍遙散: Dan1 zhi1 xiao1 yao2 san3/Daan1 zi1 siu1 jiu4 saan3
also called
加味逍遥散 / 加味逍遙散: Jia1 wei4 xiao1 yao2 san3/Gaa1 mei6 siu1 jiu4 saan3
(Bupleuri Radix): 柴胡: Chai2 hu2/Caai4 wu4
(Angelicae Sinensis Radix): 当归 / 當歸: Dang1 gui1/Dong1 gwai1
(Paeoniae Radix Alba): 白芍: Bai2 shao2/Baak6 zoek3
(Dry-Fried Atractylodis Macrocephalae Rhizoma): 炒白术 / 炒白術: Chao3 bai2 zhu2/Caao2 baak6 seot6
(Poria): 茯苓: Fu2 ling2/Fuk6 ling4
(Glycyrrhizae Radix Preparata): 炙甘草: Zhi4 gan1 cao3/Zek3 Gam1 cou2
(Menthae Haplocalycis Herba): 薄荷: Bo4 he2/Bok6 ho4
(Zingiberis Rhizoma Recens): 生姜 / 生薑: Sheng1 jiang1/Sang1 goeng1
(Dry-Fried Gardeniae Fructus) 炒栀子 / 炒栀子: Chao3 zhi1 zi3/Caao2 zi1 zi2
(Radicis Moutan Cortex): 牡丹皮: Mu3 dan1 pi2/Maau5 daan1 pei4

(Black Rambling Powder)
黑逍遥散 / 黑逍遙散: Hei1 xiao1 yao2 san3/Hak1 siu1 jiu4 saan3
(Bupleuri Radix): 柴胡: Chai2 hu2/Caai4 wu4
(Dry-Fried Angelicae Sinensis Radix): 炒当归 / 炒當歸: Chao3 dang1 gui1/Caau2 dong1 gwai1
(Paeoniae Radix Alba): 白芍: Bai2 shao2/Baak6 zoek3
(Atractylodis Macrocephalae Rhizoma): 白术 / 白術: Bai2 zhu2/Baak6 seot6
(Poria): 茯苓: Fu2 ling2/Fuk6 ling4
(Glycyrrhizae Radix Preparata): 炙甘草: Zhi4 gan1 cao3/Zek3 Gam1 cou2
(Menthae Haplocalycis Herba): 薄荷: Bo4 he2/Bok6 ho4
(Baked Zingiberis Rhizoma Recens): 煨姜 / 煨薑: Wei1 jiang1/Wui1 goeng1
(Rehmanniae Radix): 熟地黄: Shu2 di4 huang2/Suk6 dei6 wong4

(Support the Spleen and Soothe the Liver Decoction)
扶脾舒肝汤 / 扶脾舒肝湯: Fu2 pi2 shu1 gan1 tang1/Fu4 pei4 syu1 gon1 tong1
(Bupleuri Radix): 柴胡: Chai2 hu2/Caai4 wu4
(Paeoniae Radix Alba): 白芍: Bai2 shao2/Baak6 zoek3
(Atractylodis Macrocephalae Rhizoma): 白术 / 白術: Bai2 zhu2/Baak6 seot6
(Poria): 茯苓: Fu2 ling2/Fuk6 ling4
(Menthae Haplocalycis Herba): 薄荷: Bo4 he2/Bok6 ho4
(Zingiberis Rhizoma Recens): 生姜 / 生薑: Sheng1 jiang1/Sang1 goeng1
(Adenophorae Radix): 南沙参 / 南沙參: Nan2 sha1 shen1/Naam4 saa1 sam1
(Dry-Fried Typhae Pollen): 炒蒲黄: Chao3 pu2 huang2/Caau2 pou4 wong4
(Crinis Carbonisatus): 血余炭 / 血餘炭: Xue4 yü2 tan4/Hyut3 jyu4 taan3
(Charred Artemesiae Argyi Folium): 艾叶炭 / 艾葉炭: Ai4 ye4 tan4/Ngaai6 jip6 taan3

(Soothe Depression and Clear the Liver Drink)
疏郁清肝饮 / 疏鬱清肝飲: Shu1 yu4 qing1 gan1 tang1/So1 jyu4 cing1 gon1 jam2
(Bupleuri Radix): 柴胡: Chai2 hu2/Caai4 wu4
(Paeoniae Radix Alba): 白芍: Bai2 shao2/Baak6 zoek3
(Atractylodis Macrocephalae Rhizoma): 白术 / 白術: Bai2 zhu2/Baak6 seot6
(Poria): 茯苓: Fu2 ling2/Fuk6 ling4
(Menthae Haplocalycis Herba): 薄荷: Bo4 he2/Bok6 ho4
(Zingiberis Rhizoma Recens): 生姜 / 生薑: Sheng1 jiang1/Sang1 goeng1
(Gardeniae Fructus): 栀子 / 梔子: Zhi1 zi3/Zi1 zi2
(Leonuri Herba): 益母草: Yi4 mu3 cao3/Jik1 mou5 cou2

(Bupleurum Powder to Dredge the Liver)

柴胡疏肝散: Chai2 hu2 shu1 gan1 san3/Caai4 wu4 so1 gon1 saan3

(Vinegar-Fried Citri Reticulatae Pericarpium): 醋炒陈皮 / 醋炒陳皮: Cu4 chao3 chen2 pi2/Cou3 caau2 can4 pei4

(Bupleuri Radix): 柴胡: Chai2 hu2/Caai4 wu4

(Chuanxiong Rhizoma): 川芎: Chuan1 xiong1/Cyun1 gung1

(Dry-Fried Aurantii Fructus): 炒枳壳 / 炒枳殼: Chao3 zhi3 ke2/Caau2 zi2 hok3

(Paeoniae Radix Alba): 白芍: Bai2 shao2/Baak6 zoek3

(Glycyrrhizae Radix Preparata): 炙甘草: Zhi4 gan1 cao3/Zek3 gam1 cou2

(Cyperi Rhizoma): 香附: Xiang1 fu4/Hoeng1 fu6

(Important Formula for Painful Diarrhea)

通泻要方 / 痛瀉腰方: Tong4 xie4 yao4 fang1/Tung3 se3 jiu3 fong1

(Dry-Fried Atractylodis Macrocephalae Rhizoma): 炒白术 / 炒白術: Chao3 bai2 zhu2/Caau2 baak6 seot6

(Dry-Fried Paeoniae Radix Alba): 炒白芍: Chao3 bai2 shao2/Caau2 baak6 zoek3

(Dry-Fried Citri Reticulatae Pericarpium): 炒陈皮 / 炒陳皮: Chao3 chen2 pi2/Caau2 can4 pei4

(Saposhnikoviae Radix): 防风 / 防風: Fang2 feng2/Fong4 fung1

Regulating and Harmonizing the Intestines and Stomach Formulas

(Pinellia Drain the Heart Decoction)

半夏泻心汤 / 半夏瀉心湯: Ban4 xia4 xie4 xin1 tang1/Bun3 haa6 se2 sam1 tong1

(Pinelliae Rhizoma Preparatum): 制半夏 / 製半夏: Zhi4 ban4 xia4/Zai3 bun3 haa6

(Scutellariae Radix): 黄芩: Huang2 qin2/Wong4 kam4

(Zingiberis Rhizoma): 干姜 / 乾薑: Gan1 jiang1/Gon1 goeng1

(Ginseng Radix): 人参 / 人參: Ren2 shen1/Jan4 sam1

(Glycyrrhizae Radix Preparata): 炙甘草: Zhi4 gan1 cao3/Zek3 gam1 cou2

(Coptidis Rhizoma): 黄连 / 黃連: Huang2 lian2/Wong4 lin4

my teacher always referred to this in it's Sichuan version 川连 / 川連: Chuan1 lian2/Cyun1 lin4

(Jujubae Fructus): 大枣 / 大棗: Da4 zao3/Daai6 zou2

(Licorice Drain the Heart Decoction)

甘草泻心汤 / 甘草瀉心湯: Gan1 cao3 xie4 xin1 tang1/Gam1 cou2 se3 sam1 tong1

(Pinelliae Rhizoma Preparatum): 制半夏 / 製半夏: Zhi4 ban4 xia4/Zai3 bun3 haa6

(Scutellariae Radix): 黄芩: Huang2 qin2/Wong4 kam4

(Zingiberis Rhizoma): 干姜 / 乾薑: Gan1 jiang1/Gon1 goeng1

(Ginseng Radix): 人参 / 人參: Ren2 shen1/Jan4 sam1

(Glycyrrhizae Radix Preparata): 炙甘草: Zhi4 gan1 cao3/Zek3 gam1 cou2/dose increased to 12-15 grams from 6 grams

(Coptidis Rhizoma): 黄连 / 黃連: Huang2 lian2/Wong4 lin4

my teacher always referred to this in it's Sichuan version 川连 / 川連: Chuan1 lian2/Cyun1 lin4

(Jujubae Fructus): 大枣 / 大棗: Da4 zao3/Daai6 zou2

(Fresh Ginger Drain the Heart Decoction):

生姜泻心汤 / 生薑瀉心湯: Sheng1 jiang1 xie4 xin1 tang1/Sang1 goeng1 se3 sam1 tong1

(Pinelliae Rhizoma Preparatum): 制半夏 / 製半夏: Zhi4 ban4 xia4/Zai3 bun3 haa6

(Scutellariae Radix): 黄芩: Huang2 qin2/Wong4 kam4

(Zingiberis Rhizoma Recens): 生姜 / 生薑: Sheng1 jiang1/Sang1 goeng1

(Ginseng Radix): 人参 / 人參: Ren2 shen1/Jan4 sam1

(Glycyrrhizae Radix Preparata): 炙甘草: Zhi4 gan1 cao3/Zek3 gam1 cou2

(Coptidis Rhizoma): 黄连 / 黃連: Huang2 lian2/Wong4 lin4

my teacher always referred to this in it's Sichuan version 川连 / 川連: Chuan1 lian2/Cyun1 lin4

(Jujubae Fructus): 大枣 / 大棗: Da4 zao3/Daai6 zou2

(Zingiberis Rhizoma): 干姜 / 乾薑: Gan1 jiang1/Gon1 goeng1

(Coptis Decoction)
黄连汤 / 黄連湯: Huang2 lian2 tang1/Wong4 lin4 tong1
(Pinelliae Rhizoma Preparatum): 制半夏 / 製半夏: Zhi4 ban4 xia4/Zai3 bun3 haa6
(Cinnamomi Ramulus): 桂枝: Gui4 zhi1/Gwai3 zi1
(Zingiberis Rhizoma): 干姜 / 乾薑: Gan1 jiang1/Gon1 goeng1
(Ginseng Radix): 人参 / 人參: Ren2 shen1/Jan4 sam1
(Glycyrrhizae Radix Preparata): 炙甘草: Zhi4 gan1 cao3/Zek3 gam1 cou2
(Coptidis Rhizoma): 黄连 / 黃連: Huang2 lian2/Wong4 lin4
my teacher always referred to this in it's Sichuan version 川连 / 川連: Chuan1 lian2/Cyun1 lin4
(Jujubae Fructus): 大枣 / 大棗: Da4 zao3/Daai6 zou2

Heat Clearing Formulas
a.Clearing Heat From the Qi Division

(White Tiger Decoction)
白虎汤 / 白虎湯: Bai2 hu3 tang1/Baak6 fu2 tong1
(Gypsum Fibrosum): 石膏: Shi2 gao1/Sek6 gou1
(Anemarrhenae Rhizoma): 知母: Zhi1 mu3/Zi1 mou5
(Glycyrrhizae Radix Preparata): 炙甘草: Zhi4 gan1 cao3/Zek3 gam1 cou2
(Nonglutinous Rice): 精米: Jing1 mi3/Zing1 mai5

(Ginseng White Tiger Decoction)
人参白虎汤 / 人參白虎湯: Ren2 shen1 bai2 hu3 tang1/Jan4 sam1 baak6 fu2 tong1
(Gypsum Fibrosum): 石膏: Shi2 gao1/Sek6 gou1
(Anemarrhenae Rhizoma): 知母: Zhi1 mu3/Zi1 mou5
(Glycyrrhizae Radix Preparata): 炙甘草: Zhi4 gan1 cao3/Zek3 gam1 cou2
(Nonglutinous Rice): 精米: Jing1 mi3/Zing1 mai5
(Ginseng Radix): 人参 / 人參: Ren2 shen1/Jan4 sam1

(White Tiger Plus Atractylodis Decoction)
白虎加苍术汤 / 白虎加蒼術湯: Bai2 hu3 jia1 cang1 zhu2 tang1/Baak6 fu2 gaa1 cong1 seot6 tong1
(Gypsum Fibrosum): 石膏: Shi2 gao1/Sek6 gou1
(Anemarrhenae Rhizoma): 知母: Zhi1 mu3/Zi1 mou5
(Glycyrrhizae Radix Preparata): 炙甘草: Zhi4 gan1 cao3/Zek3 gam1 cou2
(Nonglutinous Rice): 精米: Jing1 mi3/Zing1 mai5
(Atractylodis Rhizoma): 苍术 / 蒼術: Cang1 zhu2/Cong1 seot6

(White Tiger Plus Cinnamon Decoction)

白虎加桂枝汤 / 白虎加桂枝湯: Bai2 hu3 jia1 gui4 zhi1 tang1/Baak6 fu2 gaa1 Gwai3 zi1 tong1
(Gypsum Fibrosum): 石膏: Shi2 gao1/Sek6 gou1
(Anemarrhenae Rhizoma): 知母: Zhi1 mu3/Zi1 mou5
(Glycyrrhizae Radix Preparata): 炙甘草: Zhi4 gan1 cao3/Zek3 gam1 cou2
(Nonglutinous Rice): 精米: Jing1 mi3/Zing1 mai5
(Cinnamomi Ramulus): 桂枝: Gui4 zhi1/Gwai3 zi1

(White Tiger Order the Qi Decoction)
白虎承气汤 / 白虎承氣湯: Bai2 hu3 cheng2 qi4 tang1/Baak6 fu2 sing4 hei3 tong1
(Gypsum Fibrosum): 石膏: Shi2 gao1/Sek6 gou1
(Anemarrhenae Rhizoma): 知母: Zhi1 mu3/Zi1 mou5
(Glycyrrhizae Radix Preparata): 炙甘草: Zhi4 gan1 cao3/Zek3 gam1 cou2
(Nonglutinous Rice): 精米: Jing1 mi3/Zing1 mai5
(Rhei Radix et Rhizoma): 大黄: Da4 huang2/Daai6 wong4
(Natrii Sulfas): 磁硝: Mang2 xiao1/Mong4 siu1

(Bupleurum White Tiger Decoction)
柴胡白虎汤 / 柴胡白虎湯: Chai2 hu2 bai2 hu3 tang1/Caai4 wu4 baak6 fu2 tong1
(Gypsum Fibrosum): 石膏: Shi2 gao1/Sek6 gou1
(Anemarrhenae Rhizoma): 知母: Zhi1 mu3/Zi1 mou5
(Glycyrrhizae Radix): 甘草: Gan1 cao3/Gam1 cou2
(Nonglutinous Rice): 精米: Jing1 mi3/Zing1 mai5
(Bupleurum Radix): 柴胡: Chai2 hu2/Caai4 wu4
(Scutellariae Radix): 黄芩: Huang2 qin2/Wong4 kam4
(Trichosanthis Radix): 天花粉: Tian1 hua1 fen3/Tin1 faa1 fan2
(Nelumbinis Folium Recens): 鲜荷叶 / 鮮荷葉: Xian1 he2 ye4/Sin1 ho4 jip6

(Suppress Counterflow White Tiger Decoction):
镇逆白虎汤 / 鎮逆白虎湯: Zhen4 ni4 bai2 hu3 tang1/Zan3 jik6 baak6 fu2 tong1
(Gypsum Fibrosum): 石膏: Shi2 gao1/Sek6 gou1
(Anemarrhenae Rhizoma): 知母: Zhi1 mu3/Zi1 mou5
(Pinelliae Rhizoma Preparatum): 制半夏 / 製半夏: Zhi4 ban4 xia4/Zai3 bun3 haa6
(Bambusae Caulis in Taeniam): 竹茹: Zhu2 ru2/Zuk1 jyu4

(Bamboo Leaf and Gypsum Decoction)

竹叶石膏汤 / 竹葉石膏湯: Zhu2 ye4 shi2 gao1 tang1/Zuk1 jip6 sek6 gou1 tong1

(Gypsum Fibrosum): 石膏: Shi2 gao1/Sek6 gou1

(Glycyrrhizae Radix Preparata): 炙甘草: Zhi4 gan1 cao3/Zek3 gam1 cou2

(Nonglutinous Rice): 精米: Jing1 mi3/Zing1 mai5

(Ginseng Radix): 人参 / 人參: Ren2 shen1/Jan4 sam1

(Lophatheri Herba): 淡竹叶 / 淡竹葉: Dan4 zhu2 ye4/Daam6 zuk1 jip6

(Ophiopogonis Radix): 麦门冬 / 麥門冬: Mai4 men2 dong1/Mak6 mun4 dung1

(Pinelliae Rhizoma Preparatum): 制半夏 / 製半夏: Zhi4 ban4 xia4/Zai3 bun3 haa6

(Gardenia and Prepared Soybean Decoction)

栀子豉汤 / 栀子豉湯: Zhi1 zi3 chi3 tang1/Zi1 zi2 si6 tong1

(Gardeniae Fructus): 栀子 / 栀子: Zhi1 zi3/Zi1 zi2

(Sojae Semen Preparatum): 淡豆豉: Dan4 dou4 chi3/Daam6 dau6 si6

(Gardenia, Licorice, and Prepared Soybean Decoction)

栀子甘草豉汤 / 栀子甘草豉湯: Zhi1 zi3 gan1 cao3 chi3 tang1/Zi1 zi2 gam1 cou2 si6 tong1

(Gardeniae Fructus): 栀子 / 栀子: Zhi1 zi3/Zi1 zi2

(Sojae Semen Preparatum): 淡豆豉: Dan4 dou4 chi3/Daam6 dau6 si6

(Glycyrrhizae Radix): 甘草: Gan1 cao3/Gam1 cou2

(Clear Epidemics and Overcome Toxicity Drink)
清瘟败毒饮 / 清瘟敗毒飲: Qing1 wen1 bai4 du2 yin3/Cing1 wan1 baai6 duk6 jam2
(Gypsum Fibrosum): 石膏: Shi2 gao1/Sek6 gou1
(Rehmanniae Radix): 生地黄: Sheng1 di4 huang2/Sang1 dei6 wong4
(Coptidis Rhizoma): 黄连 / 黃連: Huang2 lian2/Wong4 lin4 my teacher always referred to this in its Sichuan version 川连 / 川連: Chuan1 lian2/Cyun1 lin4
(Bubali Cornu): 水牛角: Shui3 niu2 jiao3/Seoi2 ngau4 gok3
(Gardeniae Fructus): 栀子 / 栀子: Zhi1 zi3/Zi1 zi2
(Platycodi Radix): 桔梗: Jie2 geng3/Gat1 gang2
(Scutellariae Radix): 黄芩: Huang2 qin2/Wong4 kam4
(Anemarrhenae Rhizoma): 知母: Zhi1 mu3/Zi1 mou5
(Paeoniae Radix Rubra): 赤芍: Chi4 shao2/Cek3 zoek3
(Scrophulariae Radix): 玄参 / 玄參: Xuan2 shen1/Jyun4 sam1
(Forsythiae Fructus): 连翘 / 連翹: Lian2 qiao2/Lin4 kiu4
(Lophatheri Herba): 淡竹叶 / 淡竹葉: Dan4 zhu2 ye4/Daam6 zuk1 jip6
(Glycyrrhizae Radix): 甘草: Gan1 cao3/Gam1 cou2
(Moutan Cortex): 牡丹皮: Mu3 dan1 pi2/Maau5 daan1 pei4

b. Constructive-Clearing and Blood-Cooling Formulas

(Rhinoceros and Rehmannia Decoction)
犀角地黄汤 / 犀角地黃湯: Xi1 jiao3 di4 huang2 tang1/Sai1 gok3 dei6 wong4 tong1
(Rhinocerotis Cornu): 犀角: Xi1 jiao3/Sai1 gok3
now usually replaced with (Bubali Cornu): 水牛角: Shui3 niu2 jiao3/Seoi2 ngau4 gok3
(Rehmanniae Radix): 生地黄: Sheng1 di4 huang2/Sang1 dei6 wong4
(Paeoniae Radix Rubra): 赤芍: Chi4 shao2/Cek3 zoek3
(Moutan Cortex): 牡丹皮: Mu3 dan1 pi2/Maau5 daan1 pei4

(Clear the Nutritive-Level Decoction)

清营汤 / 清營湯: Qing1 ying2 tang1/Cing1 jing4 tong1

(Bubali Cornu): 水牛角: Shui3 niu2 jiao3/Seoi2 ngau4 gok3

(Scrophulariae Radix): 玄参 / 玄參: Xuan2 shen1/Jyun4 sam1

(Rehmanniae Radix): 生地黄: Sheng1 di4 huang2/Sang1 dei6 wong4

(Ophiopogonis Radix): 麦门冬 / 麥門冬: Mai4 men2 dong1/Mak6 mun4 dung1

(Lonicerae Flos): 金银花 / 金銀花: Jin1 yin2 hua1/Gam1 ngan4 faa1

(Forsythiae Fructus): 连翘 / 連翹: Lian2 qiao2/Lin4 kiu4

(Coptidis Rhizoma): 黄连 / 黃連: Huang2 lian2/Wong4 lin4 My teacher always referred to this medicinal in its Sichuan version 川连 / 川連: Chuan1 lian2/Cyun1 lin4

c.Heat-Clearing and Toxin-Resolving Formulas

(Coptis Resolve Toxins Decoction)

黄连解毒汤 / 黃連解毒湯: Huang2 lian2 jie3 du2 tang1/Wong4 lin4 gaai2 duk6 tong1

(Coptidis Rhizoma): 黄连 / 黃連: Huang2 lian2/Wong4 lin4

my teacher always referred to this medicinal in its Sichuan version 川连 / 川連: Chuan1 lian2/Cyun1 lin4

(Scutellariae Radix): 黄芩: Huang2 qin2/Wong4 kam4

(Phellodendri Cortex): 黄柏: Huang1 bai3/Wong4 paak3

(Gardeniae Fructus): 栀子 / 梔子: Zhi1 zi3/Zi1 zi2

(Aconite Accessory Root Infusion to Drain the Epigastrium)

附子泻心汤 / 附子瀉心湯: Fu4 zi3 xie4 xin1 tang1/Fu6 zi2 se3 sam1 tong1

(Rhei Radix et Rhizoma): 大黄: Da4 huang2/Daai6 wong4

(Coptidis Rhizoma): 黄连 / 黃連: Huang2 lian2/Wong4 lin4 my teacher always referred to this medicinal in its Sichuan form 川连 / 川連: Chuan1 lian2/Cyun1 lin4

(Scutellariae Radix): 黄芩: Huang2 qin2/Wong4 kam4

(Aconiti Radix Lateralis Preparata): 制附子 / 製附子: Zhi4 fu4 zi3/Zai3 fu6 zi2

(Universal Benefit Drink to Eliminate Toxin)

普济消毒饮 / 普濟消毒飲: Pu3 ji4 xiao1 du2 yin3/Pou2 zai3 siu1 duk6 jam2

(Scutellariae Radix): 黄芩: Huang2 qin2/Wong4 kam4

(Coptidis Rhizoma):): 黄连 / 黃連: Huang2 lian2/Wong4 lin4

my teacher always referred to this medicinal in its Sichuan version 川连 / 川連: Chuan1 lian2/Cyun1 lin4

(Ginseng Radix): 人参 / 人參: Ren2 shen1/Jan4 sam1

(Arctii Fructus): 牛蒡子: Niu2 bang4 zi3/Ngau4 bong2 zi2

(Forsythiae Fructus): 连翘 / 連翹: Lian2 qiao2/Lin4 kiu4

(Menthae Haplocalycis Herba): 薄荷: Bo4 he2/Bok6 ho4

(Dry-Fried Bombyx Batryticatus): 炒僵蚕 / 炒僵蠶: Chao3 Jiang1 can2/Goeng1 caam4

(Scrophulariae Radix): 玄参 / 玄參: Xuan2 shen1/Jyun4 sam1

(Lasiophaera/Calvatia): 马勃 / 馬勃: Ma3 bo2/Maa5 but6

(Isatidis/Baphicacanthis Radix): 板蓝根 / 板藍根: Ban3 lan2 gen1/Baan2 laam4 gan1

(Five Ingredient Drink to Eliminate Toxin)

五味消毒饮 / 五味消毒飲: Wu3 wei4 xiao1 du2 yin3/Ng5 mei6 siu1 duk6 jam2

(Lonicerae Flos): 金银花 / 金銀花: Jin1 yin2 hua1/Gam1 ngan4 faa1

(Taraxaci Herba): 蒲公英: Pu2 gong1 ying1/Pou4 gung1 jing1

(Violae Herba): 紫花地丁: Zi3 hua1 di4 ding1/Zi2 faa1 dei6 ding1

(Chrysanthemi Indici Flos): 野菊花: Ye3 ju2 hua1/Je5 guk1 faa1

(Semiaquilegiae Radix): 天葵子: Tian1 kui2 zi3/Tin1 kwai4 zi2

(Cool the Diaphragm Powder)

凉膈散 / 涼膈散: Liang2 ge2 san3/Loeng4 gaak3 saan3

(Rhei Radix et Rhizoma): 大黄: Da4 huang2/Daai6 wong4

(Natrii Sulfas): 硭硝: Mang2 xiao1/Mong4 siu1

(Glycyrrhizae Radix): 甘草: Gan1 cao3/Gam1 cou2

(Scutellariae Radix): 黄芩: Huang2 qin2/Wong4 kam4

(Gardeniae Fructus): 栀子 / 梔子: Zhi1 zi3/Zi1 zi2

(Forsythiae Fructus): 连翘 / 連翹: Lian2 qiao2/Lin4 kiu4

(Menthae Haplocalycis Herba): 薄荷: Bo4 he2/Bok6 ho4

(Lophatheri Herba): 淡竹叶 / 淡竹葉: Dan4 zhu2 ye4/Daam6 zuk1 jip6

(Warming and Clearing Drink)

温清饮 / 溫清飲: Wen1 qing1 yin3/Wan1 cing1 jam2

(Coptidis Rhizoma): 黄连 / 黃連: Huang2 lian2/Wong4 lin4

my teacher always referred to this medicinal in its Sichuan version 川连 / 川連: Chuan1 lian2/Cyun1 lin4

(Scutellariae Radix): 黄芩: Huang2 qin2/Wong4 kam4

(Phellodendri Cortex): 黄柏: Huang1 bai3/Wong4 paak3

(Gardeniae Fructus): 栀子 / 梔子: Zhi1 zi3/Zi1 zi2

(Angelicae Sinensis Radix): 当归 / 當歸: Dang1 gui1/Dong1 gwai1

(Paeoniae Radix Alba): 白芍: Bai2 shao2/Baak6 zoek3

(Rehmanniae Radix): 熟地黄 / 熟地黃: Shu2 di4 huang2/Suk6 dei6 wong4

(Chuanxiong Rhizoma): 川芎: Chuan1 xiong1/Cyun1 gung1

(Three Yellows Gypsum Decoction)

三黄石膏汤 / 三黃石膏湯: San1 huang2 shi2 gao1 tang1/Saam1 wong4 sek6 gou1 tong1

(Coptidis Rhizoma): 黄连 / 黃連: Huang2 lian2/Wong4 lin4

my teacher always referred to this medicinal in its Sichuan version 川连 / 川連: Chuan1 lian2/Cyun1 lin4

(Scutellariae Radix): 黄芩: Huang2 qin2/Wong4 kam4

(Phellodendri Cortex): 黄柏: Huang1 bai3/Wong4 paak3

(Gardeniae Fructus): 栀子 / 梔子: Zhi1 zi3/Zi1 zi2

(Gypsum Fibrosum): 石膏: Shi2 gao1/Sek6 gou1

(Scrophulariae Radix): 玄参 / 玄參: Xuan2 shen1/Jyun4 sam1

(Anemarrhenae Rhizoma): 知母: Zhi1 mu3/Zi1 mou5

(Glycyrrhizae Radix): 甘草: Gan1 cao3/Gam1 cou2

(Four-Valiant Decoction for Well-Being)

四妙勇安汤 / 四妙勇安湯: Si4 miao4 yong3 an1 tang1/Sei3 miu6 jung5 on1 tong1

(Lonicerae Flos): 金银花 / 金銀花: Jin1 yin2 hua1/Gam1 ngan4 faa1

(Scrophulariae Radix): 玄参 / 玄參: Xuan2 shen1/Jyun4 sam1

(Angelicae Sinensis Radix): 当归 / 當歸: Dang1 gui1/Dong1 gwai1

(Glycyrrhizae Radix): 甘草: Gan1 cao3/Gam1 cou2

Heat-Clearing and Summerheat-Dispelling Formulas

(Clear the Collaterals Drink)
清络饮 / 清絡飲: Qing1 luo4 yin3/Cing1 lok3 jam2
(Lonicerae flos Recens): 鲜金银花 / 鮮金銀花: Xian1 jin1 yin2 hua1/Sin1 gam1 ngan4 faa1
(Lablab Flos Recens): 鲜扁豆花 / 鮮扁豆花: Xian1 bian3 dou4 hua1/Sin1 bin2 dau6 faa1
(Citrulli Exocarpium): 西瓜: Xi1 gua1/Sai1 gwaa1
(Luffae Pericarpium): 丝瓜络 / 絲瓜絡: Si1 gua1 luo4/Si1 gwaa1 lok3
(Nelumbinis Folium Recens): 鲜荷叶 / 鮮荷葉: Xian1 he2 ye4/Sin1 ho4 jip6
(Lophateri Herba Recens): 鲜淡竹叶 / 鮮淡竹葉: Xian1 dan4 zhu2 ye4/Sin1 daam6 zuk1 jip6

(Augment the Primal Powder)
益元散: Yi4 yuan2 san3/Jik1 jyun4 saan3
(Talcum): 滑石: Hua2 shi2/Waat6 sek6
(Glycyrrhizae Radix): 甘草: Gan1 cao3/Gam1 cou2
(Cinnabaris): 朱砂: Zhu1 sha1/Zyu1 saa1

(Cinnamon and Poria Sweet Dew Drink)
桂苓甘露饮 / 桂苓甘露飲: Gui4 ling2 gan1 lu4 yin3/Gwai3 ling4 gam1 lou6 jam2
(Talcum): 滑石: Hua2 shi2/Waat6 sek6
(Glycyrrhizae Radix Preparata): 炙甘草: Zhi4 gan1 cao3/Zek3 gam1 cou2
(Gypsum Fibrosum): 石膏: Shi2 gao1/Sek6 gou1
(Glauberitum): 寒水石: Han2 shui3 shi2/Hon4 seoi2 sek6
(Cinnamomi Cortex): 肉桂: Rou4 gui4/Juk6 gwai3
(Polyporus): 猪苓 / 豬苓: Zhu1 ling2/Zyu1 ling4
(Alismatis Rhizoma): 泽泻 / 澤瀉: Ze3 xie4/Zaak6 se3
(Atractylodis Macrocephalae Rhizoma): 白术 / 白術: Bai2 zhu2/Baak6 seot6

(Clear Summerheat and Augment the Qi Decoction)
清暑益气汤 / 清暑益氣湯: Qing1 shu3 yi4 qi4 tang1/Cing1 syu2 jik1 hei3 tong1
(Astragali Radix): 黄芪 / 黃耆: Huang2 qi2/Wong4 kei4 my teacher always
referred to this medicinal as 北芪 / 北耆
(Ginseng Radix): 人参 / 人參: Ren2 shen1/Jan4 sam1
(Atractylodis Rhizoma): 苍术 / 蒼術: Cang1 zhu2/Cong1 seot6
(Atrctylodis Macrocephalae Rhizoma): 白术 / 白術: Bai2 zhu2/Baak6 seot6
(Ophiopogonis Radix): 麦门冬 / 麥門冬: Mai4 men2 dong1/Mak6 mun4 dung1
(Schisandrae Fructus): 五味子: Wu3 wei4 zi3/Ng5 mei6 zi2
(Puerariae Radix): 葛根: Ge2 gen1/Got3 gan1
(Citri Reticulatae Pericarpium): 陈皮 / 陳皮: Chen2 pi2/Can4 pei4
(Citri Reticulatae Viride Pericarpium): 青皮: Qing1 pi2/Cing1 pei4
(Angelicae Sinensis Radixis Corpus): 当归身 / 當歸身: Dang1 gui1 shen1/Dong1
gwai1 san1
(Cimicifugae Rhizoma): 升麻: Sheng1 ma2/Sing1 maa4
(Alismatis Rhizoma): 泽泻 / 澤瀉: Ze2 xie4/Zaak6 se3
(Wine-Fried Phellodendri Cortex): 酒炒黄柏: Jiu3 chao3 huang2 bai3/Zau2 caau2
wong4 paak3
(Dry-Fried Massa Medicata Fementata): 炒神曲 / 炒神麴: Chao3 shen2
qü1/Caau2 san4 kuk1
(Glycyrrhizae Radix Preparata): 炙甘草: Zhi4 gan1 cao3/Zek3 gam1 cou2

(Six to One Powder)
六一散: Liu4 yi1 san3/Luk6 jat1 saan3
(Talcum): 滑石: Hua2 shi2/Waat6 sek6
(Glycyrrhizae Radix): 甘草: Gan1 cao3/Gam1 cou2

(Green Jade Powder/Jasper Powder)
碧玉散: Bi4 yü4 san3/Bik1 juk6 saan3
(Talcum): 滑石: Hua2 shi2/Waat6 sek6
(Glycyrrhizae Radix): 甘草: Gan1 cao3/Gam1 cou2
(Indigo Naturalis): 青黛: Qing1 dai4/Cing1 doi6

(Cock-Waking Powder/Mint Powder)
鸡苏散 / 雞蘇散: Ji1 su1 san3/Gai1 sou1 saan3
(Talcum): 滑石: Hua2 shi2/Waat6 sek6
(Glycyrrhizae Radix): 甘草: Gan1 cao3/Gam1 cou2
(Menthae Haplocalycis Herba): 薄荷: Bo4 he2/Bok6 ho4

Viscera and Bowel Heat-Clearing Formulas

(Ephedra, Apricot Kernel, Licorice, and Gypsum Decoction)
麻杏石甘汤 / 麻杏石甘湯: Ma2 xing4 shi2 gan1 tang1/Maa4 hang6 sek6 gam1 tong1
(Ephedrae Herba): 麻黄: Ma2 huang2/Maa4 wong4
(Armeniacae Semen): 杏仁: Xing4 ren2/Hang6 jan6
(Glycyrrhizae Radix Preparata): 炙甘草: Zhi4 gan1 cao3/Zek3 gam1 cou2
(Gypsum Fibrosum): 石膏: Shi2 gao1/Sek6 gou1

(Maidservant from Yue Decoction)
越婢汤 / 越婢湯: Yue4 bi4 tang1/Jyut6 pei5 tong1
(Ephedrae herba): 麻黄: Ma2 huang2/Maa4 wong4
(Gypsum Fibrosum): 石膏: Shi2 gao1/Sek6 gou1
(Zingiberis Rhizoma Recens): 生姜 / 生薑: Sheng1 jiang1/Saang1 goeng1
(Glycyrrhizae Radix): 甘草: Gan1 cao3/Gam1 cou2
(Jujubae Fructus): 大枣 / 大棗: Da4 zao3/Daai6 zou2

(Drain the Yellow Powder)
泻黄散 / 瀉黄散: Xie4 huang2 san3/Se3 wong4 saan3
(Gypsum Fibrosum): 石膏: Shi2 gao1/Sek6 gou1
(Gardeniae Fructus): 栀子 / 栀子: Zhi1 zi3/Zi1 zi2
(Dry-Fried Saposhikoviae Radix): 炒防风 / 炒防風: Chao3 fang2 feng1/Caau2 fong4 fung1
(Pogostemonis/Agastaches Folium): 藿香叶 / 藿香葉: Huo4 xiang1 ye4/Fok3 hoeng1 jip6
(Glycyrrhizae Radix): 甘草: Gan1 cao3/Gam1 cou2

(Clear the Stomach Powder):
清胃散: Qing1 wei4 san3/Cing1 wai6 saan3
(Coptidis Rhizoma): 黄连 / 黄連: Huang2 lian2/Wong4 lin4 my teacher always referred to this medicinal in its Sichuan version 川连 / 川連: Chuan1 lian2/Cyun1 lin4
(Cimicifugae Rhizoma): 升麻: Sheng1 ma2/Sing1 maa4
(Moutan Cortex): 牡丹皮: Mu3 dan1 pi2/Maau5 daan1 pei4
(Rehmanniae Radix): 生地黄: Sheng1 di4 huang2/Sang1 dei6 wong4
(Angelicae Sinensis Radicis Corpus): 当归身 / 當歸身: Dang1 gui1 shen1/Dong1 gwai1 san1

(Peony Decoction)

芍药汤 / 芍藥湯: Shao2 yao4 tang1/Zoek3 joek6 tong1

(Paeoniae Radix Alba): 白芍: Bai2 shao2/Baak6 zoek3

(Angelicae Sinensis Radix): 当归 / 當歸: Dang1 gui1/Dong1 gwai1

(Glycyrrhizae Radix Preparata): 炙甘草: Zhi4 gan1 cao3/Zek3 gam1 cou2

(Aucklandiae Radix): 木香: Mu4 xiang1/Muk6 hoeng1

(Arecae Semen): 槟榔 / 檳榔: Bing1 lang2/Ban1 long4

(Coptidis Rhizoma): 黄连 / 黃連: Huang2 lian2/Wong4 lin4 my teacher always referred to this medicinal in its Sichuan form 川连 / 川連: Chuan1 lian2/Cyun1 lin4

(Scutellariae Radix): 黄芩: Huang2 qin2/Wong4 kam4

(Rhei Radix et Rhizoma): 大黄: Da4 huang2/Daai6 wong4

(Cinnamomi Cortex): 肉桂: Rou4 gui4/Juk6 gwai3

(Abduct the Red Powder)

导赤散 / 導赤散: Dao3 chi4 san3/Dou6 cek3 saan3

(Rehmanniae Radix): 生地黄: Sheng1 di4 huang2/Sang1 dei6 wong4

(Akebiae Caulis): 木通: Mu4 tong1/Muk6 tung1

(Glycyrrhizae Radix Tenuis): 甘草梢: Gan1 cao3 shao1/Gam1 cou2 saau1

(Lophatheri Herba): 淡竹叶 / 淡竹葉: Dan4 zhu2 ye4/Daam6 zuk1 jip6

(Gentiana Drain the Liver Decoction)
龙胆泻肝汤 / 龍膽瀉肝湯: Long2 dan3 xie4 gan1 tang1/Lung4 daam2 se3 gon1 tong1
(Gentianae Radix): 龙胆草 / 龍膽草: Long2 dan3 cao3/Lung4 daam2 cou2
(Dry-Fried Scutellariae Radix): 炒黄芩: Chao3 huang2 qin2/Caau2 wong4 kam4
(Gardeniae Fructus): 栀子 / 梔子: Zhi1 zi3/Zi1 zi2
(Akebiae Caulis): 木通: Mu4 tong3/Muk6 tung2
(Alismatis Rhizoma): 泽泻 / 澤瀉: Ze2 xie4/Zaak6 se3
(Plantaginis Semen): 车前子 / 車前子: Che1 qian2 zi3/Ce1 cin4 zi2
(Wine-Washed Angelicae Sinensis Radix): 酒洗当归 / 酒洗當歸: Jiu3 xi3 dang1 gui1/Zau2 sai2 dong1 gwai1
(Rehmanniae Radix): 生地黄: Sheng1 di4 huang2/Sang1 dei6 wong4
(Bupleuri Radix): 柴胡: Chai2 hu2/Caai4 wu4
(Glycyrrhizae Radix): Gan1 cao3/Gam1 cou2

(Pulsatilla Decoction)
白头翁汤 / 白頭翁湯: Bai2 tou2 weng1 tang1/Baak6 tau4 jung1 tong1
(Pulsatillae Radix): 白头翁 / 白頭翁: Bai2 tou2 weng1/Baak6 tau4 jung1
(Phellodendri Cortex): 黄柏: Huang2 bai3/Wong4 paak3
(Coptidis Rhizoma): 黄连 / 黃連: Huang2 lian2/Wong4 lin4
My teacher always referred to this medicinal in its Sichuan version 川连 / 川連: Chuan1 lian2/Cyun1 lin4
(Fraxini Cortex): 秦皮: Qin2 pi2/Ceon4 pei4

(Pulsatilla, Licorice and Donkey Skin Decoction)
白头翁加甘草阿胶汤 / 白頭翁加甘草阿膠湯: Bai2 tou2 weng1 jia1 gan1 cao3 e1 jiao1 tang1/Baak6 tau4 jung4 gaa1 gam1 cou2 aa3 gaau1 tong1
(Pulsatillae Radix): 白头翁 / 白頭翁: Bai2 tou2 weng1/Baak6 tau4 jung1
(Phellodendri Cortex): 黄柏: Huang2 bai3/Wong4 paak3
(Coptidis Rhizoma): 黄连 / 黃連: Huang2 lian2/Wong4 lin4
My teacher always referred to this medicinal in its Sichuan version 川连 / 川連: Chuan1 lian2/Cyun1 lin4
(Fraxini Cortex): 秦皮: Qin2 pi2/Ceon4 pei4
(Asini Corii Colla): 阿胶 / 阿膠: E1 jiao1/Aa3 gaau1
(Glycyrrhizae Radix): 甘草: Gan1 cao3/Gam1 cou2

(Jade Woman Decoction)
玉女煎: Yü4 nü3 jian1/Juk6 neoi5 zin1
(Gypsum Fibrosum): 石膏: Shi2 gao1/Sek6 gou1
(Rehmanniae Radix Preparata): 熟地黄: Shu2 di4 huang2/Suk6 dei6 wong4
(Anemarrhenae Rhizoma): 知母: Zhi1 mu3/Zi1 mou5
(Ophiopogonis Radix): 麦门冬 / 麥門冬: Mai4 men2 dong1/Mak6 mun4 dung1
(Achyranthis Radix): 牛膝: Niu2 xi1/Ngau4 sat1 My teacher always wrote this "cow seven" or 牛七: Niu2 qi1/Ngau4 cat1

(Reed Decoction)
苇茎汤 / 葦莖湯: Wei3 jing1 tang1/Wai5 ging3 tong1
(Phragmititis Caulis): 苇茎 / 葦莖: Wei3 jing1/Wai5 ging3
(Coicis Semen): 薏苡仁: Yi4 yi3 ren2/Ji3 ji5 jan4
(Benincasae Semen): 冬瓜子: Dong1 gua1 zi3/Dung1 gwaa1 zi2
(Persicae Semen): 桃仁: Tao2 ren2/Tou4 jan4

(Drain the White Powder)
泻白散 / 瀉白散: Xie4 bai2 san3/Se3 baak6 saan3
(Dry-Fried Mori Cortex): 炒桑白皮: Chao3 sang1 bai2 pi2/Caau2 song1 baak6 pei4
(Lycii Cortex): 地骨皮: Di4 gu3 pi2/Dei6 gwat1 pei4
(Glycyrrhizae Radix Preparata): 炙甘草: Zhi4 gan1 cao3/Zek3 gam1 cou2
(Nonglutinous rice): 精米: Jing1 mi3/Zing1 mai5

(Kudzu, Scutellaria, and Coptis Decoction)
葛根芩连汤 / 葛根芩連湯: Ge2 gen1 qin2 lian2 tang1/Got3 gan1 kam4 lin4 tong1
(Puerariae Radix): 葛根: Ge2 gen1/Got3 gan1
(Scutellariae Radix): 黄芩: Huang2 qin2/Wong4 kam4
(Coptidis Rhizoma): 黄连 / 黃連: Huang2 lian2/Wong4 lin4 my teacher always referred to this medicinal in its Sichuan version 川连 / 川連: Chuan1 lian2/Cyun1 lin4
(Glycyrrhizae Radix Preparata): 炙甘草: Zhi4 gan1 cao3/Zek3 gam1 cou2

(Drain the Epigastrium Decoction)
泻心汤 / 瀉心湯: Xie4 xin1 tang1/Se3 sam1 tong1
(Rhei Radix et Rhizoma): 大黄: Da4 huang2/Daai6 wong4
(Coptidis Rhizoma): 黄连 / 黃連: Huang2 lian2/Wong4 lin4 my teacher always referred to this medicinal in its Sichuan version 川连 / 川連: Chuan1 lian2/Cyun1 lin4
(Scutellariae Radix): 黄芩: Huang2 qin2/Wong4 kam4

(Left Metal Pill):
左金丸: Zuo3 jin1 wan2/Zo2 gam1 jyun2
(Coptidis Rhizoma): 黄连 / 黃連: Huang2 lian2/Wong4 lin4 my teacher always referred to this medicinal in its Sichuan version 川连 / 川連: Chuan1 lian2/Cyun1 lin4
(Evodiae Fructus): 吴茱萸 / 吳茱萸: Wu2 zhu1 yü2/Ng4 zyu1 jyu4

Vacuity Heat Clearing Formulas

(Artemisia Annuae and Tryonicis Carapax Decoction)
青蒿鳖甲通 / 青蒿鱉甲湯: Qing1 hao1 bie1 jia3 tang1/Cing1 hou1 bit3 gaap3 tong1
(Artemisiae Annuae Herba): 青蒿: Qing1 hao1/Cing1 hou1
(Tryonicis Carapax): 鳖甲 / 鱉甲: Bie1 jia3/Bit3 gaap3
(Rehmanniae Radix): 生地黄: Sheng1 di4 huang2/Sang1 dei6 wong4
(Anemarrhenae Rhizoma): 知母: Zhi1 mu3/Zi1 mou5
(Moutan Cortex): 牡丹皮: Mu3 dan1 pi2/Maau5 daan1 pei4

(Cool the Bones Powder)
清骨散: Qing1 gu3 san3/Cing1 gwat1 saan3
(Stellariae Radix): 银柴胡 / 銀柴胡: Yin2 chai2 hu2/Ngan4 caai4 wu4
(Anemarrhenae Rhizoma): 知母: Zhi1 mu3/Zi1 mou5
(Picrorhizae Rhizoma): 胡黄连 / 胡黃連: Hu2 huang2 lian2/Wu4 wong4 lin4
(Lycii Cortex): 地骨皮: Di4 gu3 pi2/Dei6 gwat1 pei4
(Artemisiae Annuae Herba): 青蒿: Qing1 hao1/Cing1 hou1
(Gentianae Macrophyllae Radix): 秦艽: Qin2 jiao1/Ceon4 gau2
(Vinegar-Fried Trionycis Carapax): 醋炒鳖甲 / 醋炒鱉甲: Cu4 chao3 bie1 jia3/Cou3 caau2 bit3 gaap3
(Glycyrrhizae Radix): 甘草: Gan1 cao3/Gam1 cou2

(Tangkuei and Six-Yellows Decoction)

当归六黄汤 / 當歸六黄湯: Dang1 gui1 liu4 huang2 tang1/Dong1 gwai1 luk6 wong4 tong1

(Angelicae Sinensis Radix): 当归 / 當歸: Dang1 gui1/Dong1 gwai1

(Rehmanniae Radix): 生地黄: Sheng1 di4 huang2/Sang1 dei6 wong4

(Rehmanniae Radix Preparata): 熟地黄: Shu2 di6 huang2/Suk6 dei6 wong4

(Coptidis Rhizoma): 黄连 / 黄連: Huang2 lian2/Wong4 lin4 my teacher always referred to this medicinal in its Sichuan version 川连 / 川連: Chuan1 lian2/Cyun1 lin4

(Scutellariae Radix): 黄芩: Huang2 qin2/Wong4 kam4

(Phellodendri Cortex): 黄柏: Huang2 bai3/Wong4 paak3

(Astragali Radix): 黄芪 / 黃耆: Huang2 qi2/Wong4 kei4 my teacher referred to this medicinal as 北芪: Bak1 kei4.

Center-Warming and Cold Dispelling Formulas

(Rectify the Center Pills)

理中丸: Li3 zhong1 wan2/Lei5 zung1 jyun2

(Ginseng Radix): 人参 / 人參: Ren2 shen1/Jan4 sam1

(Zingiberis Rhizoma): 干姜 / 乾薑: Gan1 jiang1/Gon1 goeng1

(Glycyrrhizae Radix Preparata): 炙甘草: Zhi4 gan1 cao3/Zek3 gam1 cou2

(Atractylodis Macrocephalae Rhizoma): 白术 / 白術: Bai2 zhu2/Baak6 seot6

(Astragalus and Cinnamon Twig Five-Substance Decoction)

黄芪桂枝五物汤 / 黃耆桂枝五物湯: Huang2 qi2 gui4 zhi1 wu3 wu4 tang1/Wong4 kei4 gwai3 zi1 ng5 mat6 tong1

(Astragali radix): 黄芪 / 黃耆: Huang2 qi2/Wong4 kei4 my teacher referred to this medicinal as 北芪: Bak1 kei4.

(Paeoniae Radix Alba): 白芍: Bai2 shao2/Baak6 zoek3

(Cinnamomi Ramulus): 桂枝: Gui4 zhi1/Gwai3 zi1

(Zingiberis Rhizoma Recens): 生姜 / 生薑: Sheng1 jiang1/Sang1 goeng1

(Jujubae Fructus): 大枣 / 大棗: Da4 zao3/Daai6 zou2

(Tangkuei Decoction for Frigid Extremities)
当归四逆汤 / 當歸四逆湯: Dang1 gui1 si4 ni4 tang1/Dong1 gwai1 sei3 jik6 tong1
(Angelicae sinensis Radix): 当归 / 當歸: Dang1 gui1/Dong1 gwai1
(Paeoniae Radix Alba): 白芍: Bai2 shao2/Baak6 zoek3
(Cinnamomi Ramulus): 桂枝: Gui4 zhi1/Gwai3 zi1
(Asari Herba): 细辛 / 細辛: Xi4 xin1/Sai3 san1
(Glycyrrhizae Radix Preparata): 炙甘草: Zhi4 gan1 cao3/Zek3 gam1 cou2
(Jujubae Fructus): 大枣 / 大棗: Da1 zao3/Daai6 zou2
(Akebiae Caulis): 木通: Mu4 tong1/Muk6 tung1

(Clove and Evodia Rectify the Center Decoction
丁萸理中汤 / 丁萸理中湯: Ding1 yü2 li3 zhong1 tang1/Ding1 jyu4 lei5 zung1 tong1
(Ginseng Radix): 人参 / 人參: Ren2 shen1/Jan4 sam1
(Zingiberis Rhizoma): 干姜 / 乾薑: Gan1 jiang1/Gon1 goeng1
(Glycyrrhizae Radix): 炙甘草: Zhi4 gan1 cao3/Zek3 gam1 cou2
(Atractylodis Macrocephalae Rhizoma): 白术 / 白術: Bai2 zhu2/Baak6 seot6
(Caryophylli Flos): 丁香: Ding1 xiang1/Ding1 hoeng1
(Evodiae Fructus): 吴茱萸 / 吳茱萸: Wu2 zhu1 yü2/Ng4 zyu1 jyu4

(Rectify the Center and Transform Phlegm Pills)
理中化痰丸: Li3 zhong1 hua4 tan2 wan2/Lei5 zung1 faa3 taam4 jyun2
(Ginseng Radix): 人参 / 人參: Ren2 shen1/Jan4 sam1
(Zingiberis Rhizoma): 干姜 / 乾薑: Gan1 jiang1/Gon1 goeng1
(Glycyrrhizae Radix Preparata): 炙甘草: Zhi4 gan1 cao3/Zek3 gam1 cou2
(Atractylodis Macrocephalae Rhizoma): 白术 / 白術: Bai2 zhu2/Baak6 seot6
(Pinelliae Rhizoma Preparatum): 制半夏 / 製半夏: Zhi4 ban4 xia4/Zai3 bun3 haa6
(Poria): 茯苓: Fu2 ling2/Fuk6 ling4

(Rectify the Center and Quiet Roundworms Pills)
理中安蛔丸: Li3 zhong1 an1 hui2 wan2/Lei5 zung1 on1 wui4 jyun2
(Ginseng Radix): 人参 / 人參: Ren2 shen1/Jan4 sam1
(Zingiberis Rhizoma): 干姜 / 乾薑: Gan1 jiang1/Gon1 goeng1
(Atractylodis Macrocephalae Rhizoma): 白术 / 白術: Bai2 zhu2/Baak6 seot6
(Zanthoxyli Pericarpium): 川椒: Chuan1 jiao1/Cyun1 ziu1
(Mume Fructus): 乌梅 / 烏梅：Wu1 mei2/Wu1 mui4
(Poria): 茯苓: Fu2 ling2/Fuk6 ling4

(Coptis Rectifying Decoction)
连理汤 / 連理湯: Lian2 li3 tang1/Lin4 lei5 tong1
(Ginseng Radix): 人参 / 人參: Ren2 shen1/Jan4 sam1
(Zingiberis Rhizoma): 干姜 / 乾薑: Gan1 jiang1/Gon1 goeng1
(Glycyrrhizae Radix): 炙甘草: Zhi4 gan1 cao3/Zek3 gam1 cou2
(Atractylodis Macrocephalae Rhizoma): 白术 / 白術: Bai2 zhu2/Baak6 seot6
(Coptidis Rhizoma): 黄连 / 黃連: Huang2 lian2/Wong4 lin4
My teacher always referred to this medicinal in its Sichuan form: 川连 / 川連: Chuan1 lian2/Cyun1 lin4

(Aconite Rectify the Center Pill)
附子理中丸: Fu4 zi3 li3 zhong1 wan2/Fu6 zi2 lei5 zung1 jyun2
(Panacis Ginseng Radix): 人参 / 人參: Ren2 shen1/Jan4 sam1
(Zingiberis Rhizoma): 干姜 / 乾薑: Gan1 jiang1/Gon1 goeng1
(Glycyrrhizae Radix Praeparata): 炙甘草: Zhi4 gan1 cao3/Zek3 gam1 cou2
(Atractylodis Macrocephalae Rhizoma): 白术 / 白術: Bai2 zhu2/Baak6 seot6
(Aconiti Radix Lateralis Praeparata): 制附子 / 製附子: Zhi4 fu4 zi3/Zai3 fu6 zi2

(Cinnamon and Aconite Rectify the Center Decoction)
桂附理中汤 / 桂附理中湯: Gui4 fu4 li3 zhong1 tang1/Gwai3 fu6 lei5 zung1 tong1
(Panacis Ginseng Radix): 人参 / 人參: Ren2 shen1/Jan4 sam1
(Zingiberis Rhizoma): 干姜 / 乾薑: Gan1 jiang1/Gon1 goeng1
(Glycyrrhizae Radix Praeparata): 炙甘草: Zhi4 gan1 cao3/Zek3 gam1 cou2
(Atractylodis Macrocephalae Rhizoma): 白术 / 白術: Bai2 zhu2/Baak6 seot6
(Cinnamomi Cortex): 肉桂: Rou4 gui4/Juk6 gwai3
(Aconiti Radix Lateralis Praeparata): 制附子 / 製附子: Zhi4 fu4 zi3/Zai3 fu6 zi2

(Immature Aurantium Rectify the Center Pills)
枳实理中丸 / 枳實理中丸: Zhi3 shi2 li3 zhong1 wan2/Zi2 sat6 lei5 zung1 jyun2
(Ginseng Radix): 人参 / 人參: Ren2 shen1/Jan4 sam1
(Zingiberis Rhizoma): 干姜 / 乾薑: Gan1 jiang1/Gon1 goeng1
(Glycyrrhizae Radix Preparata): 炙甘草: Zhi4 gan1 cao3/Zek3 gam1 cou2
(Atractylodis Macrocephalae Rhizoma): 炒白术 / 炒白術: Chao3 bai2 zhu2/Caau2 baak6 seot6
(Aurantii Fructus Immaturus): 枳实 / 枳實: Zhi3 shi2/Zi2 sat6
(Poria): 茯苓: Fu2 ling2/Fuk6 ling4

(Evodia Decoction)
吴茱萸汤 / 吳茱萸湯: Wu2 zhu1 yü2 tang1/Ng4 zyu1 jyu4 tong1
(Evodiae Fructus): 吴茱萸 / 吳茱萸: Wu2 zhu1 yü2/Ng4 zyu1 jyu4
(Zingiberis Rhizoma Recens): 生姜 / 生薑: Sheng1 jiang1/Sang1 goeng1
(Ginseng Radix): 人参 / 人參: Ren2 shen1/Jan4 sam1
(Jujubae Fructus): 大枣 / 大棗: Da4 zao3/Daai6 zou2

(Minor Construct the Middle Decoction)
小建中汤 / 小建中湯: Xiao3 jian4 zhong1 tang1/Siu2 gin3 zung1 tong1
(Maltosum): 饴糖 / 飴糖: Yi2 tang2/Ji4 tong4
(Cinnamomi Ramulus): 桂枝: Gui4 zhi1/Gwai3 zi1
(Paeoniae Radix Alba): 白芍: Bai2 shao2/Baak6 zoek3
(Glycyrrhizae Radix Preparata): 炙甘草: Zhi4 gan1 cao3/Zek3 gam1 cou2
(Zingiberis Rhizoma Recens): 生姜 / 生薑: Sheng1 jiang1/Sang1 goeng1
(Jujubae Fructus): 大枣 / 大棗: Da4 zao3/Daai6 zou2

(Astragalus Decoction to Construct the Middle)
黄芪建中汤 / 黃耆建中湯: Huang2 qi2 jian4 zhong1 tang1/Wong4 kei4 gin3 zung1 tong1
(Maltosum): 饴糖 / 飴糖: Yi2 tang2/Ji4 tong4
(Cinnamomi Ramulus): 桂枝: Gui4 zhi1/Gwai3 zi1
(Paeoniae Radix Alba): 白芍: Bai2 shao2/Baak6 zoek6
(Glycyrrhizae Radix): 甘草: Gan1 cao3/Gam1 cou2
(Zingiberis Rhizoma Recens): 生姜 / 生薑: Sheng1 jiang1/Sang1 goeng1
(Jujubae Fructus): 大枣 / 大棗: Da4 zao3/Daai6 zou2
(Astragali Radix): 黄芪 / 黃耆: Huang2 qi2/Wong4 kei4 my teacher always referred to this medicinal as 北芪 / 北耆: Bei3 qi2/Bak1 kei4.

(Licorice and Ginger Decoction)
甘草干姜汤 / 甘草乾薑湯: Gan1 cao3 gan1 jiang1 tang1/Gam1 cou2 gon1 goeng1 tong1
(Glycyrrhizae Radix Preparata): 炙甘草: Zhi4 gan1 cao3/Zek3 gam1 cou2
(Zingiberis Rhizoma Preparata): 炮姜 / 炮薑: Pao2 jiang1/Paau3 goeng1

(Major Construct the Middle Decoction)
大建中汤 / 大建中湯: Da4 jian4 zhong1 tang1/Daai6 gin3 zung1 tong1
(Zanthoxyli Pericarpium): 花椒: Hua1 jiao1/Faa1 ziu1
(Zingiberis Rhizoma): 干姜 / 乾薑: Gan1 jiang1/Gon1 goeng1
(Ginseng Radix): 人参 / 人參: Ren2 shen1/Jan4 sam1
(Maltosum): 饴糖 / 飴糖: Yi2 tang2/Ji4 tong4

Yang-Returning and Counterflow-Stemming Formulas

(Four Counterflows Decoction)
四逆汤 / 四逆湯: Si4 ni4 tang1/Sei3 jik6 tong1
(Aconiti Radix Lateralis Praeparata): 制附子 / 製附子: Zhi4 fu4 zi3/Zai3 fu6 zi2
(Zingiberis Rhizoma): 干姜 / 乾薑: Gan1 jiang1/Gon1 goeng1
(Glycyrrhizae Radix Preparata): 炙甘草: Zhi4 gan1 cao3/Zek3 gam1 cou2

(Four Counterflows Plus Ginseng Decoction)
四逆加人参汤 / 四逆人參湯: Si4 ni4 jia1 ren2 shen1 tang1/Sei3 jik6 gaa1 jan4 sam1 tong1
(Aconiti Radix Lateralis Praeparata): 制附子 / 製附子: Zhi4 fu4 zi3/Zai3 fu6 zi2
(Zingiberis Rhizoma): 干姜 / 乾薑: Gan1 jiang1/Gon1 goeng1
(Glycyrrhizae Radix Preparata): 炙甘草: Zhi4 gan1 cao3/Zek3 gam1 cou2
(Ginseng Radix): 人参 / 人參: Ren2 shen1/Jan4 sam1

(Unblock the Pulse Decoction for Frigid Extremities)
通脉四逆汤 / 通脈四逆湯: Tong1 mai4 si4 ni4 tang1/Tung1 mak6 sei3 jik6 tong1
(Glycyrrhizae Radix Preparata): 炙甘草: Zhi4 gan1 cao3/Zek3 gam1 cou2
(Aconiti Radix Lateralis Preparata): 制附子 / 製附子: Zhi4 fu4 zi3/Zai3 fu6 zi2
(Zingiberis Rhizoma): 干姜 / 乾薑: Gan1 jiang1/Gon1 goeng1

(White Penetrating Decoction)
白通汤 / 白通湯: Bai2 tong1 tang1/Baak6 tung1 tong1
(Allii Fistulosi Bulbus): 葱白 / 蔥白: Cong1 bai2/Cung1 baak6
(Zingiberis Rhizoma): 干姜 / 乾薑: Gan1 jiang1/Gon1 goeng1
(Aconiti Radix Lateralis Preparata): 制附子 / 製附子: Zhi4 fu4 zi3/Zai3 fu6 zi2

(Unaccompanied Ginseng Decoction)
独参汤 / 獨參湯: Du2 shen1 tang1/Duk6 san1 tong1
(Ginseng Radix): 人参 / 人參: Ren2 shen1/Jan4 sam1

(Ginseng and Aconite Accessory Root Decoction)
参附汤 / 參附湯: Shen1 fu4 tang1/Sam1 fu6 tong1
(Ginseng Radix): 人参 / 人參: Ren2 shen1/Jan4 sam1
(Aconiti Radix Lateralis Preparata): 制附子 / 製附子: Zhi4 fu4 zi3/Zai3 fu6 zi2

Formulas that Treat External Abscesses and Sores

(Balmy Yang Decoction)
阳和汤 / 陽和湯: Yang2 he2 tang1/Joeng4 wo6 tong1
(Rehmanniae Radix Preparata): 熟地黄: Shu2 di4 huang2/Suk6 dei6 wong4
(Cervi Cornus Colla): 鹿角胶 / 鹿角膠: Lu4 jiao3 jiao1/Luk6 gok3 gaau1
(Cinnamomi Cortex): 肉桂: Rou4 gui4/Juk6 gwai3
(Zingiberis Rhizoma Preparata): 炮姜 / 炮薑: Pao2 jiang1/Paau3 goeng1
(Sinapis Semen): 白芥子: Bai2 jie4 zi3/Baak6 gaai3 zi2
(Ephedrae Herba): 麻黄: Ma2 huang2/Maa4 wong4
(Glycyrrhizae Radix): 甘草: Gan1 cao3/Gam1 cou2

(Five-Ingredient Drink to Eliminate Toxin)
五味消毒饮 / 五味消毒飲: Wu3 wei4 xiao1 du2 yin3/Ng5 mei6 siu1 duk6 jam2
(Lonicerae Flos): 金银花 / 金銀花: Jin1 yin2 hua1/Gam1 ngan4 faa1
(Taraxici Herba): 蒲公英 / 蒲公英: Pu2 gong1 ying1/Pou4 gung1 jing1
(Violae Herba): 紫花地丁: Zi3 hua1 di4 ding1/Zi2 faa1 dei6 ding1
(Chrysanthemi Indici Flos): 野菊花: Ye3 ju2 hua1/Je5 gu1 faa1
(Semiaquilegiae Radix): 天葵子: Tian1 kui2 zi3/Tin1 kwai4 zi2

(Immortals' Formula for Sustaining Life)
仙方活命饮 / 仙方活命飲: Xian1 fang1 huo2 ming4 yin3/Sin1 fong1 wut6 ming6 jam2
(Lonicerae Flos): 金银花 / 金銀花: Jin1 yin2 hua1/Gam1 ngan4 faa1
(Glycyrrhizae Radix): 甘草: Gan1 cao3/Gam1 cou2
(Fritillariae Thunbergii Bulbus): 浙贝母 / 浙貝母: Zhe4 bei4 mu3/Zit3 bui3 mou5
(Trichosanthis Radix): 天花粉: Tian1 hua1 fen3/Tin1 faa1 fan2
(Angelicae Sinensis Radicis Cauda): 当归尾 / 當歸尾: Dang1 gui1 wei3/Dong1 gwai1 mei5
(Paeoniae Radix Rubra): 赤芍: Chi4 shao2/Cek3 zoek3
(Olibanum): 乳香: Ru3 xiang1/Jyu5 hoeng1
(Myrrha): 没药 / 沒藥: Mo4 yao4/Mut6 joek6
(Saposhnikoviae Radix): 防风 / 防風: Fang2 feng1/Fong4 fung1
(Angelicae Dahuricae Radix): 白芷: Bai2 zhi3/Baak6 zi2
(Manitis Squama): 穿山甲: Chuan1 shan1 jia3/Cyun1 saan1 gaap3
(Gleditsiae Spina): 皂角刺: Zao4 jiao3 ci4/Zou6 gok3 ci3
(Citri Reticulatae Pericarpium): 陈皮 / 陳皮: Chen2 pi2/Can4 pei4

(Six Divine Pill)
六神丸: Liu4 shen2 wan2/Luk6 san4 jyun2
(Bovis Calculus): 牛黄: Niu2 huang2/Ngau4 wong4
(Margarita): 珍珠: Zhen1 zhu1/Zan1 zyu1
(Bufonis Venenum): 蟾酥: Chan2 su1/Sim4 sou1
(Realgar): 雄黄: Xiong2 huang2/Hung4 wong4
(Borneolum): 冰片: Bing1 pian4/Bing1 pin3
(Moschus): 麝香: She4 xiang1/Se6 hoeng1

Channel-Warming and Cold-Scattering Formulas

(Dang Gui Four Counterflows Decoction)
当归四逆汤 / 當歸四逆湯: Dang1 gui1 si4 ni4 tang1/Dong1 gwai1 sei3 jik6 tong1
(Angelicae Sinensis Radix): 当归 / 當歸: Dang1 gui1/Dong1 gwai1
(Cinnamomi Ramulus): 桂枝: Gui4 zhi1/Gwai3 zi1
(Paeoniae Radix Alba): 白芍: Bai2 shao2/Baak6 zoek3
(Asari Herba): 细辛 / 細辛: Xi4 xin1/Sai3 sam1
(Glycyrrhizae Radix Preparata): 炙甘草: Zhi4 Gan1 cao3/Zek3 gam1 cou2
(Akebiae Caulis): 木通: Mu4 tong1/Muk6 tung2
(Jujubae Fructus): 大枣 / 大棗: Da4 zao3/Daai6 zou2

(Dang Gui Four Counterflows Plus Evodia and Uncooked Ginger Decoction)
当归四逆加吴茱萸生姜汤 / 當歸四逆加吳茱萸生薑湯
Dang1 gui1 si4 ni4 jia1 wu2 zhu1 yu2 sheng1 jiang1 tang1
Dong1 gwai1 sei3 jik6 gaa1ng4 zyu1 jyu4 sang1 goeng1 tong1
(Angelicae Sinensis Radix): 当归 / 當歸: Dang1 gui1
(Cinnamomi Ramulus): 桂枝: Gui4 zhi1/Gwai3 zi1
(Paeoniae Radix Alba): 白芍: Bai2 shao2/Baak6 zoek3
(Asari Herba): 细辛 / 細辛: Xi4 xin1/Sai3 sam1
(Glycyrrhizae Radix Preparata): 炙甘草: Zhi4 Gan1 cao3/Zek3 gam1 cou2
(Akebiae Caulis): 木通: Mu4 tong1/Muk6 tung2
(Jujubae Fructus): 大枣 / 大棗: Da4 zao3/Daai6 zou2
(Zingiberis Rhizoma Recens): 生姜 / 生薑: Sheng1 jiang1/Sang1 goeng1
(Evodiae Fructus): 吴茱萸 / 吳茱萸: Wu2 zhu1 yü2/Ng4 zyu1 jyu4

Supplementing and Boosting Formulas
Qi-Supplementing Formulas

(Four Gentlemen Decoction)
四君子汤 / 四君子湯: Si4 jun1 zi3 tang1/Sei3 gwan1 zi2 tong1
(Ginseng Radix): 人参 / 人參: Ren2 shen1/Jan4 sam1
(Atractylodis Macrocephalae Rhizoma): 白术 / 白術: Bai2 zhu2/Baak6 seot6
(Poria): 茯苓: Fu2 ling2/Fuk6 ling4
(Glycyrrhizae Radix Preparata): 炙甘草: Zhi4 gan1 cao3/Zek3 gam1 cou2

(Extraordinary Merit Powder)
异功散 / 異功散: Yi4 gong1 san3/Ji6 gung1 saan3
also called:
(Five Flavors Extraordinary Merit Powder)
五味异功散 / 五味異功散: Wu3 wei4 yi4 gong1 san3/Ng5 mei6 ji6 gung1 saan3
(Ginseng Radix): 人参 / 人參: Ren2 shen1/Jan4 sam1
(Atractylodis Macrocephalae Rhizoma): 白术 / 白術: Bai2 zhu2/Baak6 seot6
(Poria): 茯苓: Fu2 ling2/Fuk6 ling4
(Glycyrrhizae Radix Preparata): 炙甘草: Zhi4 gan1 cao3/Zek3 gam1 cou2
(Citri Reticulatae Pericarpium): 陈皮 / 陳皮: Chen2 pi2/Can4 pei4

(Six Gentlemen Decoction)
六君子汤 / 六君子湯: Liu4 jun1 zi3 tang1/Luk6 gwan1 zi2 tong1
(Ginseng Radix): 人参 / 人參: Ren2 shen1/Jan4 sam1
(Atractylodis Macrocephalae Rhizoma): 白术 / 白術: Bai2 zhu2/Baak6 seot6
(Poria): 茯苓: Fu2 ling2/Fuk6 ling4
(Glycyrrhizae Radix Preparata): 炙甘草: Zhi4 gan1 cao3/Zek3 gam1 cou2
(Citri Reticulatae Pericarpium): 陈皮 / 陳皮: Chen2 pi2/Can4 pei4
(Pinelliae Rhizoma Preparatum): 制半夏 / 製半夏: Zhi4 ban4 xia4/Zai3 bun3 haa6
sometimes the six gentlemen are augmented by adding:
(Zingiberis Rhizoma Recens): 生姜 / 生薑: Sheng1 jiang1/Sang1 goeng1
(Jujubae Fructus): 大枣 / 大棗: Da4 zao3/Daai6 zou2

(Amomum and Aucklandia Six Gentlemen Decoction)
香砂六君子汤 / 香砂六君子湯: Xiang1 sha1 liu4 jun1 zi3 tang1/Hoeng1 saa1 luk6 gwan1 zi2 tong1
(Ginseng Radix): 人参 / 人參: Ren2 shen1/Jan4 sam1
(Atractylodis Macrocephalae Rhizoma): 白术 / 白術: Bai2 zhu2/Baak6 seot6
(Poria): 茯苓: Fu2 ling2/Fuk6 ling4
(Glycyrrhizae Radix Preparata): 炙甘草: Zhi4 gan1 cao3/Zek3 gam1 cou2
(Citri Reticulatae Pericarpium): 陈皮 / 陳皮: Chen2 pi2/Can4 pei4
(Pinelliae Rhizoma Preparatum): 制半夏 / 製半夏: Zhi4 ban4 xia4/Zai3 bun3 haa6
(Zingiberis Rhizoma Recens): 生姜 / 生薑: Sheng1 jiang1/Sang1 goeng1
(Jujubae Fructus): 大枣 / 大棗: Da4 zao3/Daai6 zou2
(Aucklandiae Radix): 木香: Mu4 xiang1/Muk6 hoeng1
(Amomi Fructus): 砂仁: Sha1 ren2/Saa1 jan4

(Ginseng, Poria and Atractylodes Powder)
参苓白术散 / 參苓白術散: Shen1 ling2 bai2 zhu2 san3/San1 ling4 baak6 seot6 saan3
(Ginseng Radix): 人参 / 人參: Ren2 shen1/Jan4 sam1
(Atractylodis Macrocephalae Rhizoma): 白术 / 白術: Bai2 zhu2/Baak6 seot6
(Poria): 茯苓: Fu2 ling2/Fuk6 ling4
(Glycyrrhizae Radix Preparata): 炙甘草: Zhi4 gan1 cao3/Zek3 gam1 cou2
(Dry-Fried Lablab Semen Album): 炒扁豆: Chao3 bian3 dou4/Caau2 bin2 dau2
(Dioscoreae Rhizoma): 山药 / 山藥: Shan1 yao4/Saan1 joek6
(Amomi Fructus): 砂仁: Sha1 ren2/Saa1 jan4
(Nelumbinis Semen): 莲子 / 蓮子: Lian2 zi3/Lin4 zi2
(Dry-Fried Platycodi Radix): 炒桔梗: Chao3 jie2 geng3/Caau2 gat1 gang2
(Coicis Semen): 薏苡仁: Yi4 yi3 ren2/Ji3 ji5 jan4

(Jade Windscreen Powder)
玉屏风散 / 玉屏風散: Yü4 ping2 feng1 san3/Juk6 ping4 fung1 saan3
(Honey-Prepared Astragali Radix): 蜜炙黄芪 / 蜜炙黃耆: Mi4 zhi4 huang2 qi2/Mat6 zek3 wong4 kei4 my teacher always referred to this medicinal as 北芪 / 北耆: Bei3 qi2/Bak1 kei4.
(Atractylodis Macrocephalae Rhizoma): 白术 / 白術: Bai2 zhu2/Baak6 seot6
(Saposhnikoviae Radix): 防风 / 防風: Fang2 feng1/Fong4 fung1

(Ginseng and Gecko Powder)

人参蛤蚧散 / 人參蛤蚧散: Ren2 shen1 ge2 jie4 san3/Jan4 sam1 gap3 gaai3 saan3

(Gecko): 蛤蚧: Ge2 jie4/Gap3 gaai3

(Ginseng Radix): 人参 / 人參: Ren2 shen1/Jan4 sam1

(Poria): 茯苓: Fu2 ling2/Fuk6 ling4

(Mori Cortex): 桑白皮: Sang1 bai2 pi2/Song1 baak6 pei4

(Armeniacae Semen): 杏仁: Xing4 ren2/Hang6 jan4

(Fritillariae Cirrhosae Bulbus): 川贝母 / 川貝母: Chuan1 bei4 mu3/Cyun1 bui3 mou5

(Anemarrhenae Rhizoma): 知母: Zhi1 mu3/Zi1 mou5

(Glycyrrhizae Radix Preparata): 炙甘草: Zhi4 gan1 cao3/Zek3 gam1 cou2

(Pinellia Draining Six Gentlemen Decoction)

半泻六君子汤 / 半瀉六君子湯: Ban4 xie4 liu4 jun1 zi3 tang1/Bun3 se3 luk6 gwan1 zi2 tong1

(Ginseng Radix): 人参 / 人參: Ren2 shen1/Jan4 sam1

(Atractylodis Macrocephalae Rhizoma): 白术 / 白術: Bai2 zhu2/Baak6 seot6

(Poria): 茯苓: Fu2 ling2/Fuk6 ling4

(Glycyrrhizae Radix Preparata): 炙甘草: Zhi4 gan1 cao3/Zek3 gam1 cou2

(Citri Reticulatae Pericarpium): 陈皮 / 陳皮: Chen2 pi2/Can4 pei4

(Pinelliae Rhizoma Preparatum): 制半夏 / 製半夏: Zhi4 ban4 xia4/Zai3 bun3 haa6

(Scutellariae Radix): 黄芩: Huang2 qin2/Wong4 kam4

(Coptidis Rhizoma): 黄连 / 黃連: Huang2 lian2/Wong4 lin4

My teacher always referred to this medicinal in its Sichuan form: 川连 / 川連: Chuan1 lian2/Cyun1 lin4

(Ostreae Concha): 牡蛎 / 牡蠣: Mu3 li4/Maau5 lai6

(Aucklandia and Amomum Nourish the Stomach Decoction)

香砂養胃汤 / 香砂養胃湯: Xiang1 sha1 yang3 wei4 tang1/Hoeng1 saa1 joeng5 wai6 tong1

(Ginseng Radix): 人参 / 人參: Ren2 shen1/Jan4 sam1

(Atractylodis Macrocephalae Rhizoma): 白术 / 白術: Bai2 zhu2/Baak6 seot6

(Atractylodis Rhizoma): 苍术 / 蒼術: Cang1 zhu2/Cong1 seot6

(Poria): 茯苓: Fu2 ling2/Fuk6 ling4

(Glycyrrhizae Radix Preparata): 炙甘草: Zhi4 gan1 cao3/Zek gam1 cou2

(Citri Reticulatae Pericarpium): 陈皮 / 陳皮: Chen2 pi2/Can4 pei4

(Zingiberis Rhizoma Recens): 生姜 / 生薑: Sheng1 jiang1/Sang1 goeng1

(Amomi Fructus Rotundus): 白豆蔻: Bai2 dou4 kou4/Baak6 dau6 kau3

(Jujubae Fructus): 大枣 / 大棗: Da4 zao3/Daai6 zou2

(Aucklandiae Radix): 木香: Mu4 xiang1/Muk6 hoeng1

(Amomi Fructus): 砂仁: Sha1 ren2/Saa1 jan4
(Ginger Juice Fried Magnoliae Officinalis Cortex): 姜汁炒厚朴 / 薑汁炒厚朴:
Jiang1 zhi1 chao3 hou4 po4/Goeng1 zap1 caau2 hau5 pok3

(Dividing and Dispersing Decoction):
分消汤 / 分消湯: Fen1 xiao1 tang1/Fan1 siu1 tong1
(Atractylodis Rhizoma): 苍术 / 蒼術: Cang1 zhu2/Cong1 seot6
(Atractylodis Macrocephalae Rhizoma): 白术 / 白術: Bai2 zhu2/Baak6 seot6
(Poria): 茯苓: Fu2 ling2/Fuk6 ling4
(Citri Reticulatae Pericarpium): 陈皮 / 陳皮: Chen2 pi2/Can4 pei4
(Magnoliae Officinalis Cortex): 厚朴: Hou4 po4/Hau5 pok3
(Cyperi Rhizoma): 香附: Xiang1 fu4/Hoeng1 fu6
(Polyporus): 猪苓 / 豬苓: Zhu1 ling2/Zyu1 ling4
(Alismatis Rhizoma): 泽泻 / 澤瀉: Ze2 xie4/Zaak6 se3
(Aurantii fructus Immaturus): 枳实 / 枳實: Zhi3 shi2/Zi2 sat6
(Arecae Pericarpium): 大腹皮: Da4 fu4 pi2/Daai6 fuk1 pei4
(Amomi Fructus): 砂仁: Sha1 ren2/Saa1 jan4
(Aucklandiae Radix): 木香: Mu4 xiang1/Muk6 hoeng1
(Junci Medulla): 灯心草: Deng1 xin1 cao3/Dang1 sam1 cou2
(Zingiberis Rhizoma Recens): 生姜 / 生薑: Sheng1 jiang1/Sang1 goeng1

(Qian's Atractylodes Powder)
钱氏白术散 / 錢氏白術散: Qian2 shi4 bai2 zhu2 san3/Cin4 si6 baak6 soet6
saan3
(Ginseng Radix): 人参 / 人參: Ren2 shen1/Jan4 sam1
(Atractylodis Macrocephalae Rhizoma): 白术 / 白術: Bai2 zhu2/Baak6 seot6
(Poria): 茯苓: Fu2 ling2/Fuk6 ling4
(Glycyrrhizae Radix): 甘草: Gan1 cao3/Gam1 cou2
(Puerariae Radix): 葛根: Ge2 gen1/Got3 gan1
(Pogostemonis Herba): 藿香: Huo4 xiang1/Fok3 hoeng1
(Aucklandiae Radix): 木香: Mu4 xiang1/Muk6 hoeng1

(Eight Treasure Decoction)

八珍汤 / 八珍湯: Ba1 zhen1 tang1/Baat3 zan1 tong1

(Ginseng Radix): 人参 / 人參: Ren2 shen1/Jan4 sam1

(Atractylodis Macrocephalae Rhizoma): 白术 / 白術: Bai2 zhu2/Baak6 seot6

(Poriae): 茯苓: Fu2 ling2/Fuk6 ling4

(Glycyrrhizae Radix Preparata): 炙甘草: Zhi4 gan1 cao3/Zek3 gam1 cou2

(Angelicae Sinensis Radix): 当归 / 當歸: Dang1 gui1/Dong1 gwai1

(Rehmanniae Radix Praeparata): 熟地黄: Shu2 di4 huang2/Suk6 dei6 wong4

(Paeoniae Radix Alba): 白芍: Bai2 shao2/Baak6 zoek3

(Chuanxiong Rhizoma): 川芎: Chuan1 xiong1/Cyun1 gung1

(Prepared Licorice Decoction)

炙甘草汤 / 炙甘草湯: Zhi4 gan1 cao3 tang1/Zek3 gam1 cou2 tong1

(Glycyrrhizae Radix Preparata): 炙甘草: Zhi4 gan1 cao3

(Ginseng Radix): 人参 / 人參: Ren2 shen1/Jan4 sam1

(Cinnamomi Ramulus): 桂枝: Gui4 zhi1/Gwai3 zi1

(Rehmanniae Radix): 生地黄: Sheng1 di4 huang2/Sang1 dei4 wong4

(Ophiopogonis Radix): 麦门冬 / 麥門冬: Mai4 men2 dong1/Mak6 mun4 dung1

(Asini Corii Colla): 阿胶 / 阿膠: E1 jiao1/Aa3 gaau1

(Cannabis Semen): 火麻仁: Huo3 ma2 ren2/Fo2 maa4 jan4

(Zingiberis Rhizoma Recens): 生姜 / 生薑: Sheng1 jiang1/Sang1 goeng1

(Jujubae Fructus): 大枣 / 大棗: Da4 zao3/Daai6 zou2

(All-Inclusive Great Tonifying Decoction)

十全大补汤 / 十全大補湯: Shi2 quan2 da4 bu3 tang1/Sap6 cyun4 daai6 bou2 tong1

(Ginseng Radix): 人参 / 人參: Ren2 shen1/Jan4 sam1

(Atractylodis Macrocephalae Rhizoma): 白术 / 白術: Bai2 zhu2/Baak6 seot6

(Poria): 茯苓: Fu2 ling2/Fuk6 ling4

(Glycyrrhizae Radix Preparata): 炙甘草: Zhi4 gan1 cao3/Zek3 gam1 cou2

(Rehmanniae Radix Preparata): 熟地黄: Shu2 di4 huang2/Suk6 dei6 wong4

(Paeoniae Radix Alba): 白芍: Bai2 shao2/Baak6 zoek3

(Angelicae Sinensis Radix): 当归 / 當歸: Dang1 gui1/Dong1 gwai1

(Chuanxiong Rhizoma): 川芎: Chuan1 xiong1/Cyun1 gung1

(Cinnamomi Cortex): 肉桂: Rou4 gui1/Juk6 gwai3

(Astragali Radix): 黄芪 / 黃耆: Huang2 qi2/Wong4 kei4 my teacher always referred to this medicinal as 北芪 / 北耆: Bei3 qi2/Bak1 kei4.

(Ginseng Decoction to Nourish Luxuriance)

人参养荣汤 / 人参養榮湯: Ren2 shen1 yang3 rong2 tang1/Jan4 sam1 joeng5 wing4 tong1

(Paeoniae Radix Alba): 白芍: Bai2 shao2/Baak6 zoek3

(Angelicae Sinensis Radix): 当归 / 當歸: Dang1 gui1/Dong1 gwai1

(Citri Reticulatae Pericarpium): 陈皮 / 陳皮: Chen2 pi2/Can4 pei4

(Astragali Radix): 黄芪 / 黃耆: Huang2 qi2/Wong4 kei4 my teacher always referred to this medicinal as 北芪 / 北耆: Bei3 qi2/Bak1 kei4.

(Cinnamomi Cortex): 肉桂: Rou4 gui4

(Ginseng Radix): 人参 / 人參: Ren2 shen1/Jan4 sam1

(Atractylodis Macrocephalae Rizoma): 白术 / 白術: Bai2 zhu2/Baak6 seot6

(Glycyrrhizae Radix Preparata): 炙甘草: Zhi4 gan1 cao3/Zek3 gam1 cou2

(Rehmanniae Radix Preparata): 熟地黄: Shu2 di4 huang2/Suk6 dei6 wong4

(Shisandrae Fructus): 五味子: Wu3 wei4 zi3/Ng5 mei6 zi2

(Poria): 茯苓: Fu2 ling2/Fuk6 ling4

(Dry-Fried Polygalae Radix): 炒远志/炒遠志: Chao3 yuan3 zhi4/Caau2 jyun5 zi3

(Zingiberis Rhizoma Recens): 生姜 / 生薑: Sheng1 jiang1/Sang1 goeng1

(Jujubae Fructus): 大枣 / 大棗: Da4 zao3/Daai6 zou2

(Taishan Bedrock Powder)

泰山盘石散 / 泰山磐石散: Tai4 shan1 pan2 shi2 san3/Taai3 saan1 pun4 sek6 saan3

(Ginseng Radix): 人参 / 人參: Ren2 shen1/Jan4 sam1

(Astragali Radix): 黄芪 / 黃耆: Huang2 qi2/Wong4 kei4 My teacher always referred to this as 北芪: Bei3 qi2/Bak1 kei4.

(Atractylodis Macrocephalae Rhizoma): 白术 / 白術: Bai2 zhu2/Baak6 seot6

(Glycyrrhizae Radix Preparata): 炙甘草: Zhi4 gan1 cao3/Zek3 gam1 cou2

(Angelicae Sinensis Radix): 当归 / 當歸: Dang1 gui1/Dong1 gwai1

(Chuanxiong Rhizoma): 川芎: Chuan1 xiong1/Cyun1 gung1

(Paeoniae Radix Alba): 白芍: Bai2 shao2/Baak6 zoek3

(Rehmanniae Radix Preparata): 熟地黄: Shu2 di4 huang2/Suk6 dei6 wong4

(Dipsaci Radix): 续断 / 續斷: Xü4 duan4/Zuk6 dyun6

(Scutellariae Radix): 黄芩: Huang2 qin2/Wong4 kam4

(Amomi Fructus): 砂仁: Sha1 ren2/Saa1 jan4

(Glutinous Rice): 糯米: Nuo4 mi3/No6 mai5

(Fleeceflower Root and Ginseng Drink)

何人饮 / 何人飲: He2 ren2 yin3/Ho4 jan4 jam2

(Polygoni Multiflori Radix): 何首乌 / 何首烏: He2 shou3 wu1/Ho4 sau2 wu1

(Ginseng Radix): 人参 / 人參: Ren2 shen1/Jan4 sam1

(Angelicae Sinensis Radix): 当归 / 當歸: Dang1 gui1/Dong1 gwai1

(Citri Reticulatae Pericarpium): 陈皮 / 陳皮: Chen2 pi2/Can4 pei4

(Baked Zingiberis Rhizoma Recens): 煨姜 / 煨薑: Wei1 jiang1/Wui1 goeng1

(Supplement the Center and Boost the Qi Decoction)

补中益气汤 / 補中益氣湯: Bu3 zhong1 yi4 qi4 tang1/Bou2 zung1 jik1 hei3 tong1

(Astragali Radix): 黄芪 / 黃耆: Huang2 qi2/Wong4 Kei4 My teacher always referred to this as 北芪: Bei3 qi2/Bak1 kei4.

(Atractylodis Macrocephalae Rhizoma): 白术 / 白術: Bai2 zhu2/Baak6 seot6

(Ginseng Radix): 人参 / 人參: Ren2 shen1/Jan4 sam1

(Wine-Washed Angelicae Sinensis Radix): 酒洗当归 / 酒洗當歸: Jiu3 xi3 dang1 gui1/Zau2 sai2 dong1 gwai1

(Citri Reticulatae Pericarpium): 陈皮 / 陳皮: Chen2 pi2/Can4 pei4

(Glycyrrhizae Radix Praeparata): 炙甘草: Zhi4 gan1 cao3/Zek3 gam1 cou2

(Cimicifugae Rhizoma): 升麻: Sheng1 ma2/Sing1 maa4

(Bupleuri Radix): 柴胡: Chai2 hu2/Caai4 wu4

(Regulate the Center and Boost the Qi Decoction)

调中益气汤 / 調中益氣湯: Tiao2 zhong1 yi4 qi4 tang1/Tiu4 zung1 jik1 hei3 tong1

(Astragali Radix): 黄芪 / 黃耆: Huang2 qi2/Wong4 Kei4 My teacher always referred to this as 北芪: Bei3 qi2/Bak1 kei4.

(Atractylodis Rhizoma): 苍术 / 蒼術: Cang1 zhu2/Cong1 seot6

(Ginseng Radix): 人参 / 人參: Ren2 shen1/Jan4 sam1

(Citri Reticulatae Pericarpium): 陈皮 / 陳皮: Chen2 pi2/Can4 pei4

(Aucklandiae Radix): 木香: Mu4 xiang1/Muk6 hoeng1

(Glycyrrhizae Radix Preparata): 炙甘草: Zhi4 gan1 cao3/Zek3 gam1 cou2

(Cimicifugae Rhizoma): 升麻: Sheng1 ma2/Sing1 maa4

(Bupleuri Radix): 柴胡: Chai2 hu2/Caai4 wu4

(Modified Supplement the Center and Boost the Qi Decoction)

加减补中益气汤 / 加減補中益氣湯: Jia1 jian3 bu3 zhong1 yi4 qi4 tang/Gaa1 gaam2 bou2 zung1 jik1 hei3 tong1

(Astragali Radix): 黄芪 / 黃耆: Huang2 qi2/Wong4 Kei4 My teacher always referred to this as 北芪: Bei3 qi2/Bak1 kei4.

(Atractylodis Macrocephalae Rhizoma): 白术 / 白術: Bai2 zhu2/Baak6 seot6

(Ginseng Radix): 人参 / 人參: Ren2 shen1/Jan4 sam1

(Citri Reticulatae Pericarpium): 陈皮 / 陳皮: Chen2 pi2/Can4 pei4

(Glycyrrhizae Radix Preparata): 炙甘草: Zhi4 gan1 cao3/Zek3 gam1 cou2
(Cimicifugae Rhizoma): 升麻: Sheng1 ma2/Sing1 maa4
(Bupleuri Radix): 柴胡: Chai2 hu2/Caai4 wu4
(Asini Corii Colla): 阿胶 / 阿膠: E1 jiao1/Aa3 gaau1
(Artemisiae Argyii Folium): 艾叶 / 艾葉: Ai4 ye4/Ngaai6 jip6

(Generate the Pulse Powder)
生脉散 / 生脈散: Sheng1 mai4 san3/Sang1 mak6 saan3
(Ginseng Radix): 人参 / 人參: Ren2 shen1/Jan4 sam1
(Ophiopogonis Radix): 麦门冬 / 麥門冬: Mai4 men2 dong1/Mak6 mun4 dung1
(Schisandrae Fructus): 五味子: Wu3 wei4 zi3/Ng5 mei6 zi2

(Tonify the Lungs Decoction)
补肺汤 / 補肺湯: Bu3 fei4 tang1/Bou2 fai3 tong1
(Ginseng Radix): 人参 / 人參: Ren2 shen1/Jan4 sam1
(Astragali Radix): 黄芪 / 黃耆: Huang2 qi2/Wong4 kei4 my teacher always referred to this medicinal as 北芪 / 北耆: Bei3 qi2/Bak1 kei4.
(Rehmanniae Radix Preparata): 熟地黄: Shu2 di4 huang2/Suk6 dei6 wong4
(Schisandrae Fructus): 五味子: Wu3 wei4 zi3/Ng5 mei6 ji2
(Asteris Radix): 紫菀: Zi3 wan3/Zi2 jyun2
(Mori Cortex): 桑白皮: Sang1 bai2 pi2/Song1 baak6 pei4

Blood-Supplementing Formulas

(Four Materials Decoction)
四物汤 / 四物湯: Si4 wu4 tang1/Sei3 mat6 tong1
(Angelicae Sinensis Radix): 当归 / 當歸: Dang1 gui1/Dong1 gwai1
(Rehmanniae Radix Praeparata): 熟地黄: Shu2 di4 huang2/Suk6 dei6 wong4
(Paeoniae Radix Alba): 白芍: Bai2 shao2/Baak6 zoek3
(Chuanxiong Rhizoma): 川芎: Chuan1 xiong1/Cyun1 gung1

(Persica and Carthamus Four Materials Decoction)
桃红四物汤 / 桃仁紅四物湯: Tao2 hong2 si4 wu4 tang1/Tou4 hung4 sei3 mat6 tong1
(Angelicae Sinensis Radix): 当归 / 當歸: Dang1 gui1/Dong1 gwai1
(Rehmanniae Radix Praeparata): 熟地黄: Shu2 di4 huang2/Suk6 dei6 wong4
(Paeoniae Radix Alba): 白芍: Bai2 shao2/Baak6 zoek3
(Chuanxiong Rhizoma): 川芎: Chuan1 xiong1/Cyun1 gung1
(Persicae Semen): 桃仁: Tao2 ren2/Tou4 jan4
(Carthami Flos): 红花 / 紅花: Hong2 hua1/Hung4 faa1

(Sage-Like Healing Decoction)

圣愈汤 / 聖愈湯: Sheng4 yü4 tang1/Sing3 jyu6 tong1

(Angelicae Sinensis Radix): 当归 / 當歸: Dang1 gui1/Dong1 gwai1

(Rehmanniae Radix Praeparata): 熟地黄: Shu2 di4 huang2/Suk6 dei6 wong4

(Rehmanniae Radix): 生地黄: Sheng1 di4 huang2

(Paeoniae Radix Alba): 白芍: Bai2 shao2/Baak6 zoek3

(Chuanxiong Rhizoma): 川芎: Chuan1 xiong1/Cyun1 gung1

(Ginseng Radix): 人参 / 人參: Ren2 shen1/Jan4 sam1

(Astragali Radix): 黄芪 / 黃耆: Huang2 qi2/Wong4 kei4 My teacher always referred to this as 北芪: Bei3 qi2/Bak1 kei4.

(Ginger and Cinnamon Four Materials Decoction)

姜桂四物汤 / 薑桂四物湯: Jiang1 gui4 si4 wu4 tang1/Goeng1 gwai3 sei3 mat6 tong1

(Angelicae Sinensis Radix): 当归 / 當歸: Dang1 gui1/Dong1 gwai1

(Rehmanniae Radix Praeparata): 熟地黄: Shu2 di4 huang2/Suk6 dei6 wong4

(Paeoniae Radix Alba): 白芍: Bai2 shao2/Baak6 zoek3

(Chuanxiong Rhizoma): 川芎: Chuan1 xiong1/Cyun1 gung1

(Cinnamomi Cortex): 肉桂: Rou4 gui4/Juk6 gwai3

(Zingiberis Rhizoma Praeparatum): 炮姜 / 炮薑: Pao2 jiang1/Paau4 goeng1

(Three Yellows Four Materials Decoction)

三黄四物汤 / 三黃四物湯: San1 huang2 si4 wu4 tang1/Saam1 wong4 sei3 mat6 tong1

(Angelicae Sinensis Radix): 当归 / 當歸: Dang1 gui1/Dong1 gwai1

(Rehmanniae Radix Praeparata): 熟地黄: Shu2 di4 huang2/Suk6 dei6 wong4

(Paeoniae Radix Alba): 白芍: Bai2 shao2/Baak6 zoek3

(Chuanxiong Rhizoma): 川芎: Chuan1 xiong1/Cyun1 gung1

(Scutellariae Radix): 黄芩: Huang2 qin2/Wong4 kam4

(Coptidis Rhizoma): 黄连 / 黃連: Huang2 lian2/Wong4 lin4 My teacher always referred to this medicinal in its Sichuan form: 川连 / 川連: Chuan1 lian2/Cyun1 lin4

(Rhei Radix et Rhizoma): 大黄: Da4 huang2/Daai6 wong4

(Scutellaria and Coptis Four Materials Decoction)

芩连四物汤 / 芩連四物湯: Qin2 lian2 si4 wu4 tang1/Kam4 lin4 sei3 mat6 tong1

(Angelicae Sinensis Radix): 当归 / 當歸: Dang1 gui1/Dong1 gwai1

(Rehmanniae Radix): 生地黄: Sheng1 di4 huang2/Sang1 dei6 wong4

(Paeoniae Radix Alba): 白芍: Bai2 shao2/Baak6 zoek3

(Chuanxiong Rhizoma): 川芎: Chuan1 xiong1/Cyun1 gung1

(Scutellariae Radix): 黄芩: Huang2 qin2/Wong4 kam4

(Coptidis Rhizoma): 黄连 / 黄連: Huang2 lian2/Wong4 lin4 My teacher always referred to this medicinal in its Sichuan form: 川连 / 川連: Chuan1 lian2/Cyun1 lin4

(Ophiopogonis Radix): 麦门冬 / 麥門冬: Mai4 men2 dong1/Mak6 mun4 dung1

(Peony and Licorice Decoction)

芍药甘草汤 / 芍藥甘草湯: Shao2 yao4 gan1 cao3 tang1/Zoek3 joek6 gam1 cou2 tong1

(Paeoniae Radix Alba): 白芍: Bai2 shao2/Baak6 zoek3

(Glycyrrhizae Radix Preparata): 炙甘草: Zhi4 gan1 cao3/Zek3 gam1 cou2

(Chinese Angelica Six Yellows Decoction)

当归六黄汤 / 當歸六黃湯: Dang1 gui1 liu4 huang2 tang1/Dong1 gwai1 luk6 wong4 tong1

(Angelicae Sinensis Radix): 当归 / 當歸: Dang1 gui1/Dong1 gwai1

(Rehmanniae Radix Praeparata): 熟地黄: Shu2 di4 huang2/Suk6 dei6 wong4

(Rehmanniae Radix): 生地黄: Sheng1 di4 huang2/Sang1 dei6 wong4

(Paeoniae Radix Alba): 白芍: Bai2 shao2/Baak6 zoek3

(Ligustici Wallici Rhizoma): 川芎: Chuan1 xiong1/Cyun1 gung1

(Astragali Radix): 黄芪 / 黃耆: Huang2 qi2/Wong4 kei4 My teacher always referred to this as 北芪: Bei3 qi2/Bak1 kei4.

(Scutellariae Radix): 黄芩: Huang2 qin2/Wong4 kam4

(Coptidis Rhizoma): 黄连 / 黃連: Huang2 lian2/Wong4 lin4 My teacher always referred to this medicinal in its Sichuan form: 川连 / 川連: Chuan1 lian2/Cyun1 lin4

(Phellodendri Cortex): 黄柏: Huang2 bai2/Wong4 paak3

(Supplement the Liver Decoction)
补肝汤 / 補肝湯: Bu3 gan1 tang1/Bou2 gon1 tong1
(Angelicae Sinensis Radix): 当归 / 當歸: Dang1 gui1/Dong1 gwai1
(Rehmanniae Radix Praeparata): 熟地黄: Shu2 di4 huang2/Suk6 dei6 wong4
(Paeoniae Radix Alba): 白芍: Bai2 shao2/Baak6 zoek3
(Chuanxiong Rhizoma): 川芎: Chuan1 xiong1/Cyun1 gung1
(Zizyphi Spinosae Semen): 酸枣仁 / 酸棗仁: Suan1 zao3 ren2/Syun1 zou2 jan4
(Chaenomelis Fructus): 木瓜: Mu4 gua1/Muk6 gwaa1
(Glycyrrhizae Radix Preparata): 炙甘草: Zhi4 gan1 cao3/Zek3 gam1 cou2

(Jade Candle Powder)
玉烛散 / 玉燭散: Yü4 zhu2 san3/Juk6 zuk1 saan3
(Angelicae Sinensis Radix): 当归 / 當歸: Dang1 gui1/Dong1 gwai1
(Rehmanniae Radix Praeparata): 熟地黄: Shu2 di4 huang2/Suk6 dei6 wong4
(Paeoniae Radix Alba): 白芍: Bai2 shao2/Baak6 zoek3
(Chuanxiong Rhizoma): 川芎: Chuan1 xiong1/Cyun1 gung1
(Rhei Radix et Rhizoma): 大黄: Da4 huang2/Daai6 wong4
(Natrii Sulfas): 硭硝: Mang2 xiao1/Mong4 siu1
(Glycyrrhizae Radix): 甘草: Gan1 cao3/Gam1 cou2

(Chinese Angelica and Peony Powder)
当归芍药散 / 當歸芍藥散: Dang1 gui1 shao2 yao4 san3/Dong1 gwai1 zoek3 joek6 saan3
(Angelicae Sinensis Radix): 当归 / 當歸: Dang1 gui1/Dong1 gwai1
(Paeoniae Radix Alba): 白芍: Bai2 shao2/Baak6 zoek3
(Chuanxiong Rhizoma): 川芎: Chuan1 xiong1/Cyun1 gung1
(Atractylodis Macrocephalae Rhizoma): 白术 / 白術: Bai2 zhu2/Baak6 seot6
(Poria): 茯苓: Fu2 ling2/Fuk6 ling4
(Alismatis Rhizoma): 泽泻 / 澤瀉: Ze2 xie4/Zaak6 se3

(Tangkuei Decoction to Tonify the Blood)
当归补血汤 / 當歸補血湯: Dang1 gui1 bu3 xue4 tang1/Dong1 gwai1 bou2 hyut3 tong1
(Astragali Radix): 黄芪 / 黃耆: Huang2 qi2/Wong4 kei4 my teacher always referred to this medicinal as 北芪 / 北耆: Bei3 qi2/Bak1 kei4.
(Wine-Washed Angelicae Sinensis Radix): 酒洗当归 / 酒洗當歸: Jiu3 xi3 dang1 gui1/Zau2 sai2 dong1 gwai1

(Mutton Stew with Tangkuei and Fresh Ginger Decoction)

当归生姜羊肉汤 / 當歸生薑羊肉湯: Dang1 gui1 sheng1 jiang1 yang2 rou4 tang1/Dong1 gwai1 sang1 goeng1 joeng4 juk6 tong1

(Angelicae Sinensis Radix): 当归 / 當歸: Dang1 gui1/Dong1 gwai1

(Zingiberis Rhizoma Recens): 生姜 / 生薑: Sheng1 jiang1/Sang1 goeng1

(Mutton): 羊肉: Yang2 rou4/Joeng4 juk6

(Artemisia Argyium and Cyperus Warm the Palace Decoction)

艾附暖宫丸 / 艾附暖宮丸: Ai4 fu4 nuan3 gong1 wan2/Ngaai6 fu6 nyun5 gung1 jyun2

(Artemisiae Argyi Folium): 艾叶 / 艾葉: Ai4 ye4/Ngaai6 jip6

(Wine-Fried Rehmanniae Radix): 酒炒生地黄: Jiu3 chao3 sheng1 di4 huang2/Zau2 caau2 sang1 dei6 wong4

(Wine-Fried Paeoniae Radix Alba): 酒炒白芍: Jiu3 chao3 bai2 shao2/Zau2 caau2 baak6 zoek3

(Chuanxiong Rhizoma): 川芎: Chuan1 xiong1/Cyun1 gung1

(Vinegar-Fried Cyperi Rhizoma): 醋炒香附: Cu4 chao3 xiang1 fu4/Cou3 caau2 hoeng1 fu6

(Zanghoxyli Pericarpium): 花椒: Hua1 jiao1/Faa1 ziu1

(Astragali Radix): 黄芪 / 黃耆: Huang1 qi2 My teacher always referred to this as 北芪: Bei3 qi2/Bak1 kei4.

(Evodiae Fructus): 吴茱萸 / 吳茱萸: Wu2 zhu1 yü2/Ng4 zyu1 jyu4

(Cinnamomi Cortex): 肉桂: Rou4 gui4/Juk6 gwai3

(Dipsaci Radix): 续断 / 續斷: Xü4 duan4/Zuk6 dyun6

(Added Flavors Four Materials Decoction)

加味四物汤 / 加味四物湯: Jia1 wei4 si4 wu4 tang1/Gaa1 mei6 sei3 mat6 tong1

(Angelicae Sinensis Radix): 当归 / 當歸: Dang1 gui1/Dong1 gwai1

(Rehmanniae Radix Praeparata): 熟地黄: Shu2 di4 huang2/Suk6 dei6 wong4

(Paeoniae Radix Alba): 白芍: Bai2 shao2/Baak6 zoek3

(Chuanxiong Rhizoma): 川芎: Chuan1 xiong1/Cyun1 gung1

(Ophiopogonis Radix): 麦门冬 / 麥門冬: Mai4 men2 dong1/Mak6 mun4 dung1

(Phellodendri Cortex): 黄柏: Huang2 bai2/Wong4 paak3

(Atractylodis Rhizoma): 苍术 / 蒼術: Cang1 zhu2/Cong1 seot6

(Eucommiae Cortex): 杜仲: Du4 zhong4/Dou6 zung6

(Schisandrae Fructus): 五味子: Wu3 wei4 zi3/Ng5 mei6 zi2

(Ginseng Radix): 人参 / 人參: Ren2 shen1/Jan4 sam1

(Coptidis Rhizoma): 黄连 / 黃連: Huang2 lian2/Wong4 lin4 My teacher always referred to this medicinal in its Sichuan form: 川连 / 川連: Chuan1 lian2/Cyun1 lin4

(Anemarrhenae Rhizoma): 知母: Zhi1 mu3/Zi1 mou5

(Achyranthis Radix): 牛膝: Niu2 xi1/Ngau4 sat1 My teacher always wrote this "cow seven" or 牛七: Niu2 qi1/Ngau4 cat1

(Tangkuei and Spatholobus Decoction)

当归鸡血藤汤 / 當歸雞血藤湯: Dang1 gui1 ji1 xue4 teng2 tang1/Dong1 gwai1 gai1 hyut3 tang4 tong1

(Angelicae Sinensis Radix): 当归 / 當歸: Dang1 gui1/Dong1 gwai1

(Rehmanniae Radix Praeparata): 熟地黄: Shu2 di4 huang2/Suk6 dei6 wong4

(Paeoniae Radix Alba): 白芍: Bai2 shao2/Baak6 zoek3

(Longan Arillus): 龙眼肉 / 龍眼肉: Long2 yan3 rou4/Lung4 ngaan5 juk6

(Salviae Miltiorrhizae Radix): 丹参 / 丹參: Dan1 shen1/Daan1 sam1

(Spatholobi Caulis): 鸡血藤 / 雞血藤: Ji1 xue4 teng2/Gai1 hyut3 tang4

(Lotus and Pearl Drink)

莲珠饮 / 蓮珠飲: Lian2 zhu1yin3/Lin4 zyu1 jam2

(Angelicae Sinensis Radix): 当归 / 當歸: Dang1 gui1/Dong1 gwai1

(Rehmanniae Radix Praeparata): 生地黄: Sheng1 di4 huang2/Sang1 dei6 wong4

(Paeoniae Radix Alba): 白芍: Bai2 shao2/Baak6 zoek3

(Chuanxiong Rhizoma): 川芎: Chuan1 xiong1/Cyun1 gung1

(Cinnamomi Cassiae Ramulus): 桂枝: Gui4 zhi1/Gwai zi1

(Poria): 茯苓: Fu2 ling2/Fuk6 ling4

(Atractylodis Macrocephalae Rhizoma): 白术 / 白術: Bai2 zhu1/Baak6 seot6

(Glycyrrhizae Radix): 甘草: Gan1 cao3/Gam1 cou2

(Restore the Spleen Decoction)

归脾汤 / 歸脾湯: Gui1 pi2 tang1/Gwai1 pei4 tong1

(Ginseng Radix): 人参 / 人參: Ren2 shen1/Jan4 sam1

(Dry-Fried Astragali Radix): 炒黄芪 / 炒黃耆: Chao3 huang2 qi2/Caau2 wong4 kei4 My teacher always referred to this as 北芪: Bei3 qi2/Bak1 kei4.

(Atractylodis Macrocephalae Rhizoma): 白术 / 白術: Bai2 zhu2/Baak6 seot6

(Paradicis Poriae Cocos Sclerotium): 茯苓: Fu2 ling2/Fuk6 ling4

(Longanae Arillus): 龙眼肉 / 龍眼肉: Long2 yan3 rou4/Lung4 ngaan5 juk6

(Dry-Fried Zizyphi Spinosae Semen): 炒酸枣仁 / 炒酸棗仁: Chao3 suan1 zao3 ren2/Caau2 syun1 zou2 jan4

(Auklandiae Radix): 木香: Mu4 xiang1/Muk6 hoeng1

(Glycyrrhizae Radix Preparata): 炙甘草 / 炙甘草: Zhi4 gan1 cao3/Zek3 gam1 cou2

(Angelicae Sinensis Radix): 当归 / 當歸: Dang1 gui1/Dong1 gwai1

(Processed Polygalae Radix): 制远志 / 製遠志: Zhi4 yuan3 zhi4/Zai3 jyun5 zi3

(Zingiberis Rhizoma Recens): 生姜 / 生薑: Sheng1 jiang1/Sang1 goeng1

(Jujubae Fructus): 大枣 / 大棗: Da4 zao3/Daai6 zou2

Yin-Supplementing Formulas

(Six Flavors Rehmannia Pills)
六味地黄丸: Liu4 wei4 di4 huang2 wan2/Luk6 mei6 dei6 wong4 jyun2
(Rehmanniae Radix): 熟地黄: Shu2 di4 huang2/Suk6 dei6 wong4
(Corni Fructus): 山茱萸 / 山茱萸: Shan1 zhu1 yü2/Saan1 zyu1 jyu4
(Dioscoreae Rhizoma): 山药 / 山藥: Shan1 yao4/Saan1 joek6
(Alismatis Rhizoma): 泽泻 / 澤瀉: Ze2 xie4/Zaak6 se3
(Poria): 茯苓: Fu2 ling2/Fuk6 ling4
(Moutan Cortex): 牡丹皮: Mu3 dan1 pi2/Maau5 daan1 pei4

(Improve Vision Pill With Rehmannia)
明目地黄丸: Ming2 mu4 di4 huang2 wan2/Ming4 muk6 dei6 wong4 jyun2
(Rehmanniae Radix Preparata): 熟地黄: Shu2 di4 huang2/Suk6 dei6 wong4
(Rehmanniae Radix): 生地黄: Sheng1 di4 huang2/Sang1 dei6 wong4
(Dioscoreae Rhizoma): 山药 / 山藥: Shan1 yao4/Saan1 joek6
(Alismatis Rhizoma): 泽泻 / 澤瀉: Ze2 xie4/Zaak6 se3
(Corni Fructus): 山茱萸: Shan1 zhu1 yü2/Saan1 zyu1 jyu4
(Moutan Cortex): 牡丹皮: Mu3 dan1 pi2/Maau5 daan1 pei4
(Bupleuri Radix): 柴胡: Chai2 hu2/Caai4 wu4
(Poriae Sclerotium Pararadicis): 茯神: Fu2 shen2/Fuk6 san4
(Angelicae Sinensis Radix): 当归 / 當歸: Dang1 gui1/Dong1 gwai1
(Schisandrae Fructus): 五味子: Wu3 wei4 zi3/Ng5 mei6 zi2

(Restore the Left [Kidney] Pill)

左归丸／佐歸丸: Zuo3 gui1 wan2/Zo2 gwai1 jyun2

(Rehmanniae Radix Preparata): 熟地黄: Shu2 di4 huang2/Suk6 dei6 wong4

(Dry-Fried Dioscoreae Rhizoma): 炒山药／炒山藥: Chao3 shan1 yao4/Caau2 saan1 joek6

(Lycii Fructus): 枸杞子: Gou3 qi3 zi3/Gau2 gei2 zi2-my teacher always referred to this as 杞子: Gei2 zi2

(Corni Fructus): 山茱萸: Shan1 zhu1 yü2/Saan1 zyu1 jyu4

(Wine-Prepared Cyathulae Radix): 酒川牛膝: Jiu3 chuan1 niu2 xi1/Zau2 cyun1 ngau4 sat1 My teacher always wrote this "cow seven" or 牛七: Niu2 qi1/Ngau4 cat1

(Cuscutae Semen): 菟丝子／菟絲子: Tu4 si1 zi3/Tou3 si1 zi2

(Cerbi Cornus Colla): 鹿角胶／鹿角膠: Lu4 jiao3 jiao1/Luk6 gok3 gaau1

(Testudinis Plastri Colla): 龟板胶／龜板膠: Gui1 ban3 jiao1/Gwai1 baan2 gaau1

(Restore the Left [Kidney] Drink)

左归饮／佐歸飲: Zuo3 gui1 yin3/Zo2 gwai1 jam2

(Rehmanniae Radix Preparata): 熟地黄: Shu2 di4 huang2/Suk6 dei6 wong4

(Dioscoreae Rhizoma): 山药／山藥: Shan1 yao4/Saan1 joek6

(Lycii Fructus): 枸杞子: Gou3 qi3 zi3/Gau2 gei2 zi2-my teacher always referred to this as 杞子: Gei2 zi2

(Poria): 茯苓: Fu2 ling2/Fuk6 ling4

(Corni Fructus): 山茱萸: Shan1 zhu1 yü2/Saan1 zyu1 jyu4

(Glycyrrhizae Radix Preparata): 炙甘草: Zhi4 gan1 cao3/Zek3 gam1 cou2

(Great Tonify the Yin Pill)

大补阴丸／大補陰丸: Da4 bu3 yin1 wan2/Daai6 bou2 jam1 jyun2

(Rehmanniae Radix Preparata): 熟地黄: Shu2 di4 huang2/Suk6 dei6 wong4

(Crisp Testudinis Plastrum): 酥龟板／酥龜板: Su1 gui1 ban3/Sou1 gwai1 baan2

(Dry-Fried Phellodendri Cortex): 炒黄柏: Chao3 huang1 bai3/Caau2 wong4 paak3

(Wine-Fried Anemarrhenae Rhizoma): 酒炒知母／酒炒知母: Jiu3 chao3 Zhi1 mu3/Jau2 caau2 zi1 mou5

(Hidden Tiger Pill)

虎潜丸 / 虎潛丸: Hu2 qian2 wan2/Fu2 cim4 jyun2

(Wine-Fried Phellodendri Cortex): 酒炒黄柏 / 酒炒黃柏: Jiu2 chao3 huang2 bai3/Zau2 caau2 wong4 paak3

(Wine-Fried Anemarrhenae Rhizoma): 酒炒知母 / 酒炒知母: Jiu3 chao3 Zhi1 mu3/Jau2 caau2 zi1 mou5

(Rehmanniae Radix Preparata): 熟地黄: Shu2 di4 huang2/Suk6 dei6 wong4

(Wine-Fried Tesudinis Plastrum): 酒炒龟板 / 酒炒龜板: Jiu3 chao3 gui1 ban3/Zau2 caau2 gwai1 baan2

(Paeoniae Radix Alba): 白芍: Bai2 shao2/Baak6 zoek3

(Tigris Os): 虎骨: Hu3 gu3/Fu2 gwat1

(Cynomorii Herba): 锁阳 / 鎖陽: Suo3 yang2/So2 joeng4

(Zingiberis Rhizoma): 干姜 / 乾薑: Gan1 jiang1/Gon1 goeng1

(Citri Reticulatae Pericarpium): 陈皮 / 陳皮: Chen2 pi2/Can4 pei4

(Great Creation Pill)

大造丸: Da4 zao4 wan2/Daai6 zou5 jyun2

(Hominis Placenta): 紫河车 / 紫河車: Zi3 he2 che1/Zi2 ho4 ce1

(Crisp Testudinis Plastrum): 酥龟板 / 酥龜板: Su1 gui1 ban3/Sou1 gwai1 baan2

(Phellodendri Cortex): 黄柏: Huang2 bai3/Wong4 paak3

(Eucommiae Cortex): 杜仲: Du2 zhong4/Dou6 zung6

(Achyranthis Radix): 牛膝: Niu2 xi1/Ngau4 sat1 My teacher always wrote this "cow seven" or 牛七: Niu2 qi1/Ngau4 cat1

(Ophiopogonis Radix): 麦门冬 / 麥門冬: Mai4 men2 dong1/Mak6 mun4 dung1

(Asparagi Radix): 天门冬 / 天門冬: Tian1 men2 dong1/Tin1 mun4 dung1

(Rehmanniae Radix): 生地黄: Sheng1 di4 huang2/Sang2 dei6 wong4

(Ginseng Radix): 人参 / 人參: Ren2 shen1/Jan4 sam1

(Linking Decoction)

一贯煎 / 一貫煎: Yi1 guan4 jian1/Jat1 gun3 zin1

(Rehmanniae Radix): 生地黄: Sheng1 di4 huang2/Sang2 dei6 wong4

(Lycii Fructus): 枸杞子: Gou3 qi3 zi3/Gau2 gei2 zi2-my teacher always referred to this as 杞子: gei2 zi2.

(Glehniae/Adenophorae Radix): 沙参 / 沙參: Sha1 shen1/Saa1 sam1

(Ophiopogonis Radix): 麦门冬 / 麥門冬: Mai4 men2 dong1/Mak6 mun4 dung1

(Angelicae Sinensis Radix): 当归 / 當歸: Dang1 gui1/Dong1 gwai1

(Toosendan Fructus): 川楝子: Chuan1 lian4 zi3/Cyun1 lin6 zi2

(Two-Solstice Pill)
二至丸: Er4 zhi4 wan2/Ji6 zi3 jyun2
(Ligustri Lucidi Fructus): 女贞子 / 女貞子: Nü3 zhen1 zi3/Neoi5 zing1 zi2
(Eclipae Herba): 墨旱莲 / 墨旱蓮: Mo4 han4 lian2/Mak6 hon4 lin4, also called 旱莲草 / 旱蓮草: Han4 lian2 cao3/Hon5 lin4 cou2

(Tonify the Lungs Decoction with Ass-Hide Gelatin)
补肺阿胶汤 / 補肺阿膠湯: Bu3 fei4 e1 jiao1 tang1/Bou2 fai3 aa3 gaau1 tong1
(Asini Corii Colla): 阿胶 / 阿膠: E1 jiao1/Aa3 gaau1
(Aristolochiae Fructus): 马兜苓 / 馬兜苓: Ma3 dou1 ling2/Maa5 dau1 ling4
(Dry-Fried Armeniacae Semen): 炒杏仁: Chao3 xing4 ren2/Caau2 hang6 jan4
(Dry-Fried Arctii Fructus): 炒牛蒡子: Chao3 niu2 bang4 zi3/Caau2 ngau4 bong2 zi2
(Dry-Fried Glutinous Rice): 炒糯米: Chao3 nuo4 mi3/Caau2 no6 mai5
Glycyrrhizae Radix Preparata): 炙甘草: Zhi3 gan1 cao3/Zek3 gam1 cou2

(Preserve Vistas Pill)
驻景丸 / 駐景丸: Zhu4 jing3 wan2/Zyu3 ging2 jyun2
(Cuscutae Semen): 菟丝子 / 菟絲子: Tu4 si1 zi3/Tou3 si1 zi2
(Rehmanniae Radix Preparata): 熟地黄: Shu2 di4 huang2/Suk6 dei6 wong4
(Plantaginis Semen): 车前子 / 車前子: Che1 qian2 zi3/Ce1 cin4 zi2

(Lycium and Chrysanthemum Rehmannia Pills)
杞菊地黄丸: Qi3 jü2 di4 huang2 wan2/gei2 guk1 dei6 wong4 jyun2
(Rehmanniae Radix): 熟地黄: Shu2 di4 huang2/Suk6 dei6 wong4
(Corni Fructus): 山茱萸: Shan1 zhu1 yü2/Saan1 zyu1 jyu4
(Dioscoreae Rhizoma): 山药 / 山藥: Shan1 yao4/Saan1 joek6
(Alismatis Rhizoma): 泽泻 / 澤瀉: Ze2 xie4/Zaak6 se3
(Poria): 茯苓: Fu2 ling2/Fuk6 ling4
(Moutan Cortex): 牡丹皮: Mu3 dan1 pi2/Maau5 daan1 pei4
(Chrysanthemi Flos): 菊花: Jü2 hua1/Guk1 faa1
(Lycii Fructus): 枸杞子: Gou3 qi3 zi3/Gau2 gei2 zi2

(Capital Qi Pills)
都气丸 / 都氣丸: Du1 qi4 wan2/Dou1 hei3 jyun2
(Schizandrae Fructus): 五味子: Wu3 wei4 zi3/Ng5 mei6 zi2
(Rehmanniae Radix): 熟地黄: Shu2 di4 huang2/Suk6 dei6 wong4
(Corni Fructus): 山茱萸: Shan1 zhu1 yü2/Saan1 zyu1 jyu4
(Dioscoreae Rhizoma): 山药 / 山藥: Shan1 yao4/Saan1 joek6
(Alismatis Rhizoma): 泽泻 / 澤瀉: Ze2 xie4/Zaak6 se3
(Poria): 茯苓: Fu2 ling2/Fuk6 ling4
(Moutan Cortex): 牡丹皮: Mu3 dan1 pi2/Maau5 daan1 pei4

(Ophiopogon and Schizandra Rehmannia Pills)
麦味地黄丸 / 麥味地黃丸: Mai4 wei4 di4 huang2 wan2/Mak6 mei6 dei6 wong4 jyun2
八仙长寿丸 / 八仙長壽丸: Ba1 xian1 chang2 shou4 wan2/baat3 sin1 coeng4 sau6 jyun2 "Eight Immortals Long Life Pills"
(Ophiopogonis Radix): 麦门冬 / 麥門冬: Mai4 men2 dong1/Mak6 mun4 dung1
(Schizandrae Fructus): 五味子: Wu3 wei4 zi3/Ng5 mei6 zi2
(Rehmanniae Radix Preparata): 熟地黄: Shu2 di4 huang2/Suk6 dei6 wong4
(Corni Fructus): 山茱萸 / 山茱萸: Shan1 zhu1 yü2/Saan1 zyu1 jyu4
(Dioscoreae Rhizoma): 山药 / 山藥: Shan1 yao4/Saan1 joek6
(Alismatis Rhizoma): 泽泻 / 澤瀉: Ze2 xie4/Zaak6 se3
(Poria): 茯苓: Fu2 ling2/Fuk6 ling4
(Moutan Cortex): 牡丹皮: Mu3 dan1 pi2/Maau5 daan1 pei4

(Anemarrhena and Phellodendron Rehmannia Pills)
知柏地黄丸: Zhi1 bai3 di4 huang2 wan2/Zi1 paak3 dei6 wong4 jyun2
(Anemarrhenae Rhizoma): 知母: Zhi1 mu3/Zi1 mou5
(Phellodendri Cortex): 黄柏: Huang2 bai2/Wong paak3
(Rehmanniae Radix Preparata): 熟地黄: Shu2 di4 huang2/Suk6 dei6 wong4
(Corni Fructus): 山茱萸 / 山茱萸: Shan1 zhu1 yü2/Saan1 zyu1 jyu4
(Dioscoreae Rhizoma): 山药 / 山藥: Shan1 yao4/Saan1 joek6
(Alismatis Rhizoma): 泽泻 / 澤瀉: Ze2 xie4/Zaak6 se3
(Poria): 茯苓: Fu2 ling2/Fuk6 ling4
(Moutan Cortex): 牡丹皮: Mu3 dan1 pi2/Maau5 daan1 pei4

(Added Flavors Rehmannia Pills)
加味六味地黄丸: Jia1 wei4 liu4 wei4 di4 huang2 wan2/Gaa1 mei6 luk6 mei6 dei6 wong4 jyun2
(Cervi Cornu Pantotrichum): 鹿茸: Lu4 rong2/Luk6 jung4
(Acanthopanacis Cortex): 五加皮: Wu3 jia1 pi2/Ng5 gaa1 pei4
(Moschus): 麝香: She4 xiang1/Se6 hoeng1

(Rehmanniae Radix Preparata): 熟地黄: Shu2 di4 huang2/Suk6 dei6 wong4
(Corni Fructus): 山茱萸 / 山茱萸: Shan1 zhu1 yü2/Saan1 zyu1 jyu4
(Dioscoreae Rhizoma): 山药 / 山藥: Shan1 yao4/Saan1 joek6
(Alismatis Rhizoma): 泽泻 / 澤瀉: Ze2 xie4/Zaak6 se3
(Poria): 茯苓: Fu2 ling2/Fuk6 ling4
(Moutan Cortex): 牡丹皮: Mu3 dan1 pi2/Maau5 daan1 pei4

(Pill for Deafness that is Kind to the Left Kidney)
耳聋左慈丸 / 耳聾佐慈丸: Er3 long2 zuo3 ci2 wan2/Ji5 lung4 zo2 ci4 jyun2
(Magenetitum): 慈石: Ci2 shi2/Ci4 sek6
(Acori Tatarinowii Rhizoma): 石菖蒲: Shi2 chang1 pu2/Sek6 coeng1 pou4
(Schizandrae Fructus): 五味子: Wu3 wei4 zi3/Ng5 mei6 zi2
(Rehmanniae Radix): 熟地黄: Shu2 di4 huang2/Suk6 dei6 wong4
(Corni Fructus): 山茱萸 / 山茱萸: Shan1 zhu1 yü2/Saan1 zyu1 jyu4
(Dioscoreae Rhizoma): 山药 / 山藥: Shan1 yao4/Saan1 joek6
(Alismatis Rhizoma): 泽泻 / 澤瀉: Ze2 xie4/Zaak6 se3
(Poria): 茯苓: Fu2 ling2/Fuk6 ling4
(Moutan Cortex): 牡丹皮: Mu3 dan1 pi2/Maau5 daan1 pei4

(Chinese Angelica and Rehmannia Drink)
当归地黄饮 / 當歸地黃飲: Dang1 gui1 di4 huang2 yin3/Dong1 gwai1 dei6 wong4 jam2
(Angelicae Sinensis Radix): 当归 / 當歸: Dang1 gui1/Dong1 gwai1
(Rehmanniae Radix Preparata): 熟地黄: Shu2 di4 huang2/Suk6 dei6 wong4
(Corni Fructus): 山茱萸 / 山茱萸: Shan1 zhu1 yü2/Saan1 zyu1 jyu4
(Dioscoreae Rhizoma): 山药 / 山藥: Shan1 yao4/Saan1 joek6
(Eucommiae Cortex): 杜仲: Du4 zhong4/Dou6 zung6
(Achyranthis Bidentatae Radix): 牛膝: Niu2 xi1/Ngau4 sat1 my teacher always referred to this as 牛七 Ngau4 cat1 "cow seven"

(Chinese Angelica and Peony Pills)
归芍地黄丸 / 歸芍地黃丸: Gui1 shao2 di4 huang2 wan2/Gwai1 zoek3 dei6 wong4 jyun2
(Angelicae Sinensis Radix): 当归 / 當歸: Dang1 gui1/Dong1 gwai1
(Paeoniae Radix Alba): 白芍: Bai2 shao2/Baak6 zoek3
(Rehmanniae Radix Preparata): 熟地黄: Shu2 di4 huang2/Suk6 dei6 wong4
(Corni Fructus): 山茱萸 / 山茱萸: Shan1 zhu1 yü2/Saan1 zyu1 jyu4
(Dioscoreae Rhizoma): 山药 / 山藥: Shan1 yao4/Saan1 joek6
(Alismatis Rhizoma): 泽泻 / 澤瀉: Ze2 xie4/Zaak6 se3
(Poria): 茯苓: Fu2 ling2/Fuk6 ling4
(Moutan Cortex): 牡丹皮: Mu3 dan1 pi2/Maau5 daan1 pei4

(Eight Flavors Rehmannia Pill)
八味地黄丸: Ba1 wei4 di4 huang2 wan2/Baat3 mei6 dei6 wong4 jyun2
(Schisandrae Fructus): 五味子: Wu3 wei4 zi3/Ng5 mei6 zi2
(Honey Prepared Astragali Radix): 炙黄芪 / 炙黃耆: Zhi4 huang2 qi2/Zek3 wong4
kei4. My teacher always referred to this as 北芪: Bei3 qi2/Bak1 kei4.
(Rehmanniae Radix Preparata): 熟地黄: Shu2 di4 huang2/Suk6 dei6 wong4
(Corni Fructus): 山茱萸 / 山茱萸: Shan1 zhu1 yü2/Saan1 zyu1 jyu4
(Dioscoreae Rhizoma): 山药 / 山藥: Shan1 yao4/Saan1 joek6
(Alismatis Rhizoma): 泽泻 / 澤瀉: Ze2 xie4/Zaak6 se3
(Poria): 茯苓: Fu2 ling2/Fuk6 ling4
(Moutan Cortex): 牡丹皮: Mu3 dan1 pi2/Maau5 daan1 pei4

Yang-Supplementing Formulas

(Golden Cabinet Kidney Qi Pills)
金匮肾气丸 / 金匱腎氣丸: Jin1 gui4 shen4 qi4 wan2/Gam1 gwai6 san6 hei3 jyun2
(Rehmanniae Radix Preparata): 生地黄: Sheng1 di4 huang2/Sang1 dei6 wong4
(Corni Fructus): 山茱萸: Shan1 zhu1 yü2/Saan1 zyu1 jyu4
(Dioscoreae Rhizoma): 山药 / 山藥: Shan1 yao4/Saan1 joek6
(Alixmatis Rhizoma): 泽泻 / 澤瀉: Ze2 xie4/Zaak6 se3
(Poria): 茯苓: Fu2 ling2/Fuk6 ling4
(Moutan Cortex): 牡丹皮: Mu3 dan1 pi2/Maau5 daan1 pei4
(Cinnamomi Ramulus): 桂枝: Gui4 zhi1/Gwai3 zi1
(Aconiti Radix Lateralis Praeparata): 炮附子: Pao2 fu4 zi3/Paau4 fu6 zi2

(Ten Supplements Pills)
十补丸 / 十補丸: Shi2 bu3 wan2/Sap6 bou2 jyun2
(Rehmanniae Radix): 熟地黄: Shu2 di4 huang2/Suk6 dei6 wong4
(Corni Fructus): 山茱萸: Shan1 zhu1 yü2/Saan1 zyu1 jyu4
(Dioscoreae Rhizoma): 炒山药 / 炒山藥: Chao3 shan1 yao4/Caau2 saan1 joek6
(Alismatis Rhizoma): 泽泻 / 澤瀉: Ze2 xie4/Zaak6 se3
(Poria): 茯苓: Fu2 ling2/Fuk6 ling4
(Moutan Cortex): 牡丹皮: Mu3 dan1 pi2/Maau5 daan1 pei4
(Cinnamomi Cortex): 肉桂: Rou4 Gui4/Juk6 gwai3
(Aconiti Radix Lateralis Praeparata): 炮附子: Pao2 fu4 zi3/Paau4 fu6 zi2
(Schisandrae Fructus): 五味子: Wu3 wei4 zi3/Ng5 mei6 zi2
(Cervi Cornu Pantotrichum): 鹿茸: Lu4 rong2/Luk6 jung4

(Seven-Treasure Special Pill for Beautiful Whiskers)

七宝美髯丹 / 七寶美髯丹: Qi1 bao3 mei3 ran2 dan1/Cat1 bou2 mei5 jim4 daan1

(Polygoni Multiflori Radix): 何首乌 / 何首烏: He2 shou3 wu1/Ho4 sau2 wu1

steam the above medicinal in black sesame seeds

(Poria): 茯苓: Fu2 ling2/Fuk6 ling4

(Poria Rubra): 赤茯苓: Chi4 fu2 ling2/Cek3 fuk6 ling4

(Achyranthis Radix): 牛膝: Niu2 xi1/Ngau4 sat1 My teacher always wrote this "cow seven" or 牛七: Niu2 qi1/Ngau4 cat1

(Wine-Washed Angelicae Sinensis Radix): 酒洗当归 / 酒洗當歸: Jiu3 xi3 dang1 gui1/Zau2 sai2 dong1 gwai1

(Lycii Fructus): 枸杞子: Gou3 qi3 zi3/Gau2 gei2 zi2-my teacher always referred to this as 杞子: gei2 zi2.

(Cuscutae Semen): 菟丝子 / 菟絲子: Tu4 si1 zi3/Tou3 si1 zi2

(Psoraleae Fructus): 补骨脂 / 補骨脂: Bu3 gu3 zhi1/Bou2 gwat1 zi1

dry fry the above ingredient with black sesame seeds

(Restore the Right [Kidney] Drink)

右归饮 / 右歸飲: You4 gui1 yin3/Jau6 gwai1 jam2

(Rehmanniae Radix Preparata): 熟地黄: Shu2 di4 huang2/Suk6 dei6 wong4

(Dry-Fried Dioscoreae Rhizoma): 炒山药 / 炒山藥: Chao3 shan1 yao4/Caau2 saan1 joek6

(Corni Fructus): 山茱萸 / 山茱萸: Shan1 zhu1 yü2/Saan1 zyu1 jyu4

(Lycii Fructus): 枸杞子: Gou3 qi3 zi3/Gau2 gei2 zi2

(Glycyrrhizae Radix Preparata): 炙甘草: Zhi4 gan1 cao3/Zek3 gam1 cou2

(Eucommiae Cortex): 杜仲: Du4 Zhong4/Dou6 zung6

(Cinnamomi Cortex): 肉桂: Rou4 gui4/Juk6 gwai3

(Aconiti Radix Lateralis Preparata): 制附子 / 製附子: Zhi4 fu4 zi3/Zai3 fu6 zi2

(Cuscuta Seed Pill)
菟丝子丸 / 菟絲子丸: Tu4 si1 zi3 wan2/Tou3 si1 zi2 jyun2
(Cuscutae Semen): 菟丝子 / 菟絲子: Tu4 si1 zi3/Tou3 si1 zi2
(Cervi Cornu Pantotrichum): 鹿茸: Lu4 rong2/Luk6 jung4
(Cistanches Herba): 肉苁蓉 / 肉蓯蓉: Rou4 cong1 rong2/Juk6 cung1 jung4
(Dioscoreae Rhizoma): 山药 / 山藥: Shan1 yao4/Saan1 joek6
(Aconiti Radix Lateralis Preparata): 制附子 / 製附子: Zhi4 fu4 zi3/Zai3 fu6 zi2
(Linderae Radix): 乌药 / 烏藥: Wu1 yao4/Wu1 joek6
(Schisandrae Fructus): 五味子: Wu3 wei4 zi3/Ng5 mei6 zi2
(Mantidis Ootheca): 桑螵蛸: Sang1 piao1 xiao1/Song1 piu1 siu1
(Alpiniae Oxyphyllae Fructus): 益智仁: Yi4 zhi4 ren2/Jik1 zi3 jan4
(Calcined Ostrae Concha): 煅牡蛎 / 煅牡蠣: Duan4 mu3 li4/Dyun3 maau5 lai6
(Gigeriae Galli Endothelium Corneum): 鸡内金 / 雞內金: Ji1 nei4 jin1/Gai1 noi6 gam1

(Special Pill to Aid Fertility)
赞育丹 / 贊育丹: Zan4 yü4 dan1/Zaan3 juk6 daan1
(Aconiti Radix Lateralis Preparata): 制附子 / 製附子: Zhi4 fu4 zi3/Zai3 fu6 zi2
(Cinnamomi Cortex): 肉桂: Rou4 gui4/Juk6 gwai3
(Cistanches Herba): 肉苁蓉 / 肉蓯蓉: Rou4 cong1 rong2/Juk6 cung1 jung4
(Morindae Officinalis Radix): 巴戟天: Ba1 ji3 tian1/Baa1 gik1 tin1
(Epimedii Herba): 淫羊藿: Yin2 yang2 huo4/Jam4 joeng4 fok3
(Cnidii Fructus): 蛇床子: She2 chuang2 zi3/Se4 cong4 zi2
(Allii Tuberosi Semen): 韭子: Jiu3 zi3/Gau2 zi2
(Curculiginis Rhizoma): 仙茅: Xian1 mao2/Sin1 maau4
(Corni Fructus): 山茱萸 / 山茱萸: Shan1 zhu1 yü2/Saan1 zyu1 jyu4
(Eucommiae Cortex): 杜仲: Du4 Zhong4/Dou6 zung6
(Rehmanniae Radix Preparata): 熟地黄: Shu2 di4 huang2/Suk6 dei6 wong4
(Angelicae Sinensis Radix): 当归 / 當歸: Dang1 gui1/Dong1 gwai1
(Lycii Fructus): 枸杞子: Gou3 qi3 zi3/Gau2 gei2 zi2-my teacher always referred to this as 杞子: gei2 zi2.
(Atractylodis Macrocephalae Rhizoma): 白术 / 白術: Bai2 zhu2/Baak6 soet6

(Rehmannia Drink)
地黄饮子 / 地黃飲子: Di4 huang2 yin3 zi3/Dei6 wong4 jam2 zi2
(Rehmanniae Radix Preparata): 熟地黄: Shu2 di4 huang2/Suk6 dei6 wong4
(Corni Fructus): 山茱萸 / 山茱萸: Shan1 zhu1 yü2/Saan1 zyu1 jyu4
(Wine-Prepared Cistanches Herba): 酒苁蓉 / 酒蓯蓉: Jiu3 cong1 rong2/Zau2 cung1 jung4
(Morindae Officinalis Radix): 巴戟天: Ba1 ji3 tian1/Baa1 gik1 tin1
(Baked Aconiti Radix Lateralis): 炮附子: Pau2 fu4 zi3/Paau4 fu6 zi2

(Cinnamomi Cortex): 肉桂: Rou4 gui4/Juk6 gwai3

(Dendrobii Herba): 石斛: Shi2 hu2/Sek6 huk6

(Poria): 茯苓: Fu2 ling2/Fuk6 ling4

(Dry-Fried Schisandrae Fructus): 炒五味子: Chao3 wu3 wei4 zi3/Caau2 ng5 mei6 zi2

(Prepared Ophopogonis Radix): 制麦门冬 / 製麥門冬: Zhi4 mai4 men2 dong1/Zai3 mak6 mun4 dung1

(Acori Tatarinowii Rhizoma): 石菖蒲: Shi2 chang1 pu2/Sek6 coeng1 pou4

(Polygalae Radix): 远志 / 遠志: Yuan3 zhi4/Jyun4 zi3

(Aid the Living Kidney Qi Pills)

济生肾气丸 / 濟生腎氣丸: Ji4 sheng1 shen1 qi4 wan2/Zai3 sang1 san6 hei3 jyun2

(Achyranthis Bidentatae Radix): 川牛膝: Chuan1niu2 xi1/Cyun1 ngau4 sat1 My teacher always wrote this "cow seven" or 牛七: Niu2 qi1/Ngau4 cat1

(Plantaginis Semen): 车前子 / 車前子: Che1 qian2 zi3/Ce1 cin4 zi2

(Rehmanniae Radix Preparata): 熟地黄: Shu2 di4 huang2/Suk6 dei6 wong4

(Corni Fructus): 山茱萸 / 山茱萸: Shan1 zhu1 yü2/Saan1 zyu1 jyu4

(Dioscoreae Rhizoma): 山药 / 山藥: Shan1 yao4/Saan1 joek6

(Alismatis Rhizoma): 泽泻 / 澤瀉: Ze2 xie4/Zaak6 se3

(Poria): 茯苓: Fu2 ling2/Fuk6 ling4

(Moutan Cortex): 牡丹皮: Mu3 dan1 pi2/Maau5 daan1 pei4

(Cinnamomi Cortex): 肉桂: Rou4 gui4/Juk6 gwai3

(Aconiti Radix Lateralis Praeparata): 附子: Fu4 zi3/Fu6 zi2

(Two Immortals Decoction)

二仙汤 / 二仙湯: Er4 xian1 tang1/Ji6 sin1 tong1

(Curculiginis Rhizoma): 仙茅: Xian1 mao2/Sin1 maau4

(Epimedii Herba): 仙灵脾 / 仙靈脾: Xian1 ling1 pi2/Sin1 ling4 pei4 or 淫羊霍: Yin2 yang2 huo4/Jam4 joeng4 fok3

(Morindae Officinalis Radix): 巴戟天: Ba1 ji3 tian1/Baa1 gik1 tin1

(Phellodendri Cortex): 黄柏: Huang2 bai2/Wong4 paak3

(Anemarrhenae Rhizoma): 知母: Zhi1 mu3/Zi1 mou5

(Restore the Right [Kidney] Pill)

右归丸 / 右歸丸: You4 gui1 wan2/Jau6 gwai1 jyun2

(Aconiti Radix Lateralis Preparata): 制附子: Zhi4 fu4 zi3/Zai3 fu6 zi2

(Cinnamomi Cortex): 肉桂: Rou4 gui4/Juk6 gwai3

(Cervi Cornus Colla): 鹿角胶 / 鹿角膠: Lu4 jiao3 jiao1/Luk6 gok3 gaau1

(Rehmanniae Radix Preparata): 熟地黄: Shu2 di4 huang2/Suk6 dei6 wong4

(Corni Fructus): 山茱萸: Shan1 zhu1 yü2/Saan1 zyu1 jyu4

(Dry-Fried Lycii Fructus): 炒枸杞子: Chao3 gou3 qi3 zi3/Caau2 gau2 gei2 zi2

(Cuscutae Semen): 菟丝子 / 菟絲子: Tu4 si1 zi3/Tou3 si1 zi2

(Eucommiae Cortex): 杜仲: Du4 zhong4/Dou6 zung6

(Angelicae Sinensis Radix): 当归 / 當歸: Dang1 gui1/Dong1 gwai1

(Dry-Fried Dioscoreae Rhizoma): 炒山药 / 炒山藥: Chao3 shan1 yao4/Caau2 saan1 joek6

Spirit-Quieting Formulas
a. Heavy, Settling, Spirit-Quieting Formulas

(Cinnabar Quiet the Spirit Pills)
朱砂安神丸: Zhu1 sha1 an1 shen2 wan2/Zyu1 saa1 on1 san4 jyun2

(Cinnabar): 朱砂: Zhu1 sha1/Zyu1 saa1

(Coptidis Rhizoma): 黄连 / 黃連: Huang2 lian2/Wong4 lin4 My teacher always referred to this medicinal in its Sichuan form: 川连 / 川連: Chuan1 lian2/Cyun1 lin4

(Angelicae Sinensis Radix): 当归 / 當歸: Dang1 gui1/Dong1 gwai1

(Rehmanniae Radix): 生地黄: Sheng1 di4 huang2/Sang1 dei6 wong4

(Glycyrrhizae Radix Preparata): 炙甘草: Zhi4 gan1 cao3/Zek3 gam1 cou2

(Magnetite and Cinnabar Pill)
磁朱丸: Ci2 zhu1 wan2/Ci4 zyu1 jyun2

(Magnetitum): 磁石: Ci2 shi2/Ci4 sek6

(Cinnabaris): 朱砂: Zhu1 sha1/Zyu1 saa1

(Massa Dedicata Fementata): 神曲 / 神麴: Shen2 qu1/San4 kuk1

b. Enriching and Nourishing Spirit-Quieting Formulas

(Zizyphus Spinosa Decoction)
酸枣仁汤 / 酸棗仁湯: Suan1 zao3 ren2 tang1/Syun1 zou2 jan4 tong1

(Zizyphi Spinosae Semen): 酸枣仁 / 酸棗仁: Suan1 zao3 ren2/Syun1 zou2 jan4

(Glycyrrhizae Radix): 甘草: Gan1 cao3/Gam1 cou2

(Anemarrhenae Rhizoma): 知母: Zhi1 mu3/Zi1 mou5

(Poria): 茯苓: Fu2 ling2/Fuk6 ling4

(Chuanxiong Radix): 川芎: Chuan1 xiong1/Cyun1 gung1

(Emperor of Heaven's Special Pill to Tonify the Heart)
天王补心丹 / 天王補心丹: Tian1 wang2 bu3 xin1 dan1/Tin1 wong4 bou2 sam1 tong1
(Rehmanniae Radix): 生地黄: Sheng1 di4 huang2/Sang1 dei6 wong4
(Ginseng Radix): 人参 / 人參: Ren2 shen1 /Jan4 sam1
(Aparagi Radix): 天门冬 / 天門冬: Tian1 men2 dong1/Tin1 mun4 dung1
(Ophiopogonis Radix): 麦门冬 / 麥門冬: Mai4 men2 dong1/Mak6 mun4 dung1
(Scrophulariae Radix): 玄参 / 玄參: Xuan2 shen1/Jyun4 sam1
(Salviae Miltiorrhizae Radix): 丹参: Dan1 shen1/Daan1 sam1
(Poria): 茯苓: Fu2 ling2/Fuk6 ling4
(Wine-Washed Angelicae Sinensis Radix): 酒洗当归 / 酒洗當歸: Jiu3 xi3 dang1 gui1/Zau2 sai2 dong1 gwai1
(Schisandrae Fructus): 五味子: Wu3 wei4 zi3/Ng5 mei6 zi2
(Platycladi Semen): 柏子仁: Bai3 zi3 ren2/Paak3 zi2 jan4
(Dry-Fried Ziziphi Spinosae Semen): 炒酸枣仁 / 炒酸棗仁: Chao3 suan1 zao3 ren2/Caau2 syun1 zou2 jan4
(Platycodi Radix): 桔梗: Jie2 geng3/Gat1 gang2
(Cinnabaris): 朱砂: Zhu1 sha1/Zyu1 saa1

(Settle the Emotions Pill)
定志丸: Ding4 zhi4 wan2/Ding6 zi3 jyun2
(Ginseng Radix): 人参 / 人參: Ren2 shen1/Jan4 sam1
(Poria): 茯苓: Fu2 ling2/Fuk6 ling4
(Acori Tatainowii Rhizoma): 石菖蒲: Shi2 chang1 pu2/Sek6 coeng1 pou4
(Polygalae Radix): 远志: Yuan3 zhi4/Jyun5 zi3

(Coptis and Ass-Hide Gelatin Decoction)
黄连阿胶汤 / 黃連阿膠湯: Huang2 lian2 e1 jiao1 tang1/Wong4 lin4 aa3 gaau1 tong1
(Coptidis Rhizoma): 黄连 / 黃連: Huang2 lian2/Wong4 lin4 my teacher always referred to this medicinal in its Sichuan form 川连 / 川連: Chuan1 lian2/Cyun1 lin4
(Scutellariae Radix): 黄芩: Huang2 lian2/Wong4 kam4
(Asini Corii Colla): 阿胶 / 阿膠: E1 jiao1/Aa3 gaau1
(Paeoniae Radix Alba): 白芍: Bai2 shao2/Baak6 zoek3
(Egg Yolk): 鸡子黄 / 雞子黃: Ji1 zi3 huang2/Gai1 zi2 wong4

(Licorice, Wheat, and Jujube Decoction)
甘麦大枣汤 / 甘麥大棗湯: Gan1 mai4 da4 zao3 tang1/Gam1 mak6 daai6 zou2 tong1
(Glycyrrhizae Radix): 甘草: Gan1 cao3/Gam1 cou2
(Tritici Fructus): 小麦 / 小麥: Xiao3 mai4/Siu2 mak6-also called 浮小麦 / 浮小麥: Fu2 xiao3 mai4/Faau4 siu2 mak6
(Jujubae Fructus): 大枣 / 大棗: Da4 zao3/Daai6 zou2

Orifice-Opening Formulas
a. Cool Opening Formulas

(Quieting the Palace Bezoar Pills)
安宫牛黄丸 / 安宫牛黃丸: An1 gong1 niu2 huang2 wan2/On1 gung1 ngau4 wong4 jyun2
(Bovis Calculus):牛黄: Niu2 huang2/Ngau4 wong4
(Curcumae Radix): 郁金 / 鬱金: Yü4 jin1/Yuk1/Wat1 gam1
(Rhinocerotis Cornu): 犀角: Xi1 jiao3/Sai1 gok3-typically replaced by (Bubali Cornu): 水牛角: Shui3 niu2 jiao3/Seoi2 ngau4 gok3
(Coptidis Rhizoma): 黄连 / 黃連: Huang2 lian2/Wong4 lin4 My teacher always referred to this medicinal in its Sichuan form: 川连 / 川連: Chuan1 lian2/Cyun1 lin4
(Scutellariae Radix): 黄芩: Huang2 qin2/Wong4 kam4
(Gardeniae Fructus): 栀子 / 栀子: Zhi1 zi3/Zi1zi2
(Cinnabaris): 朱砂: Zhu1 sha1/Zyu1 saa1
(Realgar): 雄黄: Xiong2 huang2/Hung4 wong4
(Moschus): 麝香: She4 xiang1/Se6 hoeng1
(Borneolum): 冰片: Bing1 pian4/Bing1 pin3
(Margarita): 珍珠: Zhen1 zhu1/Zan1 zyu1

(Purple Snow Special Pill)
紫雪丹: Zi3 xue3 dan1/Zi2 syut3 daan1
(Gypsum Fibrosum): 石膏: Shi2 gao1/Sek6 gou1
(Glauberitum): 寒水石: Han2 shui3 shi2/Hon4 seoi2 sek6
(Talcum): 滑石: Hua2 shi2/Waat6 sek6
(Bubali Cornu): 水牛角: Shui3 niu2 jiao3/Seoi2 ngau4 gok3
(Saigae Tataricae Cornu): 羚羊角: Ling2 yang2 jiao3/Ling4 joeng4 gok3
(Moschus): 麝香: She2 xiang1/Se6 hoeng1
(Scrophulariae Radix): 玄参 / 玄參: Xuan2 shen1/Jyun4 sam1
(Magnetitum): 磁石: Ci2 shi2/Ci4 sek6
(Cimicifugae Rhizoma): 升麻: Sheng1 ma2/Sing1 maa4
(Glycyrrhizae Radix Preparata): 炙甘草: Zhi4 gan1 cao3/Zek3 gam1 cou2

(Aucklandiae Radix): 木香: Mu4 xiang1/Muk6 hoeng1

(Aquilariae Lignum Resinatum): 沉香: Chen2 xiang1/Cam4 hoeng1

(Caryophylli Flos): 丁香: Ding1 xiang1/Ding1 hoeng1

(Cinnabaris): 朱砂: Zhu1 sha1/Zyu1 saa1

(Natrii Sulfas): 硭硝: Mang2 xiao1/Mong4 siu1

(Nitrum): 硝石: Xiao1 shi2/Siu1 sek6

(Gold): 黄金: Huang2 jin1/Wong4 gam1

(Special Pill to Restore Life)

回春丹: Hui2 chun1 dan1/Wui4 ceon1 daan1

(Bovis Calculus): 牛黄: Niu2 huang2/Ngau4 wong4

(Bambusae Concretio Sicicea): 天竺黄: Tian1 zhu2 huang2/Tin1 zuk1 wong4

(Fritillariae Cirrhosae Bulbus): 川贝母 / 川貝母: Chuan1 bei4 mu3/Cyun1 bui3 mou5

(Arisaema cum Bile): 胆南星 / 膽南星: Dan3 nan2 xing1/Daam2 naam4 sing1

(Moschus): 麝香: She4 xiang1/Se6 hoeng1

(Uncariae Ramulus cum Uncis): 钩藤 / 鉤藤: Gou1 teng2/Ngau1 tang4

(Scorpio): 全蝎: Quan2 xie1/Cyun4 hit3

(Gastrodiae Rhizoma): 天麻: Tian1 ma2/Tin1 maa4

(Bombyx Batryticatus): 白僵蚕 / 白僵蠶: Bai2 jiang1 can2/Baak6 goeng1 caam4

(Cinnabaris): 朱砂: Zhu1 sha1/Zyu1 saa1

(Rhei Radix et Rhizoma): 大黄: Da4 huang2/Daai6 wong4

(Citri Reticulatae Pericarpium): 陈皮 / 陳皮: Chen2 pi2/Can4 pei4

(Pinelliae Rhizoma Preparatum): 制半夏 / 製半夏: Zhi4 ban4 xia4/Zai3 bun3 haa6

(Amomi Fructus Rotundus): 白豆蔻: Bai2 dou4 kou4/Baak6 dau6 kau3

(Santali Albi Lignum): 檀香: Tan2 xiang1/Taan4 hoeng1

(Aucklandiae Radix): 木香: Mu4 xiang1/Muk6 hoeng1

(Aurantii Fructus): 枳壳 / 枳殼: Zhi3 ke2/Zi2 hok3

(Aquilariae Lignum Resinatum): 沉香: Chen2 xiang1/Cam4 hoeng1

(Benzoinum): 安息香: An1 xi1 xiang1/On1 sik1 hoeng1

(Borneolum): 冰片: Bing1 pian4/Bing1 pin3

(Glycyrrhizae Radix): 甘草: Gan1 cao3/Gam1 cou2

b. Warm Opening Formulas

(Liquid Styrax Pills)

苏荷香丸 / 蘇荷香丸: Su1 he2 xiang1 wan2/Sou1 hap6 hoeng1 jyun2

(Atractylodis Macrocephalae Rhizoma): 白术 / 白術: Bai2 zhu2/Baak6 seot6

(Aucklandiae Radix): 木香: Mu4 xiang1/Muk hoeng1

(Rhinocerotis Cornu): 乌犀角 / 烏犀角: Wu1 xi1jiao1/Wu1 sai1 gok3-typically replaced by (Bubali Cornu): 水牛角: Shui3 niu2 jiao3/Seoi2 ngau4 gok3

(Cyperi Rhizoma): 香附子: Xiang1 fu4 zi3/Hoeng1 fu6 zi2

 (Cinnabaris): 朱砂: Zhu1 sha1/Zyu1 saa1

(Chebulae Fructus): 诃子 / 訶子: He1 zi3/Ho1 zi2

(Santali Albi Lignum): 檀香: tan2 xiang1/Taan4 hoeng1

(Aquilariae Lignum): 沉香: Chen2 xiang1/Cam4 hoeng1

(Caryophylli Flos): 丁香: Ding1 xiang1/Ding1 hoeng1

(Piperis Longi Fructus): 荜茇 / 畢茇: Bi4 ba2/Bat1 but6

(Styrax): 苏荷香油 / 蘇荷香油: Su1 he2 xiang1 you2/Sou1 hap6 hoeng1 jau4

(Olibanum): 乳香: Ru3 xiang1/Jyu5 hoeng1

(Moschus): 麝香: She4 xiang1/Se6 hoeng1

Securing and Astringing Formulas
a. Exterior-Securing and Perspiration-Stopping Formulas

(Oyster Shell Powder)

牡蛎散 / 牡蠣散: Mu3 li4 san3/Maau5 lai6 saan3

(Astragali Radix): 黄芪 / 黃耆: Huang2 qi1/Wong4 kei4 My teacher always referred to this as 北芪: Bei3 qi2/Bak1 kei4.

(Ephedrae Radix): 麻黄根: Ma2 huang2 gen1/Maa4 wong4 gan1

(Ostreae Concha): 煅牡蛎 / 煅牡蠣: Duan4 mu3 li4/Dyun3 maau5 lai6

(Tritici Fructus Levis): 浮小麦 / 浮小麥: Fu2 xiao3 mai4/Fau4 siu2 mak6

b. Intestine-Astringing and Desertion-Stemming Formulas

(True Man Nourish the Viscera Decoction)
真人养脏汤 / 真人養藏湯: Zhen1 ren2 yang3 zang4 tang1/Zan1 jan4 joeng5 zong6 tong1
(Ginseng Radix): 人参 / 人參: Ren2 shen1/Jan4 sam1
(Angelicae Sinensis Radix): 当归 / 當歸: Dang1 gui1/Dong1 gwai1
(Dry-fried Atractylodis Macrocephalae Rhizoma): 炒白术 / 炒白術: Chao3 bai2 zhu2/Caau2 baak6 seot6
(Roasted Myristicae Semen): 煨肉豆蔻: Wei1Rou4 dou4 dou4/Wui1 juk6 dau6 kau3
(Cinnamomi Cortex): 肉桂: Rou4 gui4/Juk6 gwai3
(Glycyrrhizae Radix Preparata): 炙甘草: Zhi4 gan1 cao3/Zek3 gam1 cou2
(Paeoniae Radix Alba): 白芍: Bai2 shao2/Baak6 zoek3
(Aucklandiae Radix): 木香: Mu4 xiang1/Muk6 hoeng1
(Chebulae Fructus): 诃子 / 訶子: He1 zi3/Ho1 zi2
(Honey-prepared Papaveris Pericarpium): 蜜炙罂粟壳 / 蜜炙罌粟殼: Mi4 zhi4 ying1 su4 ke2/Mat6 zek3 aang1suk1 hok3

(Peach Blossom Decoction)
桃花汤 / 桃花湯: Tao2 hua1 tang1/Tou4 faa1 tong1
(Halloysitum Rubrum): 赤石脂: Chi4 shi2 zhi1
(Zingiberis Rhizoma): 干姜 / 乾薑: Gan1 jiang1/Gon1 goeng1
(Nonglutinous Rice): 粳米: Jing1 mi3/Gang1 mai5

(Four Spirits Pills)
四神丸: Si4 shen2 wan2/Sei3 san4 jyun2
(Myristicae Semen): 肉豆蔻: Rou4 dou4 dou4/Juk6 dau6 kau3
(Psoraleae Fructus): 补骨脂 / 補骨脂: Bu3 gu3 zhi1/Bou2 gwat1 zi1
(Schisandrae Fructus): 五味子: Wu3 wei4 zi3/Ng5 mei6 zi2
(Dry-fried Evodiae Fructus): 炒吴茱萸 / 炒吳茱萸: Chao3 wu2 zhu1 yu2/Caau2 ng4 zyu1 jyu4

c. Essence-Astringing and Loss-Stopping Formulas

(Ootheca Mantidis Powder)
桑螵蛸散: Sang1 piao1 xiao1 san3/Song1 piu1 siu1 saan3
(Mantidis Ootheca): 桑螵蛸: Sang1 piao1 xiao1/Song1 piu1 siu1
(Polygalae Radix): 远志 / 遠志: Yuan3 zhi4/Jyun5 zi3
(Acori Tatarinowii Rhizoma): 石菖蒲: Shi2 chang1 pu2/Sek6 coeng1 pou4
(Fossilia Ossis Mastodi): 龙骨 / 龍骨: Long2 gu3/Lung4 gwat1
(Ginseng Radix): 人参 / 人參: Ren2 shen1/Jan4 sam1
(Poriae Sclerotium Paradicis): 茯神: Fu2 shen2/Fuk6 san4
(Angelicae Sinensis Radix): 当归 / 當歸: Dang1 gui1/Dong1 gwai1
(Testudinis Plastrum): 制龟板 / 製龜板: Zhi4 gui1 ban3/Zai3 gwai1 baan2

(Metal Lock Pill to Stabilize the Essence)
金锁固精丸 / 金鎖固精丸: Jin1 suo3 gu4 jing1 wan2/Gam1 so2 gu3 zing1 jyun2
(Dry-Fried Astragali Complanati Semen): 炒沙苑子: Chao3 sha1 yuan4 zi3/Caau2 saa1 jyun2 zi2
(Euryales Semen): 芡实 / 芡實: Qian4 shi2/Him3 sat6
(Nelumbinis Stamen): 莲须 / 蓮鬚: Lian2 xü1/Lin4 sou1
(Calcined Fossilia Ossis Mastodi): 煅龙骨 / 煅龍骨: Duan4 long2 gu3/Dyun3 lung4 gwat1
(Calcined Ostrae Concha): 煅牡蛎 / 煅牡蠣: Duan4 mu3 li4/Dyun3 maau5 lai6

(Restrict the Fountain Pill)
缩泉丸 / 縮泉丸: Suo1 quan2 wan2/Suk1 cyun4 jyun2
(Alpiniae Oxyphyllae Fructus stir-fried in salt): 盐炒益智仁 / 鹽炒益智仁: Yan2 chao3 yi4 zhi4 ren2/Jim4 caau2 jik1 zi3 jan4
(Linderae Radix): 乌药 / 烏藥: Wu1 yao4/Wu1 joek6
(Dry-Fried Dioscoriae Rhizoma): 炒山药 / 炒山藥: Chao3 shan1 yao4/Caau2 saan1 joek6

(Cinnamon Twig Decoction plus Dragon Bone and Oyster Shell)

桂枝加龙骨牡蛎汤 / 桂枝加龍骨牡蠣湯

Gui4 zhi1 jia1 long2 gu3 mu3 li4 tang1/Gwai3 zi1 gaa1 lung4 gwat1 maau4 lai6 tong1

(Cinnamomi Ramulus): 桂枝: Gui4 zhi1/Gwai3 zi1

(Paeoniae Radix Alba): 白芍: Bai2 shao2/Baak6 zoek3

(Fossilia Ossis Mastodi): 龙骨 / 龍骨: Long4 gu3/Lung4 gwat1

(Ostreae Concha): 牡蛎 / 牡蠣: Mu3 li4/Maau5 lai6

(Zingiberis Rhizoma Recens): 生姜 / 生薑: Sheng1 jiang1/Sang1 goeng1

(Jujubae Fructus): 大枣 / 大棗: Da4 zao3/Daai6 zou2

(Glycyrrhizae Radix): 甘草: Gan1 cao3/Gam1 cou2

(Fetus Longevity Pill)

寿胎丸 / 壽胎丸: Shou4 tai1 wan2/Sau6 toi1 jyun2

(Cuscutae Semen): 菟丝子 / 菟絲子: Tu4 si1 zi3/Tou3 si1 zi2

(Taxilli Herba): 桑寄生: Sang1 ji4 sheng1/Song1 gei3 sang1

(Dipsaci Radix): 续断 / 續斷: Xü4 duan4/Zuk6 dyun6

(Asini Corii Colla): 阿胶 / 阿膠: E1 jiao1/Aa3 gaau1

d. Securing Flooding and Stopping Vaginal Discharge Formulas

(Stabilize Gushing Decoction)

固冲汤 / 固衝湯: Gu4 chong1 tang1/Gu3 cung1 tong1

(Astragali Radix): 黄芪 / 黃耆: Huang2 qi1/Wong4 kei4 My teacher always referred to this as 北芪: Bei3 qi2/Bak1 kei4.

(Atractylodis Macrocephalae Rhizoma): 炒白术 / 炒白術: Chao3 bai2 zhu2/Caau2 baak6 seot6

(Corni Fructus): 山茱萸: Shan1 zhu1 yü2/Saan1 zyu1 jyu4

(Paeoniae Radix Alba): 白芍: Bai2 shao2/Baak6 zoek3

(Calcined Ostreae Concha): 煅牡蛎 / 煅牡蠣: Duan4 mu3 li4/Dyun3 maau5 lai6

(Calcined Fossilia Ossis Mastodi): 煅龙骨 / 煅龍骨: Duan4 long2 gu3/Dyun3 lung4 gwat1

(Sepiae Endoconcha): 海螵蛸: Hai3 piao1 xiao1/Hoi2 piu2 siu1

(Galla Chinensis Galla): 五倍子: Wu3 bei4 zi3/Ng5 pui5 zi2

(Charred Trachycarpi Petiolus): 棕榈炭 / 棕櫚炭: Zong1 lü2 tan4/Zung1 leoi4 taan3

(Rubiae Radix): 茜草根: Qian4 cao3 gen1/Sin3 cou2 gan1

(End Discharge Decoction)

完带汤 / 完帶湯: Wan2 dai4 tang1/Jyun4 dai4 tang1/Jyun4 daai3 tong1

(Atractylodis Macrocephalae Rhizoma): 土炒白术 / 土炒白術: Tu3 chao3 bai2 zhu2/Tou2 caau2 baak6 seot6

(Ginseng Radix): 人参 / 人參: Ren2 shen1/Jan4 sam1

(Paeoniae Radix Alba): 酒炒白芍: Jiu3 chao3 bai2 shao2/Zau2 caau2 baak6 zoek3

(Plantaginis Semen): 车前子 / 車前子: Che1 qian2 zi3/Ce1 cin4 zi2

(Atractylodis Rhizoma): 苍术 / 蒼術: Cang1 zhu2/Cong1 seot1

(Glycyrrhizae Radix): 甘草: Gan1 cao3/Gam1 cou2

(Citri Reticulatae Pericarpium): 陈皮 / 陳皮: Chen2 pi2/Can4 pei4

(Charred Schizonepetae Spica): 荆芥穗炭 / 荊芥穗炭: Jing1 jie4 sui4 tan4/Ging1 gaai3 seoi6 taan3

(Bupleuri Radix): 柴胡: Chai2 hu2/Caai4 wu4

(Dry-fried Discoreae Rhizoma): 炒山药 / 炒山藥: Chao3 shan1 yao4/Caau2 saan1 joek6

(Change Yellow [Discharge] Decoction)

易黄汤 / 易黃湯: Yi4 huang2 tang1/Ji6 wong4 tong1/Jik6 wong4 tong1

(Dry-Fried Dioscoreae Rhizoma): 炒山药 / 炒山藥: Chao3 shan1 yao4/Caau2 saan1 joek6

(Dry-Fried Euryales Semen): 炒芡实 / 炒芡實: Chao3 qian4 shi2/Caau2 him3 sat6

(Phellodendri Cortex): 黄柏: Huang2 bai2/Wong4 paak3

(Plantaginis Semen): 车前子 / 車前子: Che3 qian2 zi3/Ce1 cin4 zi2

(Gingko Semen): 白果: Bai2 guo3/Baak6 gwo2

Qi Moving Formulas

(Escape Restraint Pills)

越鞠丸: Yue4 ju2 wan2/Jyut6 guk1 jyun2

(Cyperi Rhizoma): 香附: Xiang1 fu4/Hoeng1 fu6

(Atractylodis Rhizoma): 苍术 / 蒼術: Cang1 zhu2/Cong1 seot6

(Chuanxiong Rhizoma): 川芎: Chuan1 xiong1/Cyun1 gung1

(Gardeniae Fructus): 栀子 / 梔子: Zhi1 zi3/Zi1 zi2

(Medica Fermentata Massa): 神曲 / 神麯: Shen2 qu1/San4 kuk1

(Pinellia and Magnolia Decoction)
半夏厚朴汤 / 半夏厚朴湯: Ban4 xia4 hou4 po4 tang1/Bun3 haa6 hau5 pok3 tong1
(Pinelliae Rhizoma Preparatum): 制半夏 / 製半夏: Zhi4 ban4 xia4/Zai3 bun3 haa6
(Magnoliae Officinalis Cortex): 厚朴: Hou4 po4/Hau5 pok3
(Poria): 茯苓: Fu2 ling2/Fuk6 ling4
(Zingiberis Rhizoma Recens): 生姜 / 生薑: Sheng1 jiang1/Sang1 goeng1
(Perillae Folium): 紫苏叶 / 紫蘇葉: Zi3 su1 ye4/Zi2 sou1 jip6

(Minor Pinellia Decoction)
小半夏汤 / 小半夏湯: Xiao3 ban4 xia4 tang1/Siu2 bun3 haa6 tong1
(Pinelliae Rhizoma Preparatum): 制半夏 / 製半夏: Zhi4 ban4 xia4/Zai3 bun3 haa6
(Zingiberis Rhizoma Recens): 生姜 / 生薑: Sheng1 jiang1/Sang1 goeng1

(Four Seven Decoction)
四七汤 / 四七湯: Si4 qi1 tang1/Sei3 cat1 tong1
(Pinelliae Rhizoma Preparatum): 制半夏 / 製半夏: Zhi4 ban4 xia4/Zai3 bun3 haa6
(Magnoliae Officinalis Cortex): 厚朴: Hou4 po4/Hau5 pok3
(Poria): 茯苓: Fu2 ling2/Fuk6 ling4
(Zingiberis Rhizoma Recens): 生姜 / 生薑: Sheng1 jiang1/Sang1 goeng1
(Perillae Folium): 紫苏叶 / 紫蘇葉: Zi3 su1 ye4/Zi2 sou1 jip6

(Magnolia Bark Decoction for Warming the Middle)
厚朴温中汤 / 厚朴溫中湯: Hou4 po4 wen1 zhong1 tang1/Hau5 pok3 wan1 zung1 tong1
(Ginger magnoliae Officinalis Cortex): 姜厚朴 / 薑厚朴: Jiang1 hou4 po4/Goeng1 hau5 pok3
(Alpiniae Katsumadai Semen): 草豆蔻: Cao3 dou4 kou4/Cou2 dau6 kau3
(Citri Reticulatae Pericarpium): 陈皮 / 陳皮: Chen2 pi2/Can4 pei4
(Aucklandiae Radix): 木香: Mu4 xiang1/Muk6 hoeng1
(Zingiberis Rhizoma): 干姜 / 乾薑: Gan1 jiang1/Gon1 goeng1
(Poria): 茯苓: Fu2 ling2/Fuk6 ling4
(Glycyrrhizae Radix Preparata): 炙甘草: Zhi4 gan1 cao3/Zek3 gam1 cou2

Qi Downbearing Formulas

(Orange Peel and Caulis Bambusae Decoction)
橘皮竹茹汤/橘皮竹茹湯: Ju2 pi2 zhu2 ru2 tang1/Gwat1 pei4 zuk1 jyu4 tong1
(Citri Reticulatae Pericarpium): 橘皮: Ju2 pi2/Gwat1 pei4
(Bambusae in Taenis Caulis): 竹茹: Zhu2 ru2/Zuk1 jyu4
(Zizyphi Jujubae Fructus): 大枣 / 大棗: Da4 zao3/Daai6 zou2
(Zingiberis Rhizoma): 生姜 / 生薑: Sheng1 jiang1/Sang1 goeng1
(Glycyrrhizae Radix): 甘草: Gan1 cao3/Gam1 cou2
(Ginseng Radix): 人参 / 人參: Ren2 shen1/Jan4 sam1

(Newly Processed Orange Peel and Caulis Bambusae Decoction)
新制橘皮竹茹汤 / 新制橘皮竹茹湯: Xin1 zhi4 ju2 pi2 zhu2 ru2 tang1/San1 zai3 gwat1 pei4 zuk1 jyu4 tong1
(Citri Reticulatae Pericarpium): 橘皮: Ju2 pi2/Gwat1 pei4
(Bambusae in Taenis Caulis): 竹茹: Zhu2 ru2/Zuk1 jyu4
(Zingiberis Rhizoma): 生姜 / 生薑: Sheng1 jiang1/Sang1 goeng1
(Kaki Diospyros Calyx): 柿蒂: Shi4 di4/Ci2 dai3

Blood-Quickening and Stasis-Dispelling Formulas

(Drive Out Stasis From the Mansion of Blood Decoction)
血府逐瘀汤 / 血府逐瘀湯: Xue4 fu3 zhu2 yü1 tang1/Hyut3 fu2 zuk6 jyu1 tong1
(Persicae Semen): 桃仁: Tao2 ren2/Tou4 jan4
(Carthami Flos): 红花 / 紅花: Hong2 hua1/Hung4 faa1
(Angelicae Sinensis Radix): 当归 / 當歸: Dang1 gui1/Dong1 gwai1
(Rehmanniae Radix): 生地黄: Sheng1 di4 huang2/Sang1 dei6 wong4
(Chuanxiong Rhizoma): 川芎: Chuan1 xiong1/Cyun1 gung1
(Paeoniae Radix Rubra): 赤芍: Chi4 shao2/Cek3 zoek3
(Achyranthis Radix): 牛膝: Niu2 xi1/Ngau4 sat1 My teacher always wrote this "cow seven" or 牛七: Niu2 qi1/Ngau4 cat1
(Platycodi Radix): 桔梗: Jie2 geng3/Gat1 gang2
(Bupleuri Radix): 柴胡: Chai2 hu2/Caai4 wu4
(Aurantii Fructus): 枳壳 / 枳殼: Zhi3 ke2/Zi2 hok3
(Glycyrrhizae Radix): 甘草: Gan1 cao3/Gam1 cou2

(Sudden Smile Powder)
失笑散: Shi1 xiao4 san3/Sat1 siu3 saan3
(Trogopterori Feces): 五灵脂 / 五靈脂: Wu3 ling2 zhi1/Ng5 ling4 zi1
(Typhae Pollen): 蒲黄: Pu2 huang2/Pou4 wong4

(Engendering and Transforming Decoction)

生化汤 / 生化湯: Sheng1 hua4 tang1/Sang1 faa3 tong1

(Angelicae Sinensis Radix): 当归 / 當歸: Dang1 gui1/Dong1 gwai1

(Chuanxiong Rhizoma): 川芎: Chuan1 xiong1/Cyun1 gung1

(Persicae Semen): 桃仁: Tao2 ren2/Tou4 jan4

(Zingiberis Rhizoma Praeparata): 炮姜 / 炮薑: Pau2 jiang1/Paau4 goeng1

(Glycyrrhizae Radix): 炙甘草: Zhi4 gan1 cao3/Zek3 gam1 cou2

(Unblock the Orifices and Invigorate the Blood Decoction)

通窍活血汤 / 通竅活血湯: Tong1 qiao4 huo2 xue4 tang1/Tung1 hiu3 wut6 hyut3 tong1

(Paeoniae Radix Rubra): 赤芍: Chi4 shao2/Cek3 zoek3

(Chuanxiong Rhizoma): 川芎: Chuan1 xiong1/Cyun1 gung1

(Persicae Semen): 桃仁: Tao2 ren2/Tou4 jan4

(Carthami Flos): 红花 / 紅花: Hong2 hua1/Hung4 faa1

(Allii Fistulosi bulbus): 葱白 / 蔥白: Cong1 bai2/Cung1 baak6

(Jujubae Fructus): 大枣 / 大棗: Da4 zao3/Daai6 zou2

(Zingiberis Rhizoma Recens): 生姜 / 生薑: Sheng1 jiang1/Sang1 goeng1

(Moschus): 麝香: She4 xiang1/Se6 hoeng1

(Drive Out Stasis Below the Diaphragm Decoction)

膈下逐瘀汤 / 膈下逐瘀湯: Ge2 xia4 zhu2 yü1 tang1/Gaak3 haa6 zuk6 jyu1 tong1

(Dry-Fried Trogopterori Faeces): 炒五灵脂 / 炒五靈脂: Chao3 wu3 ling2 zhi1/Caau2 ng5 ling4 zi1

(Angelicae Sinensis Radix): 当归 / 當歸: Dang1 gui1/Dong1 gwai1

(Chuanxiong Rhizoma): 川芎: Chuan1 xiong1/Cyun1 gung1

(Persicae Semen): 桃仁: Tao2 ren2/Tou4 jan4

(Moutan Cortex): 牡丹皮: Mu3 dan1 pi2/Maau5 daan1 pei4

(Paeoniae Radix Rubra): 赤芍: Chi4 shao2/Cek3 zoek3

(Linderae Radix): 乌药 / 烏藥: Wu1 yao4/Wu1 joek6

(Corydalis Rhizoma): 延胡索: Yan2 hu2 suo3/Jin4 wu4 sok3

(Glycyrrhizae Radix): 炙甘草: Zhi4 gan1 cao3/Zek3 gam1 cou2

(Cyperi Rhizoma): 香附: Xiang1 fu4/Hoeng1 fu6

(Carthami Flos): 红花 / 紅花: Hong2 hua1/Hung4 faa1

(Aurantii Fructus): 枳壳 / 枳殼: Zhi3 ke2/Zi2 hok3

(Drive Out Stasis From the Lower Abdomen Decoction)

少腹逐瘀汤 / 少腹逐瘀湯: Shao4 fu4 zhu2 yü1 tang1/Siu2 fuk1 zuk6 jyu1 tong1

(Dry-Fried Foeniculi Fructus):炒小茴香: Chao3 xiao3 hui2 xiang1/Caau2 siu2 wui4 hoeng1

(Dry-Fried Zingiberis Rhizoma): 炒干姜 / 炒乾薑: Chao3 gan1 jiang1/Caau2 gon1 goeng1

Corydalis Rhizoma): 延胡索: Yan2 hu2 suo3/Jin4 wu4 sok3

(Angelicae Sinensis Radix): 当归 / 當歸: Dang1 gui1/Dong1 gwai1

(Chuanxiong Rhizoma): 川芎: Chuan1 xiong1/Cyun1 gung1

(Myrrha): 没药 / 沒藥: Mo4 yao4/Mut6 joek6

(Cinnamomi Cortex): 肉桂: Rou4 gui4/Juk6 gwai3

(Paeoniae Radix Rubra): 赤芍: Chi4 shao2/Cek3 zoek3

(Typhae Pollen):蒲黄: Pu2 huang2/Pou4 wong4

(Dry-Fried Trogopterori Faeces): 炒五灵脂 / 炒五靈脂: Chao3 wu3 ling2 zhi1/Caau2 ng5 ling4 zi1

(Drive Out Stasis From a Painful Body Decoction)

身痛逐瘀汤 / 身痛逐瘀湯: Shen1 tong4 zhu2 yü1 tang1/San1 tung3 zuk6 jyu1 tong1

(Gentianae Macrophyllae Radix): 秦艽: Qin2 jiao1/Ceon4 gao2

(Chuanxiong Rhizoma): 川芎: Chuan1 xiong1/Cyun1 gung1

(Persicae Semen): 桃仁: Tao2 ren2/Tou4 jan4

(Carthami Flos): 红花 / 紅花: Hong2 hua1/Hung4 faa1

(Glycyrrhizae Radix): 甘草: Gan1 cao3/Gam1 cou2

(Notopterygii Rhizoma seu Radix): 羌活: Qiang1 huo2/Goeng1 wut6

(Myrrha): 没药 / 沒藥: Mo4 yao4/Mut6 joek6

(Angelicae Sinensis Radix): 当归 / 當歸: Dang1 gui1/Dong1 gwai1

(Dry-Fried Trogopterori Faeces): 炒五灵脂 / 炒五靈脂: Chao3 wu3 ling2 zhi1/Caau2 ng5 ling4 zi1

(Pheretima): 地龙 / 地龍: Di4 long2/Dei6 lung4

(Seven-Thousandths of a Tael Powder)

七厘散 / 七釐散: Qi1 li2 san3/Cat1 lei4 saan3

(Daemonoropis Resina): 血竭: Xue4 jie2/Hyut3 kit3

(Carthami Flos): 红花 / 紅花: Hong2 hua1/Hung4 faa1

(Olibanum): 乳香: Ru3 xiang1/Jyu4 hoeng1

(Myrrha): 没药 / 沒藥: Mo4 yao4/Mut6 joek6

(Moschus): 麝香: She4 xiang1/Se6 hoeng1

(Borneolum): 冰片: Bing1 pian4/Bing1 pin3

(Catechu): 儿茶 / 兒茶: Er2 cha2/Ji4 caa4

(Floating Cinnabaris): 水飞朱砂 / 水飛硃砂: Shui3 fei1 zhu1 sha1/Seoi2 fei1 zyu1 saa1

(Revive Health by Invigorating the Blood Decoction)

复元活血汤 / 復元活血湯: Fu4 yuan2 huo2 xue4 tang1/Fuk6 jyun4 wut6 hyut3 tong1

(Angelicae Sinensis Radix): 当归 / 當歸: Dang1 gui1/Dong1 gwai1

(Persicae Semen): 桃仁: Tao2 ren2/Tou4 jan4

(Carthami Flos): 红花 / 紅花: Hong2 hua1/Hung4 faa1

(Prepared Manitis Squama): 炮山甲: Pao2 shan1 jia3/Paau4 saan1 gaap3

(Wine-Prepared Rhei Radix et Rhizoma): 酒制大黄 / 酒製大黃: Jiu3 zhi4 da4 huang2/Zau2 zai3 daai6 wong4

(Trichosanthis Radix): 天花粉: Tian1 hua1 fen3/Tin1 faa1 fan2

(Bupleuri Radix): 柴胡: Chai2 hu2/Caai4 wu4

(Glycyrrhizae Radix): 甘草: Gan1 cao3/Gam1 cou2

(Bone-Setter's Purple-Gold Special Pill)

正骨紫金丹: Zheng4 gu3 zi3 jin1 dan1/Zing3 gwat1 zi2 gam1 daan1

(Caryophylli Flos): 丁香: Ding1 xiang1/Ding1 hoeng1

(Aucklandiae Radix): 木香: Mu4 xiang1/Muk6 hoeng1

(Daemonoropis Resina): 血竭: Xue4 jie2/Hyut3 kit3

(Catechu): 儿茶 / 兒茶: Er2 cha2/Ji4 caa4

(Prepared Rhei Radix et Rhizoma): 制大黄 / 製大黃: Zhi4 da4 huang2/Zai3 daai6 wong4

(Moutan Cortex): 牡丹皮: Mu3 dan1 pi2/Maau5 daan1 pei4

(Carthami Flos): 红花 / 紅花: Hong2 hua1/Hung4 faa1

(Angelicae Sinensis Radicis Caput): 当归头 / 當歸頭: Dang1 gui1 tou2/Dong1 gwai1 tau4

(Nelumbinis Semen): 莲子 / 蓮子: Lian2 zi3/Lin4 zi2

(Poria): 茯苓: Fu2 ling2/Fuk6 ling4

(Paeoniae Radix Alba): 白芍: Bai2 shao2/Baak6 joek3

(Glycyrrhizae Radix): 甘草: Gan1 cao3/Gam1 cou2

(Trauma Pill)

跌打丸: Die1 da3 wan2/Dit3 da2 jyun2

(Angelicae Sinensis Radix): 当归 / 當歸: Dang1 gui1/Dong1 gwai1

(Chuanxiong Rhizoma): 川芎: Chuan1 xiong1/Cyun1 gung1

(Olibanum): 乳香: Ru3 xiang1/Jyu5 hoeng1

(Myrrha): 没药 / 沒藥: Mo4 yao4/Mut6 joek6

(Daemonoropis Resina): 血竭: Xue4 jie2/Hyut3 kit3

(Eupolyphaga/Stelophaga): 土鳖虫 / 土鱉蟲: Tu2 bie1 chong2/Tou2 bit3 cung4. I seem to recall my teacher referring to these as 金土鳖 / 金 土鱉: Jin1 tu2 bie1/Gam1 tou2 bit3 or even written as 金土別

(Ephedrae Herba): 麻黄: Ma2 huang2/Maa4 wong4

(Pyritum): 自然铜 / 自然銅: Zi4 ran2 tong2/Zi6 jin4 tung4

(Relax the Channels and Invigorate the Blood Decoction)

舒经活血汤 / 舒經活血湯: Shu1 jing1 huo2 xue4 tang1/Syu1 ging1 wut6 hyut3 tong1

(Paeoniae Radix Alba): 白芍: Bai2 shao2/Baak6 zoek3

(Angelicae Sinensis Radix): 当归 / 當歸: Dang1 gui1/Dong1 gwai1

(Chuanxiong Rhizoma): 川芎: Chuan1 xiong1/Cyun1 gung1

(Rehmanniae Radix): 生地黄: Sheng1 di4 huang2/Sang1 dei6 wong4

(Persicae Semen): 桃仁: Tao2 ren2/Tou4 jan4

(Atractylodis Rhizoma): 苍术 / 蒼術: Cang1 zhu2/Cong1 soet6

(Poria): 茯苓: Fu2 ling2/Fuk6 ling4

(Achyranthis Radix): 牛膝: Niu2 xi1/Ngau4 sat1 My teacher always wrote this "cow seven" or 牛七: Niu2 qi1/Ngau4 cat1

(Clematidis Radix): Wei1 ling2 lian1/Wai1 ling4 sin1

(Stephaniae Tetrandrae Radix): 汉防己 / 漢防己: Han4 fang2 ji3/Hon3 fong4 gei2

(Notopterygii Rhizoma seu Radix): Qiang1 huo2/Goeng1 wut6

(Saposhnikovae Radix): 防风 / 防風: Fang2 feng1/Fong4 fung1

(Gentianae Radix): 龙胆草 / 龍膽草: Long2 dan3 cao3/Lung4 daam2 cou2

(Angelicae Dahuricae Radix): 白芷: Bai2 zhi3/Baak6 zi2

(Citri Reticulatae Pericarpium): 陈皮 / 陳皮: Chen2 pi2/Can4 pei4

(Glycyrrhizae Radix): 甘草: Gan1 cao3/Gam1 cou2

Stop-Bleeding Formulas

(Ten Partially-Charred Substances Powder)
十灰散: Shi2 hui1 san3/Sap6 fui1 saan3
(Cirsii Japonici Herba): 大蓟 / 大薊: Da4 ji4/Daai6 gai3
(Cirsii Herba): 小蓟 / 小薊: Xiao3 ji4/Siu2 gai3
(Nelumbinis Folium): 荷叶 / 荷葉: He2 ye4/Ho4 jip6
(Platycladi Cacumen): 侧柏叶 / 側柏葉: Ce4 bai3 ye4/Zak1 paak3 jip6
(Imperatae Rhizoma): 白茅根: Bai2 mao2 gen1/Baak6 maau4 gan1
(Rubiae Radix): 茜草根: Qian4 cao3 gen1/Sin3 cou2 gan1
(Gardeniae Fructus): 栀子 / 梔子: Zhi1 zi3/Zi1 zi2
(Rhei Radix et Rhizoma): 大黄: Da4 huang2/Daai6 wong4
(Moutan Cortex): 牡丹皮: Mu3 dan1 pi2/Maau5 daan1 pei4
(Trachycarpi Petiolus): 棕榈皮 / 棕櫚皮: Zong1 lü2 pi2/Zung1 leoi4 pei4

(Yellow Earth Decoction)
黄土汤 / 黃土湯: Huang2 tu3 tang1/Wong4 tou2 tong1
(Glycyrrhizae Radix): 甘草: Gan1 cao3/Gam1 cou2
(Rehmanniae Radix): 生地黄: Sheng1 di4 huang2/Sang1 dei6 wong4
(Atractylodis Macrocephalae Rhizoma): 白术 / 白術: Bai2 zhu2/Baak6 seot6
(Baked Aconiti Radix Lateralis Praeparata): 炮附子: Pao4 fu4 zi3/Paau4 fu6 zi2
(Asini Corii Colla): 阿胶 / 阿膠: E1 jiao1/Aa3 gaau1
(Scutellariae Radix): 黄芩: Huang2 qin2/Wong4 kam4
(Terra Flava Usta): 伏龙肝 / 伏龍肝: Fu2 long2 gan1/Fuk6 lung4 gon1
this is also commonly called: 灶心土: Zao4 xin1 tu3/Zou3 sam1 tou2

(Four-Fresh Pill)
四生丸: Si4 sheng1 wan2/Sei3 sang1 jyun2
(Fresh Platycladi Cacumen): 生侧柏叶 / 生側柏葉: Sheng1 ce4 bai3 ye4/Sang1 zak1 paak3 jip6
(Rehmanniae Radix Recens): 鲜地黄 / 鮮地黃: Xian1 di4 huang2/Sin1 dei6 wong4
(Fresh Nelumbinis Folium): 生荷叶 / 生荷葉: Sheng1 he2 ye4/Sang1 ho4 jip6
(Fresh Artemisiae Argyi Folium): 生艾叶 / 生艾葉: Sheng1 ai4 ye4/Sang1 ngaai6 jip6

(Small Thistle Drink)
小蓟饮子 / 小薊飲子: Xiao3 ji4 yin3 zi3/Siu2 gai3 jam2 zi2
(Cirsii Herba): 小蓟 / 小薊: Xiao3 ji4/Siu2 gai3
(Nelumbinis Zhizomatis Nodus): 藕节 / 藕節: Ou3 jie2/Ngau5 zit3
(Dry-Fried Typhae Pollen): 炒蒲黄: Chao3 pu2 huang2/Caau2 pou4 wong4
(Rehmanniae Radix): 生地黄: Sheng1 di4 huang2/Sang1 dei6 wong4
(Talcum): 滑石: Hua2 shi2/Waat6 sek6
(Akebiae Caulis): 木通: Mu4 tong3/Muk6 tung2
(Lophatheri Herba): 淡竹叶 / 淡竹葉: Dan4 zhu2 ye4/Daam6 zuk1 jip6
(Gardeniae Fructus): 栀子 / 梔子: Zhi1 zi3/Zi1 zi2
(Angelicae Sinensis Radix): 当归 / 當歸: Dang1 gui1/Dong1 gwai1
(Glycyrrhizae Radix Preparata): 炙甘草: Zhi4 gan1 cao3/Zek3 gam1 cou2

(Sophora Flower Powder)
槐花散: Huai2 hua1 san3/Waai4 faa1 saan3
(Dry-Fried Sophorae Flos): 炒槐花: Chao3 huai2 hua1/Caau2 waai4 faa1
(Dry-Fried Platycladi Cacumen): 炒柏叶 / 炒柏葉: Chao3 bai3 ye4/Caau2 paak3 jip6
(Schizonepetae Spica): 荆芥穗 / 荊芥穗: Jing1 jie4 sui4/Ging1 gaai3 seoi6
(Bran-Fried Aurantii Fructus): 麸炒枳壳 / 麩炒枳殼: Fu1 chao3 zhi3 ke2/Fu1 caau2 zi2 hok3

(Stabilize the Menses Pill)
固经丸 / 固經丸: Gu4 jing1 wan2/Gu3 ging1 jyun2
(Prepared Testudinis Plastrum): 炙龟板 / 炙龜板: Zhi4 gui1 ban3/Zek3 gwai1 baan2
(Dry-Fried Paeoniae Radix Alba): 炒白芍: Chao3 bai2 shao2/Caau2 baak6 zoek3
(Dry-Fried Scutellariae Radix): 炒黄芩: Chao3 huang2 qin2/Caau2 wong4 kam4
(Ailanthi Cortex): 椿皮: Chun1 pi2/Ceon1 pei4
(Dry-Fried Phellodendri Cortex): 炒黄柏: Chao3 huang2 bai3/Caau2 wongk paak3
(Cyperi Rhizoma): 香附: Xiang1 fu4/Hoeng1 fu6

(Ass-Hide Gelatin and Mugwort Decoction)
胶艾汤 / 膠艾湯: Jiao1 ai4 tang1/Gaau1 ngaai6 tong1
(Asini Corii Colla): 阿胶 / 阿膠: E1 jiao1/Aa3 gaau1
(Artemisiae Argyi Folium): 艾叶 / 艾葉: Ai4 ye4/Ngaai6 jip6
(Rehmanniae Radix): 生地黄: Sheng1 di4 huang2/Sang1 dei6 wong4
(Angelicae Sinensis Radix): 当归 / 當歸: Dang1 gui1/Dong1 gwai1
(Chuanxiong Rhizoma): 川芎: Chuan1 xiong1/Cyun1 gung1
(Paeoniae Radix Alba): 白芍: Bai2 shao2/Baak6 zoek3
(Glycyrrhizae Radix): 甘草: Gan1 cao3/Gam1 cou2

External Wind Coursing and Scattering Formulas

(Ligusticum and Tea Mixed Powder)
川芎茶调散 / 川芎茶調散: Chuan1 xiong1 cha2 tiao2 san3/Cyun1 gung1 caa4 tiu4 saan3
(Chuanxiong Rhizoma): 川芎: Chuan1 xiong1/Cyun1 gung1
(Schizonepetae Herba) 荆芥穗 / 荊芥穗: Jing1 jie4 sui4/Ging1 gaai3 seoi6
(Angelicae Dahuricae Radix): 白芷: Bai2 zhi1/Baak6 zi2
(Notopterygii Rhizoma seu Radix): 羌活: Qiang1 huo2/Goeng1 wut6
(Glycyrrhizae Radix Preparata): 甘草: Gan1 cao3/Gam1cou2
(Asari Herba): 细辛 / 細辛: Xi4 xin1/Sai3 san1
(Saposhnikoviae Radix): 防风 / 防風: Fang2 feng1/Fong4 fung1
(Menthae Haplocalycis Herba): 薄荷: Bo4 he2/Bok6 ho4

(Chrysanthemum and Tea Mixed Powder)
菊花茶调散 / 菊花茶調散: Jü2 hua1 cha2 tiao2 san3/Guk1 faa1 caa4 tiu4 saan3
(Chuanxiong Rhizoma): 川芎: Chuan1 xiong1/Cyun1 gung1
(Schizonepetae Herba) 荆芥 / 荊芥: Jing1 jie4/Ging1 gaai3
(Angelicae Dahuricae Radix): 白芷: Bai2 zhi1/Baak6 zi2
(Notopterygii Rhizoma seu Radix): 羌活: Qiang1 huo2/Goeng1 wut6
(Glycyrrhizae Radix Preparata): 炙甘草: Zhi4 gan1 cao3/Zek3 gam1cou2
(Asari Herba): 细辛 / 細辛: Xi4 xin1/Sai3 san1
(Saposhnikoviae Radix): 防风 / 防風: Fang2 feng1/Fong4 fung1
(Menthae Haplocalycis Herba): 薄荷: Bo4 he2/Bok6 ho4
(Chrysanthemi Flos): 菊花: Ju2 hua1/Guk1 faa1
(Bombyx Batryticatus): 僵蚕 / 僵蠶: Jiang1 can2/Goeng1 caam4

(Xanthium Powder)
苍耳子散 / 蒼耳子散: Cang1 er3 zi3 san3/Cong1 ji5 zi2 saan3
(Xanthii Fructus): 苍耳子 / 蒼耳子: Cang1 er3 zi3/Cong1 ji5 zi2
(Magnoliae Flos): 辛夷花: Xin1 yi2 hua1/San1 ji4 faa1
(Angelicae Dahuricae Radix) 白芷: Bai2 zhi3/Baak6 zi2
(Menthae Haplocalycis Herba): 薄荷: Bo4 he2/Bok6 ho4

(Minor Invigorate the Collaterals Special Pill)
小活络丹 / 小活絡丹: Xiao3 huo2 luo4 dan1/Siu2 wut6 lok3 daan1
(Aconiti Kusnezoffi Radix Preparata): 制草乌 / 製草烏: Zhi4 cao3 wu1/Zai3 cou2 wu1
(Aconiti Radix Preparata): 制川乌 / 製川烏: Zhi4 chuan1 wu1/Zai3 cyun1 wu1
(Arisaematis Rhizoma Preparatum): 制天南星 / 製天南星: Zhi4 tian1 nan2 xing1/Zai3 tin1 naam4 sing1
(Myrrha): 没药 / 沒藥: Mo4 yao4/Mut6 joek6
(Olibanum): 乳香: Ru3 xiang1/Jyu5 hoeng1
(Pheretima): 地龙 / 地龍: Di4 long2/Dei6 lung4

(Lead to Symmetry Powder)
牵正散 / 牽正散: Qian1 zheng4 san3/Hin1 zing3 saan3
(Typhonii Rhizoma): 白附子: Bai2 fu4 zi3/Baak6 fu6 zi2
(Bombyx Batryticatus): 白僵蚕 / 白僵蠶: Bai2 jiang1 can2/Baak6 goeng1 caam4
(Scorpio): 全蝎: Quan2 xie1/Cyun4 hit3

(Eliminate Wind Powder from Orthodox Lineage)
消风散 / 消風散: Xiao1 feng1 san3/Siu1 fung1 saan3
(Schizonepetae Herba): 荆芥 / 荊芥: Jing1 jie4/Ging1 gaai3
(Saposhnikoviae Radix): 防风 / 防風: Fang2 feng1/Fong4 fung1
(Arctii Fructus): 牛蒡子: Niu2 bang4 zi3/Ngau4 bong2 zi2
(Cicadae Periostracum): 蝉蜕 / 蟬蛻: Chan2 tui4/Sim4 teoi3
(Atractylodis Rhizoma): 苍术 / 蒼術: Cang1 zhu2/Cong1 seot6
(Sophorae Flavescentis): 苦参 / 苦參: Ku3 shen1/Fu2 sam1
(Akebiae Caulis): 木通: Mu4 tong3/Muk6 tung2
(Gypsum Fibrosum): 石膏: Shi2 gao1/Sek6 gou1
(Anemarrhenae Rhizoma): 知母: Zhi1 mu3/Zi1 mou5
(Rehmanniae Radix): 生地黄: Sheng1 di4 huang2/Sang1 dei6 wong4
(Angelicae Sinensis Radix): 当归 / 當歸: Dang1 gui1/Dong1 gwai1
(Sesami Semen Nigrum): 黑脂麻 / 黑脂麻: Hei1 zhi1 ma2/Hak1 zi1 maa4
(Glycyrrhizae Radix): 甘草: Gan1 cao3/Gam1 cou2

(Eliminate Wind Drink with the Four Substances)
四物消风饮／四物消風飲: Si4 wu4 xiao1 feng1 yin3/Sei3 mat6 siu1 fung1 jam2
(Rehmanniae Radix): 生地黄: Sheng1 di4 huang2/Sang1 dei6 wong4
(Angelicae Sinensis Radix): 当归／當歸: Dang1 gui1/Dong1 gwai1
(Schizonepetae Herba): 荆芥／荊芥: Jing1 jie4/Ging1 gaai3
(Saposhnikoviae Radix): 防风／防風: Fang2 feng1/Fong4 fung1
(Paeoniae Radix Rubra): 赤芍: Chi4 shao2/Cek3 zoek3
(Chuanxiong Rhizoma): 川芎: Chuan1 xiong1/Cyun1 gung1
(Dictamni Cortex): 白鲜皮／白鮮皮: Bai2 xian3 pi2/Baak6 sin2 pei4
(Cicadae Periostracum): 蝉蜕／蟬蛻: Chan2 tui4/Sim4 teoi3
(Menthae Haplocalycis Herba): 薄荷: Bo4 he2/Bok6 ho4
(Angelicae Pubescentis Radix): 独活／獨活: Du2 huo2/Duk6 wut6
(Bupleuri Radix): 柴胡: Chai2 hu2/Caai4 wu4
(Jujubae Fructus): 大枣／大棗: Da4 zao3/Daai6 zou2

Internal Wind-Leveling and Extinguishing Formulas

(Settle the Liver and Extinguish Wind Decoction)
镇肝熄风汤／鎮肝熄風湯: Zhen4 gan1 xi1 feng1 tang1/Zan3 gon1 sik1 fung1
tong1
(Achyranthis Bidentatae Radix): 怀牛膝／懷牛膝: Huai2 niu2 xi1/Waai4 ngau4
sat1 My teacher always wrote this 牛七 or "cow-seven". Writing herb names with
easier characters is a common practice.
(Haematitum): 代赭石: Dai4 zhe3 shi2/Doi6 ze2 sek6
(Fossilia Ossis Mastodi): 龙骨／龍骨: Long2 gu3/Lung4 gwat1
(Ostreae Concha): 牡蛎／牡蠣: Mu3 li4/Maau5 lai6
(Testudinis Plastrum): 龟板／龜板: Gui1 ban3/Gwai1 baan2
(Paeoniae Radix Alba): 白芍: Bai2 shao2/Baak6 zoek3
(Scrophulariae Radix): 玄参／玄參: Xuan2 shen1/Jyun4 sam1
(Asparagi Radix): 天门冬／天門冬: Tian1 men2 dong1/Tin1 mun4 dung1
(Toosendan Fructus): 川楝子: Chuan1 lian4 zi3/Cyun1 lin6 zi2
(Hordei Fructus Germinatus): 麦芽／麥芽: Mai4 ya2/Mak6 ngaa4
(Artemisiae Herba): 茵陈蒿／茵陳蒿: Yin1 chen2 hao1/Jan1 can4 hou1
(Glycyrrhizae Radix): 甘草: Gan1 cao3/Gam1 cou2

(Gastrodia and Uncaria Drink)
天麻钩藤饮／天麻鉤藤飲: Tian1 ma2 gou1 teng2 yin3/Tin1 maa4 ngau1 tang4
jam2
(Gastrodiae Rhizoma): 天麻: Tian1 ma2/Tin1 maa4
(Uncariae Ramulus cum Uncis): 钩藤／鉤藤: Gou1 teng2/Ngau1 tang4
(Haliotidis Concha): 石决明／石決明: Shi2 jue2 ming2/Sek6 kyut3 ming4

(Gardeniae Fructus): 栀子 / 梔子: Zhi1 zi3/Zi1 zi2
(Scutellariae Radix): 黄芩: Huang2 qin2/Wong4 kam4
(Cyathulae Radix): 川牛膝: Chuan1 niu2 xi1/Cyun1 ngau4 sat1 My teacher always wrote this "cow seven" or 牛七: Niu2 qi1/Ngau4 cat1
(Eucommiae Cortex): 杜仲: Du4 zhong4/Dou6 zung6
(Leonuri Herba): 益母草: Yi4 mu3 cao3/Jik1 mou5 cou2
(Taxilli Herba): 桑寄生: Sang1 ji4 sheng1/Song1 gei3 sang1
(Polygoni Multiflori Caulis): 夜交藤: Ye4 jiao1 teng2/Je6 gaau1 tang4
(Poriae Sclerotium Pararadicis): 茯神 Fu2 shen2/Fuk6 san4

(Antelope Horn and Uncaria Decoction)
羚角钩藤汤 / 羚角鉤藤湯: Ling2 jiao3 gou1 teng2 tang1/Ling4 gok3 ngau1 tang4 tong1
also commonly known as
羚羊钩藤汤 / 羚羊鉤藤湯: Ling2 yang2 gou1 teng2 tang1/Ling4 joeng4 ngau1 tang4 tong1
(Saigae Tataricae Cornu): 羚羊角: Ling2 yang2 jiao3/Ling4 joeng4 gok3
(Uncariae Ramulus cum Uncis): 钩藤 / 鉤藤: Gou1 teng2/Ngau1 tang4
(Mori Folium): 桑叶 / 桑葉: Sang1 ye4/Song1 jip6
(Chrysanthemi Flos): Ju2 hua1/Guk1 faa1
(Paeoniae Radix Alba): 白芍: Bai2 shao2/Baak6 zoek3
(Rehmanniae Radix): 生地黄: Sheng1 di4 huang2/Sang1 dei6 wong4
(Fritillariae Cirrhosae Bulbus): 川贝母 / 川貝母: Chuan1 bei4 mu3/Cyun1 bui3 mou5
(Bambusae Caulis in Taeniam): Zhu2 ru2/Zuk1 jyu4
(Poriae Sclerotium Pararadicis): 茯神: Fu2 shen2/Fuk6 san4
(Glycyrrhizae Radix): 甘草: Gan1 cao3/Gam1 cou2

(Major Arrest Wind Pearls)
大定风珠 / 大定風珠: Da4 ding4 feng1 zhu1/Daai6 ding6 fung1 jyu1
(Egg Yolk): 鸡子黄 / 雞子黃: Ji1 zi3 huang2/Gai1 zi2 wong4
(Asini Corii Colla): 阿胶 / 阿膠: E1 jiao1/Aa3 gaau1
(Paeoniae Radix Alba): 白芍: Bai2 shao2/Baak6 zoek3
(Glycyrrhizae Radix Preparata): 炙甘草: Zhi4 gan1 cao3/Zek3 gam1 cou2
(Schisandrae Fructus): 五味子: Wu1 wei4 zi3/Ng5 mei6 zi2
(Rehmanniae Radix): 生地黄: Sheng1 di4 huang2/Sang1 dei6 wong4
(Ophiopogonis Radix): 麦门冬 / 麥門冬: Mai4 men2 dong1/Mak6 mun4 dung1
(Cannabis Semen): 火麻仁: Huo3 ma2 ren2/Fo2 maa4 jan4
(Testudinis Plastrum): 龟板 / 龜板: Gui1 ban3/Gwai1 baan2
(Trionycis Carapax): 鳖甲 / 鱉甲: Bie1 jia3/Bit3 gaap3
(Ostreae Concha): 牡蛎 / 牡蠣: Mu3 li4/Maau5 lai6

(Three-Shell Decoction to Restore the Pulse)
三甲復脉汤 / 三甲復脈湯: San1 jia3 fu4 mai4 tang1/Saam1 gaap3 fuk6 mak6 tong1
(Glycyrrhizae Radix Preparata): 炙甘草: Zhi4 gan1 cao3/Zek3 gam1 cou2
(Rehmanniae Radix): 生地黄: Sheng1 di4 huang2/Sang1 dei6 wong4
(Paeoniae Radix Alba): 白芍: Bai2 shao2/Baak6 zoek3
(Ophiopogonis Radix): 麦门冬 / 麥門冬: Mai4 men2 dong1/Mak6 mun4 dung1
(Cannabis Semen): 火麻仁: Huo3 ma2 ren2/Fo2 maa4 jan4
(Asini Corii Colla): 阿胶 / 阿膠: E1 jiao1/Aa3 gaau1
(Ostreae Concha): 牡蛎 / 牡蠣: Mu3 li4/Maau5 lai6
(Trionycis Carapax): 鳖甲 / 鱉甲: Bie1 jia3/Bit3 gaap3
(Testudinis Plastrum): 龟板 / 龜板: Gui1 ban3/Gwai1 baan2

Dryness-Treating Formulas
  a. Mildly Diffusing Dryness-Moistening Formulas

(Armeniaca and Perilla Powder)
杏苏散/杏蘇散: Xing4 su1 san3/Hang6 sou1 saan3
(Perillae Folium): 紫苏叶 / 紫蘇葉: Zi3 su1 ye4/Zi2 sou1 jip6
(Pinelliae Rhizoma Preparatum): 制半夏 / 製半夏: Zhi4 ban4 xia4/Zai3 bun3 haa6
(Poria): 茯苓: Fu2 ling2/Fuk6 ling4
(Peucedani Radix): 前胡: Qian2 hu2/Cin4 wu4
(Platycodi Radix): 桔梗: Jie2 geng3/Gat1 gang2
(Aurantii Fructus): 枳壳 / 枳殼: Zhi3 ke2/Zi2 hok3
(Glycyrrhizae Radix): 甘草: Gan1 cao3/Gam1 cou2
(Zingiberis Rhizoma Recens): 生姜 / 生薑: Sheng1 jiang1/Sang1 goeng1
(Citri Reticulatae Pericarpium): 陈皮 / 陳皮: Chen2 pi2/Can4 pei4
(Armeniacae Semen): 杏仁: Xing4 ren2/Hang6 jan4
(Jujubae Fructus): 大枣 / 大棗: Da4 zao3/Daai6 zou2

(Mulberry Leaf and Apricot Kernel Decoction)
桑杏汤 / 桑杏湯: Sang1 xing4 tang1/Song1 hang6 tong1
(Mori Folium): 桑叶 / 桑葉: Sang1 ye4/Song1 jip6
(Gardeniae Fructus): 栀子 / 梔子: Zhi1 zi3/Zi1 zi2
(Sojae Semen Preparatum): 淡豆豉: Dan4 dou4 chi3/Daam6 dau6 si6
(Armeniacae Semen): 杏仁: Xing4 ren2/Hang6 jan4
(Fritillariae Thunbergii Bulbus): 浙贝母 / 浙貝母: Zhe4 bei4 mu3/Zit3 bui3 mou5
(Glehniae/Adenophorae Radix): 沙参 / 沙參: Sha1 shen1/Saa1 sam1
(Pyri Exocarpium): 梨皮: Li2 pi2/Lei4 pei4

(Clear Dryness and Rescue the Lungs Decoction)
清燥救肺汤 / 清燥救肺湯: Qing1 zao4 jiu4 fei4 tang1/Cing1 cou3 gau3 fai3 tong1
(Mori Folium): 桑叶 / 桑葉: Sang1 ye4/Song1 jip6
(Gypsum Fibrosum): 石膏: Shi2 gao1/Sek6 gou1
(Ophiopogonis Radix): 麦门冬 / 麥門冬: Mai4 men2 dong1/Mak6 mun4 dung1
(Asini Corii Colla): 阿胶 / 阿膠: E1 jiao1/Aa3 gaau1
(Dry-Fried Sesami Semen Nigrum): 炒黑芝麻: Chao3 hei1 zhi1 ma2/Caau2 hak1 zi1 maa4
(Armeniacae Semen): 杏仁: Xing4 ren2/Hang4 jan4
(Honey-Prepared Eriobotryae Folium): 蜜炙枇杷叶 / 蜜炙枇杷葉: Mi4 zhi4 pi2 pa2 ye4/Mat6 zek3 pei4 paa4 jip6
(Ginseng Radix): 人参 / 人參: Ren2 shen1/Jan4 sam1
(Glycyrrhizae Radix): 甘草: Gan1 cao3/Gam1 cou2

(Glehnia and Ophiopogonis Decoction)
沙参麦门冬汤 / 沙參麥門冬湯: Sha1 shen1 mai4 men2 dong1 tang1/Saa1 sam1 mak6 mun4 dung1 tong1
(Glehniae/Adenophorae Radix): 沙参 / 沙參: Sha1 shen1/Saa1 sam1
(Ophiopogonis Radix): 麦门冬 / 麥門冬: Mai4 men2 dong1/Mak6 mun4 dung1
(Polygonati Odorati Rhizoma): 玉竹: Yü4 zhu2/Juk6 zuk1
(Mori Folium): 桑叶 / 桑葉: Sang1 ye4/Song1 jip6
(Trichosanthis Radix): 天花粉: Tian1 hua1 fen3/Tin1 faa1 fan2
(Lablab Semen Album): 白扁豆: Bai2 bian3 dou4/Baak6 bin2 dau6
(Glycyrrhizae Radix): 甘草: Gan1 cao3/Gam1 cou2

b. Yin-Enriching and Dryness-Moistening Formulas

(Lily Secure the Lungs Decoction)
百合固金汤 / 百合固金湯: Bai3 he2 gu4 jin1 tang1/Baak3 hap6 gu3 gam1 tong1
(Rehmanniae Radix): 生地黄: Sheng1 di4 huang2/Sang1 dei6 wong4
(Rehmanniae Radix Preparata): 熟地黄: Shu2 di4 huang2/Suk6 dei6 wong4
(Ophiopogonis Radix): 麦门冬 / 麥門冬: Mai4 men2 dong1/Mak6 mun4 dung1
(Lilii Bulbus): 百合: Bai3 he2/Baak3 hap6
(Paeoniae Radix Alba): 白芍: Bai2 shao2/Baak6 zoek3
(Angelicae Sinensis Radix): 当归 / 當歸: Dang1 gui1/Dong1 gwai1
(Fritillariae Cirrhosae Bulbus): 川贝母 / 川貝母: Chuan1 bei4 mu3/Cyun1 bui3 mou5
(Glycyrrhizae Radix): 甘草: Gan1 cao3/Gam1 cou2
(Scrophulariae Radix): 玄参 / 玄參: Xuan2 shen1/Jyun4 sam1
(Platycodi Radix): 桔梗: Jie2 geng3/Gat1 gang2

(Nourish the Yin and Clear the Lungs Decoction)
养阴清肺汤 / 養陰清肺湯: Yang3 yin1 qing1 fei4 tang1/Joeng5 jam1 cing1 fai3 tong1
(Rehmanniae Radix): 生地黄: Sheng1 di4 huang2/Sang1 dei6 wong4
(Scrophulariae Radix): 玄参 / 玄參: Xuan2 shen1/Jyun4 sam1
(Ophiopogonis Radix): 麦门冬 / 麥門冬: Mai4 men2 dong1/Mak6 mun4 dung1
(Dry-Fried Paeoniae Radix Alba): 炒白芍: Chao3 bai2 shao2/Caau2 baak6 zoek3
(Moutan Cortex): 牡丹皮: Mu3 dan1 pi2/Maau5 daan1 pei4
(Fritillariae Cirrhosae Bulbus): 川贝母 / 川貝母: Chuan1 bei4 mu3/Cyun1 bui3 mou5
(Menthae Haplocalycis Herba): 薄荷: Bo4 he2/Bok6 ho4
(Glycyrrhizae Radix): 甘草: Gan1 cao3/Gam1 cou2

(Increase the Fluids Decoction)
增液汤 / 增液湯: Zeng1 ye4 tang1/Zang1 jik6 tong1
(Scrophulariae Radix): 玄参 / 玄參: Xuan2 shen1//Jyun4 sam1
(Ophiopogonis Radix): 麦门冬 / 麥門冬: Mai4 men2 dong1/Mak6 mun4 dung1
(Rehmanniae Radix): 生地黄: Sheng1 di4 huang2/Sang1 dei6 wong4

(Jade Fluid Decoction)
玉液汤 / 玉液湯: Yü4 ye4 tang1/Juk6 jik6 tong1
(Dioscoreae Rhizoma): 山药 / 山藥: Shan1 yao4/Saan1 joek6
(Astragali Radix): 黄芪 / 黃耆: Huang2 qi2/Wong4 kei4 my teacher always referred to this medicinal as 北芪 / 北耆: Bei3 qi2/Bak1 kei4
(Anemarrhenae Rhizoma): 知母: Zhi1 mu3/Zi1 mou5
(Trichosanthis Radix): 天花粉: Tian1 hua1 fen3/Tin1 faa1 fan2
(Gigeriae Galli Endothelium Corneum): 鸡内金 / 雞內金: Ji1 nei4 jin1/Gai1 noi6 gam1
(Puerariae Radix): 葛根: Ge2 gen1/Got3 gan1
(Schisandrae Fructus): 五味子: Wu3 sei4 zi3/Ng5 mei6 zi2

Dampness-Drying and Stomach-Harmonizing Formulas

(Level the Stomach Powder)
平胃散: Ping2 wei4 san3/Ping4 wai6 saan3
(Atractylodis Rhizoma): 苍术 / 蒼術: Cang1 zhu2/Cong1 seot6
(Magnoliae Officinalis Cortex): 厚朴: Hou4 po4/Hau5 pok3
(Citri Reticulatae Pericarpium): 陈皮 / 陳皮: Chen2 pi2/Can4 pei4
(Glycyrrhizae Radix): 炙甘草: Zhi4 gan1 cao3/Zek3 gam1 cou2
(Zingiberis Rhizoma Recens): 生姜 / 生薑: Sheng1 jiang1/Sang1 goeng1
(Jujubae Fructus): 大枣 / 大棗: Da4 zao3/Daai6 zou2

(Bupleurum Leveling Decoction)
柴平汤 / 柴平湯: Chai2 ping2 tang1/Caai4 ping4 tong1
(Atractylodis Rhizoma): 苍术 / 蒼術: Cang1 zhu2/Cong1 seot6
(Magnoliae Officinalis Cortex): 厚朴: Hou4 po4/Hau5 pok3
(Citri Reticulatae Pericarpium): 陈皮 / 陳皮: Chen2 pi2/Can4 pei4
(Glycyrrhizae Radix): 甘草: Gan1 cao3/Gam1 cou2
(Bupleuri Radix): 柴平: Chai2 hu2/Caai4 wu4
(Ginseng Radix): 人参 / 人參: Ren2 shen1/Jan4 sam1
(Pinelliae Rhizoma Preparatum): 制半夏 / 製半夏: Zhi4 ban4 xia4/Zai3 bun3 haa6
(Scutellariae Radix): 黄芩: Huang2 qin2/Wong4 kam4
(Agastachis Correct the Qi Powder)
藿香正气散 / 藿香正氣散: Huo4 xiang1 zheng4 qi4 san3/Fok3 hoeng1 zing3 hei3 saan3
(Atractylodis Macrocephalae Rhizoma): 白术 / 白術: Bai2 zhu2/Baak5 seot6
(Magnoliae Officinalis Cortex): 厚朴: Hou4 po4/Hau5 pok3
(Citri Reticulatae Pericarpium): 陈皮 / 陳皮: Chen2 pi2/Can4 pei4
(Glycyrrhizae Radix Preparata): 炙甘草: Zhi4 gan1 cao3/Zek3 gam1 cou2
(Platycodonis Radix): 桔梗: Jie2 geng3/Gat1 gang2
(Pogostemis Herba): 藿香: Huo4 xiang1/Fok3 hoeng1
(Pinelliae Rhizoma Preparatum): 制半夏 / 製半夏: Zhi4 ban4 xia4/Zai3 bun3 haa6
(Perillae Folium): 紫苏叶 / 紫蘇葉: Zi3 su1 ye4/Zi2 sou1 jip6
(Angelicae Dahuricae Radix): 白芷: Bai2 zhi3/Baak6 zi2
(Arecae Pericarpium): 大腹皮: Da4 fu4 pi2/Daai6 fuk1 pei4
(Poria): 茯苓: Fu2 ling2/Fuk6 ling4

(Stomach Poria Powder)
胃苓散: Wei4 ling2 san3/Wai6 ling4 saan3
(Atractylodis Rhizoma): 苍术 / 蒼術: Cang1 zhu2/Cong1 seot6
(Magnoliae Officinalis Cortex): 厚朴: Hou4 po4/Hau5 pok3
(Citri Reticulatae Pericarpium): 陈皮 / 陳皮: Chen2 pi2/Can4 pei4
(Glycyrrhizae Radix Praeparata): 炙甘草: Zhi4 gan1 cao3/Zek3 gam1 cou2
(Zingiberis Rhizoma Recens): 生姜 / 生薑: Sheng1 jiang1/Sang1 goeng1
(Jujubae Fructus): 大枣 / 大棗: Da4 zao3/Daai6 zou2
(Poria): 茯苓: Fu2 ling2/Fuk6 ling4
(Polyporus): 猪苓: Zhu1 ling2/Zyu1 ling4
(Atractylodis Macrocephalae Rhizoma): 白术 / 白術: Bai2 zhu2/Baak6 seot6
(Alismatis Rhizoma): 泽泻 / 澤瀉: Ze2 xie4/Zaak6 se3
(Cinnamomi Ramulus): 桂枝: Gui4 zhi1/Gwai3 zi1

Heat-Clearing and Dampness-Eliminating Formulas

(Artemisia Capillaris Decoction)
茵陈蒿汤 / 茵陳蒿湯: Yin1 chen2 hao1 tang1/Jan1 can4 hou1 tong1
(Artemisiae Scopariae Herba): 茵陈蒿 / 茵陳蒿: Yin1 chen2 hao1/ Jan1 can4 hou1
(Gardeniae Fructus): 栀子 / 梔子: Zhi1 zi3/Zi1 zi2
(Rhei Radix et Rhizoma): 大黄: Da4 huang2/Daai6 wong4

(Cure Discharge Pill)
愈带丸 / 愈帶丸: Yü4 dai4 wan2/Jyu6 daai3 jyun3
(Ailanthi Cortex): 椿皮: Chun1 pi2/Ceon1 pei4
(Paeoniae Radix Alba): 白芍: Bai2 shao2/Baak6 zoek3
(Charred Alpiniae Officinarum Rhizoma): 膏凉姜灰 / 膏涼薑灰: Gao1 liang2 jiang1 hui1/Gou1 loeng4 goeng1 fui1
(Charred Phellodendri Cortex): 黄柏灰: Huang2 bai3 hui1/Wong4 paak3 fui1

(Eight Correcting Powder)

八正散: Ba1 zheng4 san3/Baat3 jing3 saan3

(Plantaginis Semen): 车前子 / 車前子: Che1 qian2 zi3/Ce1 cin4 zi2

(Dianthi Herba): 瞿麦 / 蘧麥: Qu2 mai4/Keoi4 mak6

(Polygoni Avicularis Herba): 萹蓄: Bian3 xu4/Bin1 cuk1

(Talcum): 滑石: Hua2 shi2/Waat6 sek6

(Gardeniae Fructus): 栀子 / 梔子: Zhi1 zi3/Zi1 zi2

(Glycyrrhizae Radix Praeparata): 炙甘草: Zhi4 gan1 cao3/Zek3 gam1 cou2

(Akebiae Caulis): 木通: Mu4 tong3/Muk6 tung3

(Wine-Washed Rhei Radix et Rhizoma): 酒洗大黄: Jiu3 xi3 da4 huang2/Zao2 sai2 daai6 wong4

(Junci Medulla): 灯心草 / 燈心草: Deng1 xin1 cao3/Dang1 sam1 cou2

(Two Wonders Powder)

二妙散 / 二妙散: Er4 miao4 san3/Ji6 miu6 saan3

(Dry-Fried Phellodendri Cortex): 炒黄柏: Chao3 huang2 bai2/Caau2 wong4 paak3

(Prepared Atractylodis Rhizoma): 制苍术 / 製蒼術: Zhi4 cang1 zhu2/Zai3 cong1 seot6

(Three Wonders Powder)

三妙散 / 三妙散: San1 miao4 san3/Saam1 miu6 saan3

(Wine-Fried Phellodendri Cortex): 酒炒黄柏: Jiu3 chao3 huang2 bai2/Zau2 caau2 wong4 paak3

(Atractylodis Rhizoma): 苍术 / 蒼術: Cang1 zhu2/Cong1 seot6

(Achyranthis Radix): 牛膝: Niu2 xi1/Ngau4 sat1 My teacher always wrote this "cow seven" or 牛七: Niu2 qi1/Ngau4 cat1

(Four Wonders Powder):

四妙散 / 四妙散: Si4 miao4 san3/Sei3 miu6 saan3

(Phellodendri Cortex): 黄柏: Huang2 bai2/Wong4 paak3

(Atractylodis Rhizoma): 苍术 / 蒼術: Cang1 zhu2/Cong1 seot6

(Achyranthis Radix): 牛膝: Niu2 xi1/Ngau4 sat1 My teacher always wrote this "cow seven" or 牛七: Niu2 qi1/Ngau4 cat1

(Coicis Semen): 薏苡仁: Yi4 yi3 ren2/Ji3 ji5 jan4

(Three-Seed Decoction)
三仁汤 / 三仁湯: San1 ren2 tang1/Saam1 jan4 tong1
(Armeniacae Semen): 杏仁: Xing4 ren2/Hang5 jan4
(Amomi Fructus Rotundus): 白豆蔻: Bai2 dou4 kou4/Baak6 dau6 kau3
(Magnoliae Officinalis Cortex): 厚朴: Hou4 po4/Hau5 pok3
(Pinelliae Rhizoma Preparatum): 制半夏 / 製半夏: Zhi4 ban4 xia4/Zai3 bun3 haa6
(Coicis Semen): 薏苡仁: Yi4 yi3 ren2/Ji3 ji5 jan4
(Tetrapanacis Medulla): 通草: Tong1 cao3/Tung1 cou2
(Lophatheri Herba): 淡竹叶 / 淡竹葉: Dan4 zhu2 ye4/Daam6 zuk1 jip6
(Talcum): 滑石: Hua2 shi2/Waat6 sek6

(Coptis and Magnolia Bark Drink)
连朴饮 / 連朴飲: Lian2 po4 yin3/Lin4 pok3 jam2
(Ginger Coptidis Rhizoma): 姜黄连 / 薑黃連: Jiang1 huang2 lian2/Goeng1 wong4 lin4 my teacher always referred to the basic unprocessed form of this medicinal in its Sichuan version 川连 / 川連: Chuan1 lian2/Cyun1 lin4
(Prepared Magnoliae Officinalis Cortex): 炙厚朴: Zhi4 hou4 po4/Zek3 hau5 pok3
(Gardeniae Fructus): 栀子 / 梔子: Zhi1 zi3/Zi1 zi2
(Xiangchi Dry-Fried Sojae Semen Preparatum): 炒豆豉 / 炒豆豉: Chao3 dou4 chi3/Caau2 dau6 si6
(Acori Tatarinowii Rhizoma): 石菖蒲: Shi2 chang1 pu2/Sek6 coeng1 pou4
(Pinelliae Rhizoma Preparatum): 制半夏 / 製半夏: Zhi4 ban2 xia4/Zai3 bun3 haa6
(Phragmitis Rhizoma): 芦根 / 蘆根: Lu2 gen1/Lou4 gan1

(Separate and Reduce Fullness in the Middle Pill)
中满分消丸 / 中滿分消丸: Zhong1 man3 fen1 xiao1 wan2/Zung1 mun5 fan1 siu1 jyun2
(Ginger-Fried Magnoliae Officinalis Cortex): 姜炒厚朴 / 薑炒厚朴: Jiang1 chao3 hou4 po4/Goeng1 caau2 hau5 pok3
(Dry-Fried Aurantii Fructus Immaturus): 炒枳实 / 炒枳實: Chao3 zhi3 shi2/Caau2 zi2 sat6
(Curcumae Longae Rhizoma): 姜黄 / 薑黃: Jiang1 huang2/Goeng1 wong4
(Dry-Fried Scutellariae Radix): 炒黄芩: Chao3 huang2 qin2/Caau2 wong4 kam4
(Dry-Fried Coptidis Rhizoma): 炒黄连 / 炒黃連: Chao3 huang2 lian2/Caau2 wong4 lin4 My teacher referred to the unprocessed version of this medicinal in its Sichuan version 川连 / 川連: Chuan1 lian2/Cyun1 lin4
(Zingiberis Rhizoma): 干姜 / 乾薑: Gan1 jiang1/Gon1 goeng1
(Pinelliae Rhizoma Preparatum): 制半夏 / 製半夏: Zhi4 ban4 xia4/Zai3 bun3 haa6

(Dry-Fried Anemarrhenae Rhizoma): 炒知母: Chao3 zhi1 mu3/Caau2 zi1 mou5
(Alismatis Rhizoma): 泽泻 / 澤瀉: Ze2 xie4/Zaak6 se3
(Polyporus): 猪苓 / 豬苓: Zhu1 ling2/Zyu1 ling4
(Atractylodis Macrocephalae Rhizoma): 白术 / 白術: Bai2 zhu2/Baak6 seot6
(Ginseng Radix): 人参 / 人參: Ren2 shen1/Jan4 sam1
(Glycyrrhizae Radix Preparata): 炙甘草: Zhi4 gan1 cao3/Zek3 gam1 cou2
(Citri Reticulatae Pericarpium): 陈皮 / 陳皮: Chen2 pi2/Can4 pei4
(Amomi Fructus): 砂仁: Sha1 ren2/Saa1 jan4
(Poria): 茯苓: Fu2 ling2/Fuk6 ling4

(Sweet Dew Special Pill to Eliminate Toxin)
甘露消毒丹: Gan1 lu4 xiao1 du2 dan1/Gam1 lou6 siu1 duk6 daan1
also called
普级解毒丹 / 普級解毒丹: Pu3 ji3 jie3 du2 dan1/Pou2 kap1 gaai2 duk6 daan1
(Forsythiae Fructus): 连翘 / 連翹: Lian2 qiao2/Lin4 kiu4
(Scutellariae Radix): 黄芩: Huang2 qin2/Wong4 kam4
(Menthae Haplocalycis Herba): 薄荷: Bo4 he2/Bok6 ho4
(Belamcandae Rhizoma): 射干: She4 gan1/Se6 gon1
Fritillariae Cirrhosae Bulbus): 川贝母 / 川貝母: Chuan1 bei4 mu3/Cyun1 bui3 mou5
(Talcum): 滑石: Hua2 shi2/Waat6 sek6
(Akebiae Caulis): 木通: Mu4 tong3/Muk6 tung2
(Artemisiae Scopariae Herba): 茵陈蒿 / 茵陳蒿: Yin1 chen2 hao1/Jan1 can4 hou1
(Pogostemi Herba): 藿香: Huo4 xiang1/Fok3 hoeng1
(Acori Tatarinowii Rhizoma): 石菖蒲: Shi2 chang1 pu2/Sek6 coeng1 pou4
(Amomi Fructus Rotundus): 白豆蔻: Bai2 dou4 kou4/Baak6 dau6 kau3

(Disband Painful Obstruction Decoction)
宣痹汤 / 宣痹湯: Xuan1 bi4 tang1/Syun1 bei3 tong1
(Stephaniae/Cocculi etc. Radix): 汉防己 / 漢防己: Han4 fang2 ji3/Hon3 fong4 gei2
(Armeniacae Semen): 杏仁: Xing4 ren2/Hang6 jan4
(Talcum): 滑石: Hua2 shi2/Waat6 sek6
Forsythiae Fructus): 连翘 / 連翹: Lian2 qiao2/Lin4 kiu4
(Coicis Semen): 薏苡仁: Yi4 yi3 ren2/Ji3 ji5 jan4
(Pinelliae Rhizoma Preparatum): 制半夏 / 製半夏: Zhi4 ban4 xia4/Zai3 bun3 haa6
(Bombycis Faeces): 蚕砂 / 蠶砂: Can2 sha1/Caam4 saa1
(Phaseoli Semen): 赤小豆: Chi4 xiao3 dou4/Cek3 siu2 dau2
(Gardeniae Fructus): 栀子 / 梔子: Zhi1 zi3/Zi1 zi2

(Added Flavors Two Wonders Powder)
加味二妙散: Jia1 wei4 er4 miao4 san3/Gaa1 mei6 ji6 miu6 saan3
(Phellodendri Cortex): 黄柏: Huang2 bai2/Wong4 paak3
(Atractylodis Rhizoma): 苍术 / 蒼術: Cang1 zhu2/Cong1 seot6
(Achyranthes Bidentatae Radix): 川牛膝: Chuan1 niu2 xi1/Cyun1 ngau4 sat1 My teacher always wrote this "cow seven" or 牛七: Niu2 qi1/Ngau4 cat1 My teacher always wrote this "cow seven" or 牛七: Niu2 qi1/Ngau4 cat1
(Angelicae Sinensis Radix Cauda): 当归尾 / 當歸尾: Dang1 gui1 wei3/Dong1 gwai1 mei5
(Stephaniae Tetrandrae Radix): 汉防己 / 漢防己: Han4 fang2 ji3/Hon3 fong4 gei2
(Dioscoreae Hypoglaucae Rhizoma): 萆薢: Bi4 xie4/Bei1 gaai1
(Processed Testudinis Plastrum): 制龟板 / 製龜板: Zhi4 gui1 ban3/Zai3 gwai1 baan2
(Glycyrrhizae Radix): 炙甘草: Zhi4 gan1 cao3/Zek3 gam1 cou2

Water-Disinhibiting and Dampness-Seeping Formulas

(Five Poria Powder)
五苓散: Wu3 ling2 san3/Ng5 ling4 saan3
(Poria): 茯苓: Fu2 ling2/Fuk6 ling4
(Polyporus): 猪苓 / 豬苓: Zhu1 ling2/Zyu1 ling4
(Atractylodis Macrocephalae Rhizoma): 白术 / 白術: Bai2 zhu2/Baak6 seot6
(Alismatis Rhizoma): 泽泻 / 澤瀉: Ze2 xie4/Zaak6 se3
(Cinnamomi Ramulus): 桂枝: Gui4 zhi1/Gwai3 zi1

(Polyporus Decoction)
猪苓汤 / 豬苓湯: Zhu1 ling2 tang1/Zyu1 ling4 tong1
(Polyporus): 猪苓 / 豬苓: Zhu1 ling2/Zyu1 ling4
(Poria): 茯苓: Fu2 ling2/Fuk6 ling4
(Alismatis Rhizoma): 泽泻 / 澤瀉: Ze2 xie4/Zaak6 se3
(Talcum): 滑石: Hua2 shi2/Waat6 sek6
(Asini Corii Colla): 阿胶 / 阿膠: E1 jiao1/Aa3 gaau1

(Five-Peel Powder)
五皮散: Wu3 pi2 san3/Ng5 pei4 saan3
(Mori Cortex): 桑白皮: Sang1 bai2 pi2/Song1 baak6 pei4
(Zingiberis Rhizomatis Cortex): 生姜皮 / 生薑皮: Sheng1 jiang1 pi2/Sang1 goeng1 pei4
(Poriae Cutis): 茯苓皮: Fu2 ling2 pi2/Fuk6 ling4 pei4
(Citri Reticulatae Pericarpium): 陈皮 / 陳皮: Chen2 pi2/Can4 pei4
(Arecae Pericarpium): 大腹皮: Da4 fu4 pi2/Daai6 fuk1 pei4

(Four Poria Powder)
四苓散: Si4 ling2 san3/Sei3 ling4 saan3
(Poria): 茯苓: Fu2 ling2/Fuk6 ling4
(Polyporus): 猪苓 / 豬苓: Zhu1 ling2/Zyu1 ling4
(Atractylodis Macrocephalae Rhizoma): 白术 / 白術: Bai2 zhu2/Baak6 seot6
(Alismatis Rhizoma): 泽泻 / 澤瀉: Ze2 xie4/Zaak6 se3

(Artemisia Five Poria Powder)
茵陈五苓散 / 茵陳五苓散: Yin1 chen2 wu3 ling2 san3/Jan1 can4 ng5 ling4 saan3
(Poria): 茯苓: Fu2 ling2/Fuk6 ling4
(Polyporus): 猪苓 / 豬苓: Zhu1 ling2/Zyu1 ling4
(Atractylodis Macrocephalae Rhizoma): 白术 / 白術: Bai2 zhu2/Baak6 seot6
(Alismatis Rhizoma): 泽泻 / 澤瀉: Ze2 xie4/Zaak6 se3
(Cinnamomi Ramulus): 桂枝: Gui4 zhi1/Gwai3 zi1
(Artemisiae Scopariae Herba): 茵陈蒿 / 茵陳蒿: Yin1 chen2 hao1/Jan1 can4 hou1

(Bupleurum and Poria Decoction)
柴苓汤 / 柴苓湯: Chai2 ling2 tang1/Caai4 ling4 tong1
(Poria): 茯苓: Fu2 ling2/Fuk6 ling4
(Polyporus): 猪苓: Zhu1 ling2/Zyu1 ling4
(Atractylodis Macrocephalae Rhizoma): 白术 / 白術: Bai2 zhu2/Baak6 seot6
(Alismatis Rhizoma): 泽泻 / 澤瀉: Ze2 xie4/Zaak6 se3
(Bupleuri Radix): 柴胡: Chai2 hu2/Caai4 wu4
(Scutellariae Radix): 黄芩: Huang2 qin2/Wong4 kam4
(Ginseng Radix): 人参 / 人參: Ren2 shen1/Jan4 sam1
(Pinelliae Rhizoma Preparatum): 制半夏 / 製半夏: Zhi4 ban4 xia4/Zai3 bun3 haa6
(Cinnamomi Ramulus): 桂枝: Gui4 zhi1/Gwai3 zi1
(Glycyrrhizae Radix): 甘草: Gan1 cao3/Gam1 cou2
(Zingiberis Rhizoma Recens): 生姜 / 生薑: Sheng1 jiang1/Sang1 goeng1
(Jujubae Fructus): 大枣 / 大棗: Da4 zao3/Daai6 zou2

(Stephania and Astragalus Decoction)
防己黄芪汤 / 防己黃耆湯: Fang2 ji3 huang2 qi2 tang1/Fong4 gei2 wong4 kei4 tong1
(Astragali Radix): 黄芪 / 黃耆: Huang2 qi2/Wong4 kei4 my teacher always referred to this medicinal as 北芪 / 北耆: Bei3 qi2/Bak1 kei4
(Stephaniae Tetrandrae Radix): 汉防己 / 漢防己: Han4 fang2 ji3/Hon3 fong4 gei2
(Atractylodis Macrocephalae Rhizoma): 白术 / 白術: Bai2 zhu2/Baak6 seot6
(Glycyrrhizae Radix Preparata): 炙甘草: Zhi4 gan1 cao3/Zek3 gam1 cou2
(Zingiberis Rhizoma Recens): 生姜 / 生薑: Sheng1 jiang1/Sang1 goeng1
(Jujubae Fructus): 大枣 / 大棗: Da4 zao3/Daai6 zou2

(Calm the Stomach and Poria Decoction)
胃苓汤 / 胃苓湯: Wei4 ling2 tang1/Wai6 ling4 tong1
This is a combination of Wu Ling San and Ping Wei San
(Alismatis Rhizoma): 泽泻 / 澤瀉: Ze2 xie4/Zaak6 se3
(Poria): 茯苓: Fu2 ling2/Fuk6 ling4
(Polyporus): 猪苓: Zhu1 ling2/Zyu1 ling4
(Atractylodis Macrocephalae Rhizoma): 白术 / 白術: Bai2 zhu2/Baak6 seot6
(Cinnamomi Ramulus): 桂枝: Gui4 zhi1/Gwai3 zi1
(Dry-Fried Atractylodis Rhizoma): 炒苍术 / 炒蒼術: Chao3 cang1 zhu2/Caau2 cong1 seot6
(Ginger-Fried Magnoliae Officinalis Cortex): 姜炒厚朴 / 薑炒厚朴: Jiang1 chao3 hou4 po4/Goeng1 caau2 hau5 pok3
(Citri Reticulatae Pericarpium): 陈皮 / 陳皮: Chen2 pi2/Can4 pei4
(Glycyrrhizae Radix Preparata): 炙甘草: Zhi4 gan1 cao3/Zek3 gam1 cou2
(Zingiberis Rhizoma Recens): 生姜 / 生薑: Sheng1 jiang1/Sang1 goeng1
(Jujubae Fructus): 大枣 / 大棗: Da4 zao3/Daai6 zou2

Warming and Transforming Water Dampness Formulas

(Poria, Cinnamon, Atractylodes and Licorice Decoction)
苓桂术甘汤 / 苓桂術甘湯: Ling2 gui4 zhu2 gan1 tang1/Ling4 gwai3 seot6 gam1 tong1
(Poria): 茯苓: Fu2 ling2/Fuk6 ling4
(Cinnamomi Ramulus): 桂枝: Gui4 zhi1/Gwai3 zi1
(Atractylodis Macrocephalae Rhizoma): 白术 / 白術: Bai2 zhu2/Baak6 seot6
(Glycyrrhizae Radix Preparata): 炙甘草: Zhi4 gan1 cao3/Zek3 gam1 cou2

(Powder to Take at Cock's Crow)
鸡鸣散 / 雞鳴散: Ji1 ming2 san3/Gai1 ming4 saan3
(Arecae Semen): 槟榔 / 檳榔: Bing1 lang2/Ban1 long4
(Chaenomelis Fructus): 木瓜: Mu4 gua1/Muk6 gwaa1
(Evodiae Fructus): 吴茱萸 / 吳茱萸: Wu2 zhu1 yü2/Ng4 zyu1 jyu4
(Citri Reticulatae Pericarpium): 陈皮 / 陳皮: Chen2 pi2/Can4 pei4
(Perillae Folium): 紫苏叶 / 紫蘇葉: Zi3 su1 ye4/Zi2 sou1 jip6
(Platycodi Radix): 桔梗: Jie2 geng3/Gat1 gang2
(Zingiberis Rhizoma Recens): 生姜 / 生薑: Sheng1 jiang1/Sang1 goeng1

(True Warrior Decoction)
真武汤 / 真武湯: Zhen1 wu3 tang1/Zan1 mou5 tong1
(Baked Aconiti Radix Lateralis): 炮附子 / 炮附子: Pao21 fu4 zi3/Paau4 fu6 zi2
(Atractylodis Macrocephalae Rhizoma): 白术 / 白術: Bai2 zhu2/Baak6 seot6
(Poria): 茯苓: Fu2 ling2/Fuk6 ling4
(Zingiberis Rhizoma Recens): 生姜 / 生薑: Sheng1 jiang1/Sang1 goeng1
(Paeoniae Radix Alba): 白芍: Bai2 shao2/Baak6 zoek3

(Aconite Accessory Root Decoction):
附子汤 / 附子湯: Fu4 zi3 tang1/Fu6 zi2 tong1
(Baked Aconiti Radix Lateralis): 炮附子 / 炮附子: Pao2 fu4 zi3/Paau4 fu6 zi2
(Ginseng Radix): 人参 / 人參: Ren2 shen1/Jan4 sam1
(Poria): 茯苓: Fu2 ling2/Fuk6 ling4
(Paeoniae Radix Alba): 白芍: Bai2 shao2/Baak6 zoek3

Wind-Dispelling and Dampness-Overcoming Formulas

(Angelica Pubescens and Loranthus Decoction)
独活寄生汤 / 獨活寄生湯: Du2 huo2 ji4 sheng1 tang1/Duk6 wut6 gei3 sang1 tong1
(Angelicae Pubescentis Radix): 独活 / 獨活: Du2 huo2/Duk6 wut6
(Taxilli Herba): 桑寄生: Sang1 ji4 sheng1/Song1 gei3 sang1
(Eucommiae Cortex): 杜仲: Du4 zhong4/Dou6 zung6
(Achyranthis Radix): 牛膝: Niu2 xi1/Ngau4 sat1 My teacher always wrote this "cow seven" or 牛七: Niu2 qi1/Ngau4 cat1
(Asari Herba cum Radice): 细辛 / 細辛: Xi4 xin1/Sai3 san1
(Gentianae Macrophyllae Radix): 秦艽: Qin2 jiao1/Ceon4 gao2
(Poria): 茯苓: Fu2 ling2/Fuk6 ling4
(Cinnamomi Cortex): 肉桂: Rou4 gui4/Juk6 gwai3
(Saposhnikoviae Radix): 防风 / 防風: Fang2 feng1/Fong4 fung1
(Chuanxiong Rhizoma): 川芎: Chuan1 xiong1/Cyun1 gung1

(Ginseng Radix): 人参 / 人參: Ren2 shen1/Jan4 sam1

(Glycyrrhizae Radix): 甘草: Gan1 cao3/Gam1 cou2

(Angelicae Sinensis Radix): 当归 / 當歸: Dang1 gui1/Dong1 gwai1

(Paeoniae Radix Alba): 白芍: Bai2 shao2/Baak6 zoek3

(Rehmanniae Radix): 生地黄: Sheng1 di4 huang2/Sang1 dei6 wong4

(Notopterygium Decoction to Overcome Dampness)

羌活胜湿汤 / 羌活勝濕湯: Qiang1 huo2 sheng4 shi1 tang1/Goeng1 wut6 sing3 sap1 tong1

(Notopterygii Rhizoma seu Radix): 羌活: Qiang1 huo2/Goeng1 wut6

(Angelicae Pubescentis Radix): 独活 / 獨活: Du2 huo2/Duk6 wut6

(Ligustici Rhizoma): 槁本 / 藁本: Gao3 ben3/Gou2 bun2

(Saposhikoviae Radix): 防风 / 防風: Fang2 feng1/Fong4 fung1

(Chuanxiong Rhizoma): 川芎: Chuan1 xiong1/Cyun1 gung1

(Viticis Fructus): 蔓荆子 / 蔓荊子: Man4 jing1 zi3/Maan4 ging1 zi2

(Glycyrrhizae Radix Preparata): 炙甘草: Zhi4 gan1 cao3/Zek3 gam1 cou2

(Remove Painful Obstruction Decoction)

蠲痹汤 / 蠲痹湯: Juan1 bi4 tang1/Gyun1 bei3 tong1

(Notopterygii Rhizoma seu Radix): 羌活: Qiang1 huo2/Goeng1 wut6

(Curcumae Longae Rhizoma): 姜黄 / 薑黃: Jiang1 huang2/Goeng1 wong4

(Wine-Washed Angelicae Sinensis Radix): 酒洗当归 / 酒洗當歸: Jiu3 xi3 dang1 gui1/Zau2 sai2 dong1 gwai1

(Honey-Prepared Astragali Radix): 蜜炙黄芪 / 蜜炙黃耆: Mi4 zhi4 huang2 qi2/Mat6 zek3 wong4 kei4 My teacher always referred to this as 北芪: Bei3 qi2/Bak1 kei4.

(Paeoniae Radix Alba): 白芍: Bai2 shao2/Baak6 zoek3

(Saposhikoviae Radix): 防风 / 防風: Fang2 feng1/Fong4 fung1

(Glycyrrhizae Radix Preparata): 炙甘草: Zhi4 gan1 cao3/Zek3 gam1 cou2

Dampness-Drying and Phlegm-Transforming Formulas

(Two-Aged Decoction)

二陈汤 / 二陳湯: Er4 chen2 tang1/Ji6 can4 tong1

(Pinelliae Rhizoma Preparatum): 制半夏 / 製半夏: Zhi4 ban4 xia4/Zai3 bun3 haa6

(Citri Reticulatae Exocarpium Rubrum): 橘皮: Jü2 hong2/Gwat1 hung4

(Poria): 茯苓: Fu2 ling2/Fuk6 ling4

(Glycyrrhizae Radix Preparata): 炙甘草: Zhi4 gan1 cao3/Zek3 gam1 cou2

(Zingiberis Rhizoma Recens): 生姜 / 生薑: Sheng1 jiang1/Sang1 goeng1

(Mume Fructus): 乌梅 / 烏梅: Wu1 mei2/Wu1 mui4

(Warm the Gallbladder Decoction)

温胆汤 / 溫膽湯: Wen1 dan3 tang1/Wan1 daam2 tong1

(Pinelliae Rhizoma Preparatum): 制半夏 / 製半夏: Zhi4 ban4 xia4/Zai3 bun3 haa6

(Citri Reticulatae Pericarpium): 陈皮 / 陳皮: Chen2 pi2/Can4 pei4

(Poria): 茯苓: Fu2 ling2/Fuk6 ling4

(Glycyrrhizae Radix Preparata): 炙甘草: Zhi4 gan1 cao3/Zek3 gam1 cou2

(Bambusae in Taeniis Caulis): 竹茹: Zhu2 ru2/Zuk1 jyu4

(Aurantii Fructus Immaturus): 枳实 / 枳實: Zhi3 shi2/Zi2 sat6

(Zingiberis Rhizoma Recens): 生姜 / 生薑: Sheng1 jiang1/Sang1 goeng1

(Zizyphi Jujubae Fructus): 大枣 / 大棗: Da1 zao3/Daai6 zou2

(Coptis Warm the Gallbladder Decoction)

黄连温胆汤 / 黃連溫膽湯: Huang2 lian2 wen1 dan3 tang1/Wong4 lin4 wan1 daam2 tong1

(Coptidis Rhizoma) 黄连 / 黃連: Huang2 lian2/Wong4 lin4 My teacher always referred to this medicinal in its Sichuan form: 川连 / 川連: Chuan1 lian2/Cyun1 lin4

(Pinelliae Rhizoma Preparatum): 制半夏 / 製半夏: Zhi4 ban4 xia4/Zai3 bun3 haa6

(Citri Reticulatae Pericarpium): 陈皮 / 陳皮: Chen2 pi2/Can4 pei4

(Poria): 茯苓: Fu2 ling2/Fuk6 ling4

(Glycyrrhizae Radix Preparata): 炙甘草: Zhi4 gan1 cao3/Zek3 gam1 cou2

(Bambusae Caulis in Taeniam): 竹茹: Zhu2 ru2/Zuk1 jyu4

(Aurantii Fructus Immaturus): 枳实 / 枳實: Zhi3 shi2/Zi2 sat6

(Zingiberis Rhizoma Recens): 生姜 / 生薑: Sheng1 jiang1/Sang1 goeng1

(Jujubae Fructus): 大枣 / 大棗: Da1 zao3/Daai6 zou2

(Flush Phlegm Decoction)

涤痰汤 / 滌痰湯: Di2 tan2 tang1/Dik6 taam4 tong1

(Pinelliae Rhizoma Preparatum): 制半夏 / 製半夏: Zhi4 ban4 xia4/Zai3 bun3 haa6

(Citri Reticulatae Pericarpium): 陈皮 / 陳皮: Chen2 pi2/Can4 pei4

(Acori Tatarinowii Rhizoma): 石菖蒲: Shi2 chang1 pu2/Sek6 coeng1 pou4

(Poria): 茯苓: Fu2 ling2/Fuk6 ling4

(Glycyrrhizae Radix): 甘草: Gan1 cao3/Gam1 cou2

(Bambusae Caulis in Taeniam): 竹茹: Zhu2 ru2/Zuk1 jyu4

(Aurantii Fructus Immaturus): 枳实 / 枳實: Zhi3 shi2/Zi2 sat6

(Arisaematis Rhizoma Preparatum): 制天南星 / 製天南星: Zhi4 tian1 nan2 xing1/Zai3 tin1 naam4 sing1

(Ginseng Radix): 人参 / 人參: Ren2 shen1/Jan4 sam1

(Metal and Water Six Gentlemen Decoction)

金水六君煎: Jin1 shui3 liu4 jun1 jian1/Gam1 seoi2 luk6 gwan1 zin1

(Pinelliae Rhizoma Preparatum): 制半夏 / 製半夏: Zhi4 ban4 xia4/Zai3 Bun3 haa6

(Citri Reticulatae Pericarpium): 陈皮 / 陳皮: Chen2 pi2/Can4 pei4

(Poria): 茯苓: Fu2 ling2/Fuk6 ling4

(Glycyrrhizae Radix Preparata): 炙甘草: Zhi4 gan1 cao3/Zek3 gam1 cou2

(Angelicae Sinensis Radix): 当归 / 當歸: Dang1 gui1/Dong1 gwai1

(Rehmanniae Radix): 熟地黄: Shu2 di4 huang2/Suk6 dei6 wong4

(Zingiberis Rhizoma Recens): 生姜 / 生薑: Sheng1 jiang1/Sang1 goeng1

(Aucklandia and Amomum Two Aged Decoction)

香砂二陈汤 / 香砂二陳湯: Xiang1 sha1 er4 chen2 tang1/Hoeng1 saa1 ji6 can4 tong1

(Pinelliae Rhizoma Preparatum): 制半夏 / 製半夏: Zhi4 ban4 xia4/Zai3 Bun3 haa6

(Citri Reticulatae Pericarpium): 陈皮 / 陳皮: Chen2 pi2/Can4 pei4

(Poria): 茯苓: Fu2 ling2/Fuk6 ling4

(Glycyrrhizae Radix Preparata): 炙甘草: Zhi4 gan1 cao3/Zek3 gam1 cou2

(Zingiberis Rhizoma Recens): 生姜 / 生薑: Sheng1 jiang1/Sang1 goeng1

(Mume Fructus): 乌梅 / 烏梅: Wu1 mei2/Wu1 mui4

(Aucklandiae Radix): 木香: Mu4 xiang1/Muk6 hoeng1

(Amomi Fructus): 砂仁: Sha1 ren2/Saa1 jan4

(Ginseng Radix): 人参 / 人參: Ren2 shen1/Jan4 sam1

(Atractylodes Macrocephalae Rhizoma): 白术 / 白術: Bai2 zhu2/Baak6 seot6

(Abduct Phlegm Decoction)
导痰汤 / 導痰湯: Dao3 tan2 tang1/Dou6 taam4 tong1
(Pinelliae Rhizoma Preparatum): 制半夏 / 製半夏: Zhi4 ban4 xia4/Zai3 Bun3 haa6
(Citri Reticulatae Exocarpium): 橘红 / 橘紅: Jü2 hong2/Gwat1 hung4
(Poria): 茯苓: Fu2 ling2/Fuk6 ling4
(Zingiberis Rhizoma Recens): 生姜 / 生薑: Sheng1 jiang1/Sang1 goeng1
(Aurantii Fructus Immaturus): 枳实 / 枳實: Zhi3 shi2/Zi2 sat6
(Arisaematis Rhizoma Preparatum): 制天南星 / 製天南星: Zhi4 tian1 nan2 xing1/Zai3 Tin1 naam4 sing1

(Six-Serenity Decoction)
六安煎: Liu4 an1 jian1/Luk6 on1 zin1
(Citri Reticulatae Pericarpium): 陈皮 / 陳皮: Chen2 pi2/Can4 pei4
(Pinelliae Rhizoma Preparatum): 制半夏 / 製半夏: Zhi4 ban4 xia4/Zai3 bun3 haa6
(Poria): 茯苓: Fu2 ling2/Fuk6 ling4
(Glycyrrhizae Radix Praeparata): 炙甘草: Zhi4 gan1 cao3/Zek3 gam1 cou2
(Armeniacae Semen): 杏仁: Xing4 ren2/Hang6 jan4
(Sinapis Semen): 白芥子: Bai2 jie4 zi3/Baak6 gaai3 zi2
(Zingiberis Rhizoma Recens): 生姜 / 生薑: Sheng1 jiang1/Sang1 goeng1

(Clear Dampness and Transform Phlegm Decoction)
清湿化痰汤 / 清濕化痰湯: Qing1 shi1 hua4 tan2 tang1/Cing1 sap1 faa3 taam4 tong1
(Pinelliae Rhizoma Preparatum): 制半夏 / 製半夏: Zhi4 ban4 xia4/Zai3 bun3 haa6
(Poria): 茯苓: Fu2 ling2/Fuk6 ling4
(Atractylodis Rhizoma): 苍术 / 蒼術: Cang1 zhu2/Cong1 seot6
(Arisaematis Rhizoma Preparatum): 制天南星 / 製天南星: Zhi4 tian1 nan2 xing1/Zai3 tin1 naam4 sing1
(Scutellariae Radix): 黄芩: Huang2 qin2/Wong4 kam4
(Citri Reticulatae Pericarpium): 陈皮 / 陳皮: Chen2 pi2/Can4 pei4
(Notopterygii Rhizoma Seu Radix): 羌活: Qiang1 huo2/Goeng1 wut6
(Sinapis Semen): 白芥子: Bai2 jie4 zi3/Baak6 gaai3 zi2
(Angelicae Dahuricae Radix): 白芷: Bai2 zhi3/Baak6 zi2
(Glycyrrhizae Radix): 甘草: Gan1 cao3/Gam1 cou2
(Zingiberis Rhizoma Recens): 生姜 / 生薑: Sheng1 jiang1/Sang1 goeng1
(Zingiberis Rhizoma): 干姜 / 乾薑: Gan1 jiang1/Gon1 goeng1

(Ten-Ingredient Warm Gallbladder Decoction)
十味温胆汤 / 十味溫膽湯: Shi2 wei4 wen1 dan3 tang1/Sap6 mei6 wan1 daam2 tong1
(Pinelliae Rhizoma Preparatum): 制半夏 / 製半夏: Zhi4 ban4 xia4/Zai3 bun3 haa6
(Aurantii Ructus Immaturus): 枳实 / 枳實: Zhi3 shi2/Zi2 sat6
(Citri Reticulatae Pericarpium): 陈皮 / 陳皮: Chen2 pi2/Can4 pei4
(Poria): 茯苓: Fu2 ling2/Fuk6 ling4
(Ziziphi Spinosae Semen): 酸枣仁 / 酸棗仁: Suan1 zao3 ren2/Syun1 zou2 jan4
(Polygalae Radix): 远志 / 遠志: Yuan3 zhi4/Jyun5 zi3
(Schisandrae Fructus): 五味子: Wu3 wei4 zi3/Ng5 mei6 zi2
(Rehmanniae Radix Preparata): 熟地黄: Shu2 di4 huang2/Suk6 dei6 wong4
(Ginseng Radix): 人参 / 人參: Ren2 shen1/Jan4 sam1
(Glycyrrhizae Radix): 甘草: Gan1 cao3/Gam1 cou2
(Zingiberis Rhizoma Recens): 生姜 / 生薑: Sheng1 jiang1/Sang1 goeng1
(Jujubae Fructus): 大枣 / 大棗: Da4 zao3/Daai6 zou2

(Trichosanthes Fruit and Unripe Bitter Orange Decoction)
瓜蒌枳实汤 / 瓜蔞枳實湯: Gua1 lou2 zhi3 shi2 tang1/Gwaa1 lau4 zi2 sat6 tong1
(Tricosanthes Fructus): 瓜蒌 / 瓜蔞: Gua1 lou2/Gwaa1 lau4
(Aurantii Ructus Immaturus): 枳实 / 枳實: Zhi3 shi2/Zi2 sat6
(Platycodi Radix): 桔梗: Jie2 geng3/Gat1 gang2
(Poria): 茯苓: Fu2 ling2/Fuk6 ling4
(Fritillariae Bulbus): 川贝母 / 川貝母: Chuan1 bei4 mu3/Cyun1 bui3 mou5
(Citri Reticulatae Pericarpium): 陈皮 / 陳皮: Chen2 pi2/Can4 pei4
(Gardeniae Fructus): 栀子 / 梔子: Zhi1 zi3/Zi1 zi2
(Scutellariae Radix): 黄芩: Huang2 qin2/Wong4 kam4
(Angelicae Sinensis Radix): 当归 / 當歸: Dang1 gui1/Dong1 gwai1
(Amomi Fructus): 砂仁: Sha1 ren2/Saa1 jan4
(Bambusae Caulis in Taeniam): 竹茹: Zhu2 ru2/Zuk1 jyu4
(Aucklandiae Radix): 木香: Mu4 xiang1/Muk6 hoeng1
(Glycyrrhizae Radix): 甘草: Gan1 cao3/Gam1 cou2

(Minor Decoction [for Pathogens] Stuck in the Chest)
小陷胸汤 / 小陷胸湯: Xiao3 xian4 xiong1 tang1/Siu2 haam6 hung1 tong1
(Tricosanthes Fructus): 瓜蒌 / 瓜蔞: Gua1 lou2/Gwaa1 lau4
(Coptidis Rhizoma): 黄连 / 黃連: Huang2 lian2/Wong4 lin4 my teacher always referred to this medicinal in its Sichuan version: 川连 / 川連: Chuan1 lian2/Cyun1 lin4
(Ginger-fried Pinelliae Rhizoma Preparatum): 姜半夏 / 薑半夏: Jiang1 ban4 xia4/Goeng1 bun3 haa6

(Augmented Two-Aged [Herb] Decoction)
加味二陈汤 / 加味二陳湯: Jia1 wei4 er4 chen2 tang1/Gaa1 mei6 ji6 can4 tong1
(Pinelliae Rhizoma Preparatum): 制半夏 / 製半夏: Zhi4 ban4 xia4/Zai3 bun3
haa6
(Citri Reticulatae Pericarpium): 陈皮 / 陳皮: Chen2 pi2/Can4 pei4
(Poria): 茯苓: Fu2 ling2/Fuk6 ling4
(Glycyrrhizae Radix): 甘草: Gan1 cao3/Gam1 cou2
(Zingiberis Rhizoma Recens): 生姜 / 生薑: Sheng1 jiang1/Sang1 goeng1
(Scutellariae Radix): 黄芩: Huang2 qin2/Wong4 kam4
(Coptidis Rhizoma): 黄连 / 黃連: Huang2 lian2/Wong4 lin4 my teacher always
referred to this medicinal in its Sichuan version 川连 / 川連: Chuan1 lian2/Cyun1
lin4
(Menthae Haplocalycis Herba): 薄荷: Bo4 he2/Bok ho4

Heat-Clearing and Phlegm-Transforming Formulas

(Clear the Qi and Transform Phlegm Pills)
清气化痰丸 / 清氣化痰丸: Qing1 qi4 hua4 tan2 wan2/Cing1 hei3 faa3 taam4
jyun2
(Trichosanthis Semen): 瓜萎仁 / 瓜蔞仁: Gua1 lou2 ren2/Gwaa1 lau4 jan4
(Citri Reticulatae Pericarpium): 陈皮 / 陳皮: Chen2 pi2/Can4 pei4
(Scutellariae Radix): 黄芩: Huang2 qin2/Wong4 kam4
(Armeniacae Semen): 杏仁: Xing4 ren2/Hang6 jan4
(Aurantii Fructus Immaturus): 枳实 / 枳實: Zhi3 shi2/Zi2 sat6
(Poria): 茯苓: Fu2 ling2/Fuk6 ling4
(Arisaema cum Bile): 胆南星 / 膽南星: Dan3 nan2 xing1/Daam2 naam4 sing1
(Pinelliae Rhizoma Preparatum): 制半夏 / 製半夏: Zhi4 ban4 xia4/Zai3 Bun3
haa6

(Reduce Scrofula Pill)
消瘰丸: Xiao1 luo3 wan2/Siu1 lo2 jyun2
(Scrophularae Radix): 玄参 / 玄參: Xuan2 shen1/Jyun4 sam1
(Ostreae Concha): 牡蛎 / 牡蠣:Mu3 li4/Maau5 lai6
(Fritillariae Thunbergii Bulbus): 浙贝母 / 浙貝母: Zhe4 bei4 mu3/Zit3 bui3 mou5

(Flushing Away Rolling Phlegm Pill)

滚痰丸: Gun3 tan2 wan2/Gwan2 taam4 jyun2

(Calcined Chloriti-Lapis/Micae Lapis Aureus): 煅礞石: Duan4 meng2 shi2/Dyun3 mung4 sek6

(Wine-washed Rhei Radix et Rhizoma): 酒洗大黄: Jiu3 xi3 da4 huang2/Zau2 sai2 daai6 wong4

(Wine-washed Scutellariae Radix): 酒洗黄芩: Jiu3 xi3 huang2 qin2/Zau2 sai2 wong4 kam4

(Aquilariae Lignum Resinatum): 沉香: Chen2 xiang1/Cam4 hoeng1

Dryness-Moistening and Phlegm-Transforming Formulas

(Fritillaria and Trichosanthis Powder)

贝母瓜蒌散 / 貝母瓜蔞散: Bei4 mu3 gua1 lou2 san3/Bui3 mou5 gwaa1 lau4 saan3

(Fritillariae Thunbergii Bulbus): 浙贝母 / 浙貝母: Zhe4 bei4 mu3/Zit3 bui3 mou5

(Trichosanthis Fructus): 瓜蒌 / 瓜蔞: Gua1 lou2/Gwaa1 lau4

(Trichosanthis Radix): 天花粉: Tian1 hua1 fen3/Tin1 faa1 fan2

(Poria): 茯苓: Fu2 ling2/Fuk6 ling4

(Citri Exocarpium Rubrum): 橘红 / 橘紅: Jü2 hong2/Gwat1 hung4

(Platycodi Radix): 桔梗: Jie2 geng3/Gat1 gang2

(Sargassum Decoction for the Jade Flask)

海藻玉壶汤 / 海藻玉壺湯: Hai3 zao3 yü4 hu2 tang1/Hoi2 zou2 juk6 wu4 tong1

(Sargassum): 海藻: Hai3 zao3/Hoi2 zou2

(Eckloniae Thallus): 昆布: Kun1 bu4/Kwan1 bou3

(Laminariae Thallus): 海带 / 海帶: Hai3 dai4/Hoi2 daai3

(Fritillariae Thunbergii Bulbus): 浙贝母 / 浙貝母: Zhe4 bei4 mu3/Zit3 bui3 mou5

(Pinelliae Rhizoma Preparatum): 制半夏 / 製半夏: Zhi4 ban4 xia4/Zai3 bun3 haa6

(Angelicae Pubescentis Radix): 独活 / 獨活: Du2 huo2/Duk6 wut6

(Chuanxiong Rhizoma): 川芎: Chuan1 xiong1/Cyun1 gung1

(Angelicae Sinensis Radix): 当归 / 當歸: Dang1 gui1/Dong1 gwai1

(Citri Reticulatae Viride Pericarpium): 青皮: Qing1 pi2/Cing1 pei4

(Citri Reticulatae Pericarpium): 陈皮 / 陳皮: Chen2 pi2/Can4 pei4

(Forsythiae Fructus): 连翘 / 連翹: Lian2 qiao2/Lin4 kiu4

(Glycyrrhizae Radix): 甘草: Gan1 cao3/Gam1 cou2

(Arrest Seizures Pill)
定痫丸 / 定癇丸: Ding4 xian2 wan2/Ding6 haan4 jyun2
(Gastrodiae Rhizoma): 天麻: Tian1 ma2/Tin1 maa4
(Fritillariae Cirrhosae Bulbus): 川贝母 / 川貝母: Chuan1 bei4 mu3/Cyun1 bui3 mou5
(Pinelliae Rhizoma Preparatum): 制半夏 / 製半夏: Zhi4 ban4 xia4/Zai3 bun3 haa6
(Poria): 茯苓: Fu2 ling2/Fuk6 ling4
(Poriae sclerotium Paradicis): 茯神: Fu2 shen2/Fuk6 san4
(Arisaema cum Bile): 胆南星 / 膽南星: Dan3 nan2 xing1/Daam2 naam4 sing1
(Acori Tatarinowii Rhizoma): 石菖蒲: Shi2 chang1 pu2/Sek6 coeng1 pou4
(Scorpio): 全蝎 / 全蠍: Quan2 xie1/Cyun4 hit3
(Bombyx Batryticatus): 白僵蚕 / 白僵蠶: Bai2 jiang1 can2/Baak6 goeng1 caam4
(Succinum): 琥珀: Hu3 po4/Fu2 paak3
(Junci Medulla): 灯心草 / 燈心草: Deng1 xin1 cao3/Dang1 sam1 cou2
(Citri Reticulatae Pericarpium): 陈皮 / 陳皮: Chen2 pi2/Can4 pei4
(Polygalae Radix): 远志 / 遠志: Yuan3 zhi4/Jyun5 zi3
(Salviae Miltiorrhizae Radix): 丹参 / 丹參: Dan1 shen1/Daan1 sam1
(Ophiopogonis Radix): 麦门冬 / 麥門冬: Mai4 men2 dong1/Mak6 mun4 dung1
(Cinnabaris): 朱砂: Zhu1 sha1/Zyu1 saa1

Warming and Transforming Cold Phlegm Formulas

(Poria, Licorice, Schisandra, Ginger and Asarum Decoction)
苓甘五味姜辛汤 / 苓甘五味薑辛湯: Ling2 gan1 wu3 wei4 jiang1 xin1 tang1/Ling4 gam1 ng5 mei6 goeng1 san1 tong1
(Poria): 茯苓: Fu2 ling2/Fuk6 ling4
(Glycyrrhizae Radix): 甘草: Gan1 cao3/Gam1 cou2
(Zingiberis Rhizoma): 干姜 / 乾薑: Gan1 jiang1/Gon1 goeng1
(Asari Herba): 细辛 / 細辛: Xi4 xin1/Sai3 sam1
(Schisandrae Fructus): 五味子: Wu3 wei4 zi3/Ng5 mei6 zi2

(Three-Seed Decoction to Nourish One's Parents)
三子养亲汤 / 三子養親湯: San1 zi3 yang3 qin1 tang1/Saam1 zi2 joeng5 can1 tong1
(Sinapis Semen): 白芥子: Bai2 jie4 zi3/Baak6 gaai3 zi2
(Perillae Fructus): 紫苏子 / 紫蘇子: Zi3 su1 zi3/Zi2 sou1/zi2
(Raphani Semen): 莱菔子 / 萊菔子: Lai2 fu2 zi3/Loi4 fuk6 zi2

Wind-Treating and Phlegm-Transforming Formulas

(Pinellia, Atractylodes and Gastrodia Decoction)
半夏白术天麻汤 / 半夏白術天麻湯: Ban4 xia4 bai2 zhu2 tian1 ma2 tang1/Bun3 haa6 baak6 seot6 tin1 maa4 tong1
(Pinelliae Rhizoma Preparatum): 制半夏 / 製半夏: Zhi4 ban4 xia4/Zai3 bun3 haa6
(Gastrodiae Rhizoma): 天麻: Tian1 ma2/Tin1 maa4
(Poria): 茯苓: Fu2 ling2/Fuk6 ling4
(Citri Retiuclatae Exocarpium Rubrum): 橘红 / 橘紅: Jü2 hong2/Gwat1 hung4
(Atractylodis Macrocephalae Rhizoma): 白术 / 白術: Bai2 zhu2/Baak6 seot6
(Glycyrrhizae Radix): 甘草: Gan1 cao3/Gam1 cou2
(Zingiberis Rhizoma Recens): 生姜 / 生薑: Sheng1 jiang1/Sang1 goeng1
(Jujubae Fructus): 大枣 / 大棗: Da1 zao3/Daai6 zou2

(Pinellia, Atractylodes and Gastrodia Decoction [Li Dong Yuan's Version])
半夏白术天麻汤 / 半夏白術天麻湯: Ban4 xia4 bai2 zhu2 tian1 ma2 tang1/Bun3 haa6 baak6 seot6 tin1 maa4 tong1
(Pinelliae Rhizoma): 半夏 / 半夏: Ban4 xia4/Bun3 haa6
(Gastrodiae Rhizoma): 天麻: Tian1 ma2/Tin1 maa4
(Poria): 茯苓: Fu2 ling2/Fuk6 ling4
(Citri Retiuclatae Pericarpium): 陈皮 / 陳皮: Chen2 pi2/Can4 pei4
(Atractylodis Macrocephalae Rhizoma): 白术 / 白術: Bai2 zhu2/Baak6 seot6
(Zingiberis Rhizoma): 干姜 / 乾薑: Gan1 jiang1/Gon1 goeng1
(Phellodendri Cortex): 黄柏: Huang2 bai2/Wong4 paak3
(Atractylodis Rhizoma): 苍术 / 蒼術: Cang1 zhu2/Cong1 seot6
(Ginseng Radix): 人参 / 人參: Ren2 shen1/Jan4 sam1
(Astragali Radix): 黄芪 / 黃耆: Huang2 qi2/Wong4 kei4 My teacher always referred to this as 北芪: Bei3 qi2/Bak1 kei4.
(Alismatis Rhizoma): 泽泻 / 澤瀉: Ze2 xie4/Zaak6 se3
(Hordei Fructus Germinatus): 麦芽 / 麥芽: Mai4 ya2/Mak6 ngaa4
(Massa Medicata Fermentata): 神曲 / 神麴: Shen2 qu1/San4 kuk1

(Stop Coughing Powder)
止嗽散: Zhi3 sou4 san3/Zi2 sau3 saan3
(Platycodi Radix): 桔梗: Jie2 geng3/Gat1 gang2
(Schizonepetae Herba): 荆芥 / 荊芥: Jing1 jie4/Ging1 gaai3
(Asteris Radix): 紫菀: Zi3 wan3/Zi2 jyun2
(Stemonae Radix): 百部: Bai3 bu4/Baak3 bou6
(Cynanchi Stauntonii Rhizoma): 白前: Bai2 qian2/Baak6 cin4
(Glycyrrhizae Radix): 甘草: Gan1 cao3/Gam1 cou2
(Citri Reticulatae Pericarpium): 陈皮 / 陳皮: Chen2 pi2/Can4 pei4

Formulas That Induce Vomiting
(Melon Pedicle Powder)
瓜蒂散: Gua1 di4 san3/Gwaa1 dai3 saan3
(Melo Pedicellus): 瓜蒂: Gua1 di4/Gwaa1 dai3
(Phaseoli Semen): 赤小豆: Chi4 xiao3 dou4/Cek3 siu2 dau2

Dispersing Food, Conducting Stagnation Formulas

(Protecting Harmony Pills)
保和丸: Bao3 he2 wan2/Bou2 wo6 jyun2
(Crataegi Fructus): 山楂: Shan1 zha1/Saan1 zaa1
(Massa Medicata Fermentata): 神曲 / 神麴: Shen2 qu1/San4 kuk1
(Pinelliae Rhizoma Praeparata): 制半夏 / 製半夏: Zhi4 ban4 xia4/Zai3 bun3 haa6
(Poria): 茯苓: Fu2 ling2/Fuk6 ling4
(Citri Reticulatae Pericarpium): 陈皮 / 陳皮: Chen2 pi2/Can4 pei4
(Forsythiae Fructus): 连翘 / 連翹: Lian2 qiao2/Lin4 kiu4
(Raphani Semen): 莱菔子 / 萊菔子: Lai2 fu2 zi3/Loi4 fuk6 zi2

(Unripe Bitter Orange and Atractylodes Pill)
枳术丸 / 枳術丸:Zhi3 Zhu2 Wan2/Zi2 seot6 jyun2
(Atractylodis Macrocephalae Rhizoma): 白术 / 白術: Bai2 zhu2/Baak6 seot6
(Dry-Fried Aurantii Fructus Immaturus): 炒枳实 / 炒枳實: Chao3 zhi3 shi2/Caau2 zi2 sat6
form into pills with rice fried in Nelumbinis Folium 荷叶 / 荷葉: He2 ye4/Ho4 jip6

(Unripe Bitter Orange Pill to Guide out Stagnation)

枳实导滞丸 / 枳實導滯丸: Zhi3 shi2 dao3 zhi4 wan2/Zi2 sat6 dou6 zai6 jyun2

(Dry-Fried Aurantii Fructus Immaturus): 炒枳实 / 炒枳實: Chao3 zhi3 shi2/Caau2 zi2 sat6

(Rhei Radix et Rhizoma): 大黄: Da4 huang2/Daai6 wong4

(Dry-Fried Massa Medicata Fementata): 炒神曲 / 炒神麯: Chao3 shen2 qu1/Caau2 san4 kuk1

(Poria): 茯苓: Fu2 ling2/Fuk6 ling4

(Scutellariae Radix): 黄芩: Huang2 qin2/Wong4 kam4

(Coptidis Rhizoma): 黄连 / 黃連: Huang2 lian2/Wong4 lin4 my teacher always referred to this medicinal in its Sichuan form 川连 / 川連: Chuan1 lian2/Cyun1 lin4

(Atractylodis Macrocephalae Rhizoma): 白术 / 白術: Bai2 zhu2/Baak6 seot6

(Alismatis Rhizoma): 泽泻 / 澤瀉: Ze2 xie4/Zaak6 se3

(Fat Baby Pill)

肥儿丸 / 肥兒丸: Fei2 er2 wan2/Fei4 ji4 jyun2

(Dry-Fried Massa Medicata Fementata): 炒神曲 / 炒神麯: Chao3 shen2 qu1/Caau2 san4 kuk1

(Coptidis Rhizoma): 黄连 / 黃連: Huang2 lian2/Wong4 lin4 my teacher always referred to this medicinal in its Sichuan form 川连 / 川連: Chuan1 lian2/Cyun1 lin4

(Roasted Myristicae Semen): 煨肉豆蔻: Wei1 rou4 dou4 kou4/Wui1 juk6 dau6 kau3

(Quisqualis Fructus): 使君子: Shi3 jun1 zi3/Si2 gwan1 zi2

(Dry-Fried Hordei Fructus Geminatus): 炒麦芽 / 炒麥芽: Chao3 mai4 ya2/Caau2 mak6 ngaa4

(Arecae Semen): 槟榔 / 檳榔: Bing1 lang2/Ban1 long4

(Aucklandiae Radix): 木香: Mu4 xiang1/Muk6 hoeng1

(Aucklandia and Betel Nut Pill)
木香槟榔丸 / 木香檳榔丸: Mu4 xiang1 bing1 lang2 wan2/Muk6 hoeng1 ban1 long4 jyun2
(Aucklandiae Radix): 木香: Mu4 xiang1/Muk6 hoeng1
(Arecae Semen): 槟榔 / 檳榔: Bing1 lang2/Ban1 long4
(Rhei Radix et Rhizoma): 大黄: Da4 huang2/Daai6 wong4
(Pharbitidis Semen): 牵牛子 / 牽牛子: Qian1 niu2 zi3/Hin1 ngau4 zi2
(Citri Reticulatae Viride Pericarpium): 青皮: Qing1 pi2/Cing1 pei4
(Citri Reticulatae Pericarpium): 陈皮 / 陳皮: Chen2 pi2/Can4 pei4
(Dry-Fried Cyperi Rhizoma): 炒香附: Chao3 xiang1 fu4/Caau2 hoeng1 fu6
(Dry-Fried Curcumae Rhizoma): 莪术 / 莪術: E2 zhu2/Ngo4 seot6
(Bran-Fried Aurantii Fructus): 麸炒枳壳 / 麩炒枳殼: Fu1 chao3 zhi3 ke2/Fu1 caau2 zi2 hok3
(Coptidis Rhizoma): 黄连 / 黃連: Huang2 lian2/Wong4 lin4 my teacher always referred to this medicinal in its Sichuan form 川连 / 川連: Chuan1 lian2/Cyun1 lin4
(Phellodendri Cortex): 黄柏: Huang2 bai3/Wong4 paak3

Formulas that Reduce Food Stagnation but also Tonify

(Strengthen the Spleen Pill)
健脾丸: Jian4 pi2 wan2/Gin6 pei4 jyun2
(Dry-Fried Atractylodis Macrocephalae Rhizoma): 炒白术 / 炒白術: Chao3 bai2 zhu2/Caau2 baak6 seot6
(Poria): 茯苓: Fu2 ling2/Fuk6 ling4
(Ginseng Radix): 人参 / 人參: Ren2 shen1/Jan4 sam1
(Dioscoreae Rhizoma): 山药 / 山藥: Shan1 yao4/Saan1 joek6
(Roasted Myristicae Semen): 煨肉豆蔻: Wei1 rou4 dou4 dou4/Wui1 juk6 dau6 kau3
(Crataegi Fructus): 山楂: Shan1 zha1/Saan1 zaa1
(Dry-Fried Massa Medicata Fermentata): 炒神曲/炒神麯: Chao3 shen2 qu1/Caau2 san4 guk1
(Dry-Fried Hordei Fructus Germinatus): 炒麦芽 / 炒麥芽: Chao3 mai4 ya2/Caau2 mak6 ngaa4
(Aucklandiae Radix): 木香: Mu4 xiang1/Muk6 hoeng1
(Citri Reticulatae Pericarpium): 陈皮 / 陳皮: Chen2 pi2/Can4 pei4
(Amomi Fructus): 砂仁: Sha1 ren2/Saa1 jan4
(Wine-Fried Coptidis Rhizoma): 酒炒黄连 / 酒炒黃連: Jiu3 chao3 huang2 lian2/Zau2 caau2 wong4 lin4 my teacher always referred to this medicinal in its Sichuan form 川连 / 川連: Chuan1 lian2/Cyun1 lin4
(Glycyrrhizae Radix): 甘草: Gan1 cao2

(Unripe Bitter Orange Pill to Reduce Focal Distention)
枳实消痞丸 / 枳實消痞丸: Zhi3 shi2 xiao1 pi3 wan2/Zi2 sat6 siu1 pei2 jyun2
(Aurantii Fructus Immaturus): 枳实 / 枳實: Zhi3 shi2/Zi2 sat6
(Prepared Magnoliae Officinalis): 制厚朴 / 製厚朴: Zhi4 hou4 po4/Zai3 hau5 pok3
(Coptidis Rhizoma): 黄连 / 黃連: Huang2 lian2/Wong4 lin4 my teacher always referred to this medicinal in its Sichuan form 川连 / 川連: Chuan1 lian2/Cyun1 lin4
(Pinelliae Rhizoma Preparatum): 制半夏 / 製半夏: Zhi4 ban4 xia4/Zai3 bun3 haa6
(Ginseng Radix): 人参 / 人參: Ren2 shen1/Jan4 sam1
(Atractylodis Macrocephalae Rhizoma): 白术 / 白術: Bai2 zhu2/Baak6 seot6
(Poria): 茯苓: Fu2 ling2/Fuk6 ling4
(Hordei Fructus Geminatus): 麦芽 / 麥芽: Mai4 ya2/Mak6 ngaa4
(Zingiberis Rhizoma): 干姜 / 乾薑: Gan1 jiang1/Gon1 goeng1
(Glycyrrhizae Radix Prepaerata): 炙甘草: Zhi4 gan1 cao3/Zek3 gam1 cou2

Killing Worms Formulas

(Mume Pills)
乌梅丸 / 烏梅丸: Wu1 mei2 wan2/Wu1 mui4 jyun2
(Mume Fructus): 乌梅 / 烏梅: Wu1 mei2/Wu1 mui4
(Asari Herba cum Radice): 细辛 / 細辛: Xi4 xin1/Sai3 sam1
(Zingiberis Rhizoma): 干姜 / 乾薑: Gan1 jiang1/Gon1 goeng1
(Coptidis Chinensis Rhizoma): 黄连 / 黃連: Huang2 lian2/Wong4 lin4 My teacher always referred to this medicinal in its Sichuan form: 川连 / 川連: Chuan1 lian2/Cyun1 lin4
(Angelicae Sinensis Radix): 当归 / 當歸: Dang1 gui1/Dong1 gwai1
(Aconiti Radix Lateralis Praeparata): 制附子 / 製附子: Zhi4 fu4 zi3/Zai3 fu6 zi2
(Zanthoxyli pericarpium): 花椒: Hua1 jiao1/Faa1 ziu1
(Cinnamomi Ramulus): 桂枝: Gui4 zhi1/Gwai3 zi1
(Ginseng Radix): 人参 / 人參: Ren2 shen1/Jan4 sam1
(Phellodendri Cortex): 黄柏: Huang2 bai2/Wong4 paak3

(Dissolve Parasites Pill)
化虫丸 / 化蟲丸: Hua4 chong2 wan2/Faa3 cung4 jyun2
(Carpesi Abrotanoidis Fructus): 鹤虱 / 鶴蝨: He4 shi1/Hok6 sat1
(Arecae Semen): 槟榔 / 檳榔: Bing1 lang2/Ban1 long4
(Meliae Cortex): 苦楝根皮: Ku3 lian4 gen1 pi2/Fu2 lin6 gan1 pei4
(Minium): 铅丹 / 鉛丹: Qian1 dan1/Jyun4 daan1
(Alumen): 明矾 / 明礬: Ming2 fan2/Ming4 faan4

Basic Pattern Names (138)
Lung and Large Intestine Patterns
Wind Cold Invading the Lungs
风寒犯肺 / 風寒犯肺: Feng1 han2 fan4 fei4/Fung1 hon4 faan6 fai3
Wind Heat Invading the Lungs
风热犯肺 / 風熱犯肺: Feng1 re4 fan4 fei4/Fung1 jit6 faan6 fai3
Wind Dryness Damaging the Lungs
风燥伤肺 / 風燥傷肺: Feng4 zao4 shang1 fei4/Fung1 cou3 soeng1 fai3
Summerheat Damaging the Lung Luo Vessels
暑伤肺络 / 暑傷肺絡: Shu3 shang1 Fei4 luo4/Syu2 soeng1 fai3 lok3
Phlegm Heat Depressing the Lungs
痰热郁肺 / 痰熱鬱肺: Tan2 re4 yü4 fei4/Taam4 jit6 juk1 fai3
Lung Heat Smoldering and Exuberant
肺热蕴旺 / 肺熱蘊旺: Fei4 re4 yün4 wang4/Fai3 jit6 wan2 wong6
same pattern also called:
Lung Heat Scorching the Lobes
肺热叶焦 / 肺熱傷焦: Fei4 re4 ye4 jiao1/Fai3 jit6 jip6 ziu1
Lung Heat Transmitted to the Large Intestine
肺热传大肠 / 肺熱傳大腸: Fei4 re4 chuan2 da4 chang2/Fai3 jit6 cyun4 daai6 coeng4
Damp Heat Smoldering in the Lungs
湿热蕴肺 / 濕熱蘊肺: Shi1 re4 yün4 fei4/Sap1 jit6 wan3 fai3
Phlegm Turbidity Obstructing the Lungs
痰浊阻肺 / 痰濁阻肺: Tan2 zhuo2 zu3 fei4/Taam4 zuk6 zo2 fai3
Lung Qi Vacuity
肺气虚 / 肺氣虛: Fei4 qi4 xu1/Fai3 hei3 heoi1
Lung and Spleen Qi Vacuity
肺脾气虚 / 肺脾氣虛: Fei4 pi2 qi4 xu1/Fai3 pei4 hei3 heoi1
Cold Rheum Hidden in the Lungs
寒饮伏肺 / 寒飲伏肺: Han2 yin3 fu2 fei4/Hon4 jam2 fuk6 fai3
Lung Qi Vacuity with Simultaneous Heat
肺气虚兼热 / 肺氣虛兼熱: Fei4 qi4 xu1 jian1 re4/Fai3 hei3 heoi1 gim1 jit6
Lung Dryness With Simultaneous Phlegm
肺燥兼痰 / 肺燥兼痰: Fei4 zao3 jian1 tan2/Fai3 cou3 gim1 taam4
Lung Dryness with Large Intestine Binding
肺燥大肠结 / 肺燥大腸結: Fei4 zao4 da4 chang2 jie2/Fai3 cou3 daai6 coeng4 git3
Lung Yin Vacuity
肺阴虚 / 肺陰虛: Fei4 yin1 xu1/Fai3 jam1 heoi1
this pattern also called
Lung Yin Taxation and Decline

肺阴衰劳 / 肺陰衰勞: Fei4 yin1 shuai1 lao2/Fai3 jam1 seoi1 lou4

Lung Qi and Yin Vacuity

肺气阴虚 / 肺氣陰虛: Fei4 qi4 yin1 xu1/Fai3 hei3 jam1 heoi1

Lung Qi and Yin Vacuity with Simultaneous Phlegm Heat

肺气阴虚兼痰热 / 肺氣陰虛兼痰熱

Fei4 qi4 yin1 xu1 jian1 tan2 re4/Fai3 hei3 jam1 heoi1 gim1 taam4 jit6

Lung and Kidney Yin Vacuity

肺肾阴虚 / 肺腎陰虛: Fei4 shen4 yin1 xu1/Fai3 san6 jam1 heoi1

Lung and Kidney Yang Vacuity

肺肾阳虚 / 肺腎陽虛: Fei4 shen4 yang2 xu1/Fai3 san6 joeng4 heoi1

Lung Luo Vessel Stasis and Obstruction

肺络瘀阻 / 肺絡瘀阻: Fei4 luo4 yü1 zu3/Fai3 lok3 jyu1 zo2

Intestinal Vacuity Not Securing

肠虚不固 / 腸虛不固: Chang2 xu1 bu4 gu4/Coeng4 heoi1 bat1 gu3

Large Intestine Repletion Heat

大肠实热 / 大腸實熱: Da4 chang2 shi2 re4/Daai6 coeng4 sat6 jit6

also called

Large Intestine Heat Bind

大肠热结 / 大腸熱結: Da4 chang2 re4 jie2/Daai6 coeng4 jit6 git3

Large Intestine Vacuity Cold

大肠虚寒 / 大腸虛寒: Da4 chang2 xu1 han2/Daai6 coeng4 heoi1 hon1

Large Intestine Damp Heat

大肠湿热 / 大腸濕熱: Da4 chang2 shi2 re4/Daai6 coeng4 sap6 jit6

Large Intestine Conduction and Conveyance Lose Their Duty, Dampness and Tubidity Cloud Above

大肠传导失司，湿浊上蒙 / 大腸傳導失司，濕濁上蒙

Da4 chang2 chuan2 dao3 shi1 si1/Shi1 zhuo2 shang4 meng2

Daai5 coeng4 cyun4 dou6 sat1 si1/Sap1 zuk6 soeng5 mung4

Dampness Obstructing the Intestinal Tract, Conduction and Conveyance Lose their Command

湿阻肠道，传导失司 / 濕阻腸道，傳導失司

Shi1 zu2 chang2 dao4, chuan2 dao3 shi1 si1/Sap1 zo2 coeng4 dou6, cyun4 dou6 sat1 si1

Large Intestine Humor Depletion

大肠液亏 / 大腸液虧: Da4 chang2 ye4 kui1/Daai6 coeng4 jik6 kwai1

Large Intestine Qi Stagnation

大肠气滞 / 大腸氣滯: Da4 chang2 qi4 zhi4/Daai6 coeng4 hei3 zai6

Large Intestine Stasis Heat

大肠瘀热 / 大腸瘀熱: Da4 chang2 yü1 re4/Daai6 coeng4 jyu1 jit6

Kidney and Bladder Patterns

Kidney Qi Vacuity

肾气虚 / 腎氣虛: Shen4 qi4 xu1/San6 hei3 heoi1

Kidney Qi Not Securing

肾气不固 / 腎氣不固: Shen4 qi4 bu4 gu4/San6 hei3 bat1 gu3

Kidneys Not Astringing the Intestines

肾不涩肠 / 腎不澀腸: Shen4 bu4 se4 chang2/San6 bat1 saap3 coeng4

Kidneys Not Grasping the Qi

肾不纳气 / 腎不納氣: Shen4 bu4 na4 qi4/San6 bat1 naap6 hei3

Kidney Yang Vacuity and Debility

肾阳虚衰 / 腎陽虛衰: Shen4 yang2 xu1 shuai1/San6 joeng4 heoi1 seoi1

this pattern is also called

肾阳虚 / 腎陽虛: Shen4 yang2 xu1/San6 joeng4 heoi1

or is also called Kidney Yang in decline

肾阳衰微 / 腎陽衰微: Shen4 yang2 shuai1 wei1/San6 joeng4 seoi1 mei4

Kidney Vacuity Water Spilling Over

肾虚水泛 / 腎虛水泛: Shen4 xu1 shui3 fan4/San6 heoi1 seoi2 faan3

Kidney Water Harassing the Heart

肾水扰心 / 腎水擾心: Shen4 shui3 rao3 xin1/San6 seoi2 jiu5 sam1

Kidney Yin Vacuity

肾阴虚 / 腎陰虛: Shen4 yin1 xu1/San6 jam1 heoi1

this pattern is also called Kidney yin insufficiency

肾阴不足 / 腎陰不足: Shen4 yin1 bu4 zu2/San6 jam1 bat1 zuk1

this pattern is also called Kidney yin dessication

肾阴枯涸: Shen4 yin1 ku1 he2/San6 jam1 fu1 kok3

this pattern is also called kidney yin depletion

肾阴亏虚 / 腎陰虧虛: Shen4 yin1 kui1 xu1/San6 jam4 kwai1 heoi1

Kidney Yin Vacuity Effulgent Fire

肾虚火旺 / 腎虛火旺: Shen4 xu1 huo3 wang4/San6 heoi1 fo2 wong6

Kidney Essence Insufficiency

肾精不足 / 腎精不足: Shen4 jing1 bu4 zu2/San6 zing1 bat1 zuk1

True Yin Verging on Expiry

真阴欲绝 / 真陰慾絕: Zhen1 yin1 yü4 jue2/Zan1 jam1 juk6 zyut6

Heat Wearing the True Yin

热耗真阴 / 熱耗真陰: Re4 hao4 zhen1 yin1/Jit6 hou3 zan1 jam1

Cold Dampness Damaging the Kidneys

寒湿伤肾 / 寒濕傷腎: Han2 shi1 shang1 shen4/Hon4 sap6 soeng1 san6

Kidney Qi Wandering Wind

肾气游风 / 腎氣游風: Shen4 qi4 you2 feng1/San6 hei3 jau4 fung1

Urinary Bladder Damp Heat

膀胱湿热 / 膀胱濕熱: Pang2 guang1 shi1 re4/Pong4 gwong1 sap1 jit6

Liver and Gallbladder Patterns

Liver Depression Qi Stagnation

肝郁气滞 / 肝鬱氣滯: Gan1 yü4 qi4 zhi4/Gon1 juk1 hei3 zai6

this pattern is also called Liver qi depression and binding

肝气郁结 / 肝氣鬱結: Gan1 qi4 yü4 jie2/Gon1 hei3 juk1 git3

Liver Qi Counterflowing Upward

肝气上逆 / 肝氣上逆: Gan1 qi4 shang4 ni4/Gon1 hei3 soeng5 jik6

Liver Qi Invading the Stomach

肝气犯胃 / 肝氣犯胃: Gan1 qi4 fan4 wei4/Gon1 hei3 faan6 wai6

Liver/Spleen Disharmony

肝脾不和: Gan1 pi2 bu4 he2/Gon1 pei4 bat1 wo6

this pattern is also called Liver qi exploiting the spleen

肝气乘脾 / 肝氣乘脾: Gan1 qi4 cheng2 pi2/Gon1 hei3 sing4 pei4

and also called liver qi invading the spleen

肝气犯脾 / 肝氣犯脾: Gan1 qi4 fan4 pi2/Gon1 hei3 faan6 pei4

Liver Depression Transforms into Heat

肝郁化热 / 肝鬱化熱: Gan1 yü4 hua4 re4/Gon1 juk1 faa3 jit6

also called

Liver Depression transforms into Fire

肝郁化火 / 肝鬱化火: Gan1 yü4 hua4 huo3/Gon1 juk1 faa3 fo2

Liver/Stomach Depressive Heat and Upward Counterflow

肝胃郁热上逆 / 肝胃鬱上逆: Gan1 wei4 yü4 re4 shang4 ni4/Gon1 wai6 juk1 soeng5 jik6

Liver Wind Stirring Internally

肝风内动 / 肝風內動: Gan1 feng1 nei4 dong4/Gon1 fung1 noi6 dung6

Liver Blood Insufficiency

肝血不足: Gan1 xue4 bu4 zu2/Gon1 hyut3 bat1 zuk1

Liver Blood Insufficiency Engendering Wind

肝血不足生风 / 肝血不足生風: Gan1 xue4 bu4 zu2 sheng1 feng1/Gon1 hyut3 bat1 zuk1 sang1 fung1

Liver Channel Replete Fire

肝经实火 / 肝經實火: Gan1 jing1 shi2 huo3/Gon1 ging1 sat6 fo2

Liver Fire Attacking the Lungs

肝火犯肺: Gan1 huo3 fan4 fei4/Gon1 fo2 faan6 fai3

Liver Fire Attacking the Stomach

肝火犯胃: Gan1 huo3 fan4 wei4/Gon1 fo2 faan6 wai6

Liver Yang Vacuity

肝阳虚 / 肝陽虛: Gan1 yang2 xu1/Gon1 joeng4 heoi1

Ascendant Hyperactivity of Liver Yang

肝阳上亢 / 肝陽上亢: Gan1 yang2 shang4 kang4/Gon1 joeng4 soeng5 kong3

Liver Blood and Kidney Yin Vacuity

肝血肾阴虚 / 肝血腎陰虛: Gan1 xue4 shen4 yin1 xu1/Gon1 hyut3 san6 jam1 heoi1

Liver Blood and Kidney Yang Vacuity

肝血肾阳虚 / 肝血腎陽虛: Gan1 xue4 shen4 yang2 xu1/Gon1 hyut3 san6 joeng4 heoi1

Cold Stagnating in the Liver Vessels

寒滞肝脉 / 寒滯肝脈: Han2 zhi4 gan1 mai4/Hon4 zai6 gon1 mak6

Liver/Gallbladder Damp Heat

肝胆湿热 / 肝膽濕熱: Gan1 dan3 shi1 re4/Gon1 daam2 sap1 jit6

Gallbladder Qi Vacuity and Timidity

胆气虚怯 / 膽氣虛怯: Dan3 qi4 xu1 qie4/Daam2 hei3 heoi1 hip3

Ascendant Hyperactivity of Gallbladder Fire

胆火上抗 / 膽火上抗: Dan3 huo3 shang4 kang4/Daam2 fo2 soeng5 kong3

Heart and Small Intestine Patterns

Heart Qi Vacuity

心气虚 / 心氣虛: Xin1 qi4 xu1/Sam1 hei3 heoi1

Insufficiency of Heart Blood

心血不足: Xin1 xue4 bu4 zu2/Sam1 hyut3 bat1 zuk1

Heart and Liver Blood Vacuity

心肝血虚 / 心肝血虛: Xin1 gan1 xue4 xu1/Sam1 gon1 hyut3 heoi1

Heart Yin and Blood Vacuity Sleeplessness

心阴血虚不得卧 / 心陰血虛不得臥

Xin1 yin1 xue4 xu1 bu4 de2 wo4/Sam1 jam1 hyut3 heoi1 bat1 dak1 ngo6

Heart and Spleen Dual Vacuity

心脾两虚 / 心脾兩虛: Xin1 pi2 liang3 xu1/Sam1 pei4 loeng5 heoi1

Heart and Gallbladder Qi Vacuity

心胆气虚 / 心膽氣虛: Xin1 dan3 qi4 xu1/Sam1 daam2 hei3 heoi1

Heart Yang Vacuity

心阳虚 / 心陽虛: Xin1 yang2 xu1/Sam1 joeng4 heoi1

Heart Blood Stasis and Obstruction

心血瘀阻: Xin1 xue4 yü1 zu3/Sam1 hyut3 jyu1 zo2

Phlegm Confounding the Orifices of the Heart

痰迷心窍 / 痰迷心竅: Tan2 mi2 xin1 qiao4/Taam4 mai4 sam1 hiu3

Phlegm Fire Harassing the Heart

痰热扰心 / 痰熱擾心: Tan2 re4 rao3 xin1/Taam4 jit6 jiu5 sam1

this pattern is also called phlegm fire blocking the heart

痰火闭心 / 痰火閉心: Tan2 huo3 bi4 xin1/Taam4 fo2 bai3 sam1

Heart Yang Effulgence, Yin and Blood Vacuity

心阳旺，阴血虚 / 心陽旺，陰血虛

Xin1 yang2 wang4, yin1xue4 xu1/Sam1 joeng4 wong6, jam1 hyut3 heoi1

Heart Fire Flaming Upward
心火上炎: Xin1 huo3 shang4 yan2/Sam1 fo2 soeng5 jim4

Depressive Heat in the Heart Channel
心经郁热 / 心經鬱熱: Xin1 jing1yü4 re4/Sam1 ging1 juk1 jit6

Heart Yin Vacuity
心阴虚 / 心陰虛: Xin1 yin1 xu1/Sam1 jam1 heoi1

Heart and Kidneys Not Interacting
心肾不交 / 心腎不交: Xin1 shen4 bu4 jiao1: Sam1 san6 bat1 gaau1

Small Intestine Qi Pain
小肠气痛 / 小腸氣痛: Xiao3 chang2 qi4 tong1/Siu2 coeng4 hei3 tong3

Small Intestine Replete Fire
小肠实热 / 小腸實熱: Xiao3 chang2 shi2 re4/Siu2 coeng4 sat6 jit6

Small Intestine Vacuity Cold
小肠虚寒 / 小腸虛寒: Xiao3 chang2 xu1 han2/Siu2 coeng4 heoi1 hon4

Spleen and Stomach Patterns

Food Stagnation in the Stomach Duct
食滞胃脘 / 食滯胃脘: Shi2 zhi4 wei4 wan3/Sik6 zai6 wai6 gun2

Spleen Qi Vacuity
脾气虚 / 脾氣虛: Pi2 qi4 xu1/Pei4 hei3 heoi1

Spleen Vacuity with Profuse Drooling
脾虚多涎 / 脾虛多涎: Pi2 xu1 duo1 xian2/Pei4 hoei1 do1 jin4

Spleen Qi Downward Falling
脾气下陷 / 脾氣下陷: Pi2 qi4 xia4 xian4/Pei4 hei3 haa6 haam6

Spleen Not Containing the Blood
脾不摄血 / 脾不攝血: Pi2 bu4 she4 xue4/Pei4 bat1 sip3 hyut3

Spleen Vacuity Heart Palpitations
脾虚心悸: Pi2 xu1 xin1 ji4/Pei4 heoi1 sam1 gwai3

Spleen Vacuity Qi Stagnation
脾虚气滞 / 脾虛氣滯: Pi2 xu1 qi4 zhi4/Pei4 heoi1 hei3 zai6

Spleen/Stomach Dysharmony
脾胃不和: Pi2 wei4 bu4 he2/Pei4 wai6 bat1 wo6

Spleen Vacuity with Stomach Heat
脾虚胃热 / 脾虛胃熱: Pi2 xu1 wei4 re4/Pei4 heoi1 wai6 jit6

Spleen Vacuity Reaching the Lungs
脾虚及肺 / 脾虛及肺: Pi2 xu1 ji2 fei4/Pei4 heoi1 kap6 fai3

Spleen and Stomach Vacuity Cold
脾胃虚寒 / 脾胃虛寒: Pi2 wei4 xu1 han2/Pei4 wai6 heoi1 hon4

Spleen and Kidney Yang Vacuity
脾肾阳虚 / 脾腎陽虛: Pi2 shen4 yang2 xu1/Pei4 san6 joeng4 heoi1

Spleen Vacuity Damp Encumbrance

脾虚湿困 / 脾虛濕困: Pi2 xu1 shi1 kun4/Pei4 heoi1 sap1 kwan3
Spleen Dampness Assailing the Lungs
脾湿犯肺 / 脾濕犯肺: Pi2 shi1 fan4 fei4/Pei4 sap1 faan6 fai3
Spleen/Stomach Damp Heat
脾胃湿热 / 脾胃濕熱: Pi2 wei4 shi1 re4/Pei4 wai6 sap1 jit6
Spleen Heat Copious Drool
脾热多涎 / 脾熱多涎: Pi2 re4 duo1 xian2/Pei4 jit6 do1 jin4
Stomach Qi Counterflowing Upward
胃气上逆 / 胃氣上逆: Wei4 qi4 shang4 ni4/Wai6 hei3 soeng5 jik6
Stomach Fire Bearing Upward
胃火升上: Wei4 huo3 sheng1 shang4/Wai6 fo2 sing1 soeng5
also called:
Stomach Fire Floating Upward
胃火上浮: Wei4 huo3 shang4 fu2/Wai6 fo2 soeng5 fau4
Stomach Heat and Yin Vacuity
胃热阴虚 / 胃熱陰虛: Wei4 re4 yin1 xu1/Wai6 jit6 jam1 heoi1
Stomach Yin Vacuity with Simultaneous Damp Heat
胃阴虚兼湿热 / 胃陰虛兼濕熱: Wei4 yin1 xu1 jian1 shi1 re4/Wai6 jam1 heoi1
gim1 sap1 jit6
Stomach Yin Vacuity
胃阴虚 / 胃陰虛: Wei4 yin1 xu1/Wai6 jam1 heoi1
Stomach Blood Stasis
胃血瘀: Wei4 xue4 yü1/Wai6 hyut3 jyu1

Yin/Yang Patterns
Yang Desertion
阳脱 / 陽脫: Yang2 tuo2/Joeng4 tyut3
Yin Desertion
阴脱 / 陰脫: Yin1 tuo2/Jam1 tyut3

Qi and Blood Patterns
Qi Desertion
气脱 / 氣脫: Qi4 tuo2/Hei3 tyut3
Downward Sinking of the Great Qi
大气下陷 / 大氣下陷: Da4 qi4 xia4 xian4/Daai6 hei3 haa6 haam6
Downward Sinking of the Great Qi with Yang Vacuity of the Heart and Lungs
大气下陷，心肺阳虚 / 大氣下陷，心肺陽虛
Da4 qi4 xia1 xian4, xin1 fei4 yang2 xu1/Daai6 hei3 haa6 haam6, sam1 fai3
joeng4 heoi1
Downward Sinking of the Great Qi with Qi Stagnation and Blood Stasis
大气下陷，气滞血瘀 / 大氣下陷，氣滯血瘀
Da4 qi4 xia4 xian4, qi4 zhi4 xue4 yü1/Daai6 hei3 haa6 haam6, hei3 zai6 hyut3
jyu1

Blood Vacuity
血虚 / 血虛: Xue4 xu1/Hyut3 heoi1
Blood Desertion
血脱: Xue4 tuo2/Hyut3 tyut3
Blood Stasis
血瘀: Xue4 yü1/Hyut3 jyu1
Obstruction of the Channels and Luo Vessels
经络阻滞 / 經絡阻滯: Jing1 luo4 zu3 zhi4/Ging1 lok3 zo2 zai6
Blood Stasis in the Chest
胸中血瘀: Xiong1 zhong1 xue4 yü1/Hung1 zung1 hyut3 jyu1
Stasis Binding in the Upper Abdomen
胃脘瘀结 / 胃脘瘀結: Wei4 wan3 yü1 jie1/Wai6 gun2 jyu1 git3
Stasis Binding in the Lower Abdomen
下腹瘀结 / 下腹瘀結: Xia4 fu4 yü1 jie1/Haa6 fuk1 jyu1 git3
Blood Heat
血热 / 血熱: Xue4 re4/Hyut3 jit6
Blood Heat with Blood Stasis
血热血瘀 / 血熱血瘀: Xue4 re4 xue4 yü1/Hyut3 jit6 hyut3 jyu1

Rheum and Phlegm Patterns
Spillage Rheum
溢饮 / 溢飲: Yi4 yin3/Jat6 jam2
Propping Rheum
支饮 / 支飲: Zhi1 yin3/Zi1 jam2
Suspended Rheum
悬饮 / 懸飲: Xuan2 yin3/Jyun4 jam2
Phlegm Rheum
痰饮 / 痰飲: Tan2 yin3/Taam4 jam2
Phlegm Dampness
痰湿 / 痰濕: Tan2 shi1/Taam4 sap1
Phlegm Lodged in the Chest and Rib-Side Regions
痰留胸胁 / 痰留胸脇: Tan2 liu2 xiong1 xie2/Taam4 lau4 hung1 hip3
Phlegm and Qi Obstructing Each Other
痰气交阻 / 痰氣交阻: Tan2 qi4 jiao1 zu3/Taam4 hei3 gaau1 zo2
Phlegm Pit Scrofula
痰核瘰疬/痰核瘰癧: Tan2 he2 luo3 li4/Taam4 wat6 lo2 lek6
Phlegm Nodulation with Qi and Blood Dual Vacuity
痰核兼气血两虚/痰核兼氣血兩虛
Tan2 he2 jian1 qi4 xue4 liang3 xu1/Taam4 wat6 gim1 hei3 hyut3 loeng5 heoi1
Phlegm Nodulation with Yin Vacuity and Internal Heat
痰核兼阴虚内热 / 痰核兼陰虛內熱
Tan2 he2 jian1 yin1 xu1 nei4 re4/Taam4 wat6 gim1 jam1 heoi1 noi6 jit6

Phlegm and Stasis Mutually Obstructing

痰瘀交阻: Tan2 yü1 jiao1 zu3/Taam4 jyu1 gaau1 zo2

Phlegm Turbidity Obstructing the Middle

痰浊阻中 / 痰濁阻中: Tan2 zhuo2 zu3 zhong1/Taam4 zuk6 zo2 zung1

Channel and Network Vessel Patterns

Wind Striking the Channels and Luo Vessels

风中经络 / 風中經絡: Feng1zhong1 jing1 luo4/Fung1 zung1 ging1 lok3

Dampness Striking the Channels and Luo Vessels

湿中经络 / 濕中經絡: Shi1 zhong1 jing1 luo4/Sap1 zung1 ging1 lok3

Cold Striking the Channels and Luo Vessels

寒中经络 / 寒中經絡: Han2 zhong1 jing1 luo4/Hon4 zung1 ging1 lok3

Wind Damp Impediment

风湿痹 / 風濕痺: Feng1 shi1 bi4/Fung1 sap1 bei3

Damp Heat in the Channels and Luo Vessels

经络湿热 / 經絡濕熱: Jing1 luo4 shi1 re4/Ging1 lok3 sap1 jit6

A

Acanthopanacis Cortex 26

Achyranthis Bidentatae Radix...30

Aconiti Radix Lateralis Preparata...28

 Aconiti Radix Preparata..28

Aconiti Kusnezoffi Radix Preparata...28

Acori Tatarinowii Rhizoma 31

Agkistrodon 26

Agrimoniae Herba 29

Ailanthi Cortex...33

Akebiae Caulis 27

Albiziae Cortex...31

Albiziae Flos 34

Allii Fistulosi Bulbus 21

Allii Macrostemonis Bulbus 28

Allii Sativi Bulbus..29

Alismatis Rhizoma 27

Aloe...25

Alpiniae Katsumadai Semen...27

Alpiniae Officinarum Rhizoma...28

Alpiniae Oxyphyllae Fructus 32,33

Alumen...34

Amomi Fructus...27

Amomi Fructus Rotundus 27

Ampelopsis Radix 24

Anemarrhenae Rhizoma...22

Angelicae Dahuricae Radix...21

Angelicae Pubescentis Radix 26

Angelicae Sinensis Radix...32

Aquilariae Lignum Resinatum 28

Arcae Concha 30

Arctii Fructus 21

Arecae Pericarpium 28

Arecae Semen 29

Arisaematis Rhizoma 24

Armeniacae Semen 25

Arnebiae/Lithospermi Radix..23

Artemisiae Annuae Herba..24

Artemisiae Anomalae Herba...30

Artemisiae Argyii Folium 29

Asari Radix et Rhizoma 21

Asini Corii Colla...32

Asparagi Radix...33

Artemisiae Scopariae Herba..27

Asteris Radix..25

Astragali Complanati Semen 32

Astragali Radix...31

Atractylodis Macrocephalae Rhizoma...31

Atractylodis Rhizoma 27

Aucklandiae Radix 28

Aurantii Fructus...28

Aurantii Fructus Immaturus...28

B

Bambusae Caulis in Taeniam..25

Bambusae Succus...25

Belamcandae Rhizoma..24

Benincasae Exocarpium 30

Benincasae Semen..27

Benzoinum..31

Bletillae Striatae Rhizoma..29

Bombyx Batryticatus...31

Bombycis Faeces 26

Borneolum...31

Bovis Calculus 31

Bruceae Fructus..23

Bubali Cornu 23

Buddlejae Flos 22

Bufonis Venenum...34

Bungarus Parvus 27

Bupleuri Radix...21

C

Calimina...34

Callorhini Testes et Penis 32

Camphora 34

Cannabis Semen 25

Carthami Flos..30

Caryophylli Flos 28

Cassiae Semen...22

Catechu...34

Celosiae Semen...22
Cervi Cornu Pantotrichum...32
Chaenomelis Fructus...26
Changii Radix...25
Chebulae Fructus..33
Chuanxiong Rhizoma..30
Chrysanthemi Flos..21
Chrysanthemi Incici Flos..23
Cibotii Rhizoma..32
Cicadae Periostracum...21
Cimicifugae Rhizoma...21
Cinnabaris..31
Cinnamomi Cortex...28
Cinnamomi Ramulus..21
Cirsii Herba..29
Cirsii Japonici Herba seu Radix..29
Cistanches Herba..32
Citri Reticulatae Exocarpium Rubrum...28
Citri Reticulatae Pericarpium..28
Citri Reticulatae Pericarpium Viride..28
Citri Reticulatae Semen...28
Citri Sarcodactylis Fructus..28
Citrulli Fructus..22
Clematidis Radix..26
Clerodendri Folium...26
Cnidii Fructus...34
Coicis Semen...27
Codonopsis Radix..31
Coptidis Rhizoma...22
Cordyceps..32
Corneum Gigeriae Galli Endothelium..29
Corni Fructus..33
Corydalis Rhizoma...30
Crataegi Fructus...29
Crinis Carbonisatus..29
Crotonis Fructus...26
Curculiginis Rhizoma...32
Cucurbitae Moschatae Semen..29
Curcumae Radix..30
Curcumae Longae Rhizoma..30
Curcumae Rhizoma...30
Cuscutae Semen...32
Cyathulae Radix...30
Cynanchi Atrati Radix..24

160

Cynanchi Stauntonii Rhizoma 24

Cynomorii Herba 32

Cyperi Rhizoma 28

Cyrtomii Rhizoma 24

D

Daemonoropis Resina 30

Dalbergiae Odoriferae Lignum 30

Dendrobii Herba 33

Dianthi Herba 27

Dichroae Radix 29

Dictamni Cortex 23

Dioscoreae Hypoglaucae Rhizoma 27

Dioscoreae Nipponicae Rhizoma 26

Dioscoreae Rhizoma 32

Dipsaci Radix 32

Drynariae Rhizoma 32

E

Eckloniae Thallus 25

Ecliptae Herba 33

Ephedrae Herba 21

Ephedrae Radix 34

Epimedii Herba 32

Equiseti Hiemalis Herba 21

Eriobotryae Folium 25

Erythrinae Cortex 26

Eucommiae Cortex 32

Eupatorii Herba 27

Eupolyphaga/Steleophaga 30

Euryales Semen 33

Evodiae Fructus 28

F

Farfarae Flos...25
Foeniculi Fructus...28
Forsythiae Fructus 23
Fraxini Cortex..22
Fritillariae Cirrhosae Bulbus..25
Fritillariae Thunbergii Bulbus 25

G

Galla Chinensis...33
Ganoderma Lucidum 31
Gardeniae Fructus 22
Gastrodiae Rhizoma 31
Gecko..32
Genkwa Flos 26
Gentianae Macrophyllae Radix......................................26
Gentianae Radix 22
Ginkgo Semen 33
Ginseng Radix 35
Glehniae/Adenophorae Radix 33
Glycyrrhizae Radix..32
Glauberitum 22
Gleditsiae Fructus 24
Gleditsiae Spina..24
Granati Pericarpium 33
Gypsum Fibrosum..22

H

Haematitum..31
Haliotidis Concha 31
Halloysitum Rubrum...33
Hedyotis Diffusae Herba 23
Hippocampus...32
Homalomenae Rhizoma 26

Hominis Placenta 32
Hordei Fructus Germinatus 29
Houttuyniae Herba 23

I

Illicis Pubescentis Radix 30
Imperatae Rhizoma 29
Indigo Naturalis 23
Inulae Flos 24
Isatidis Folium 23
Isatidis Radix 23

J

Juglandis Regiae Semen 32
Junci Medulla 27
Jujubae Fructus 32

K

Kaki Calyx 28
Kansui Radix 26
Knoxiae/Euphorbiae Radix 26
Kochiae Fructus 27

L

Lablab Semen Album 24
Lasiosphaera/Calvatia 23
Leonuri Herba 30
Lepidii/Descurainiae Semen 25
Ligustici Rhizoma 21
Ligustri Lucidi Fructus 33
Lilii Bulbus 33
Linderae Radix 28
Liquidambaris Fructus 30
Litchi Semen 28
Longan Arillus 32
Lobeliae Chinensis Herba 28
Lophatheri Herba 22

Lonicerae Caulis 23
Lonicerae Flos 23
Lycii Cortex 24
Lycii Fructus..32
Lycopi Herba 30
Lygodii Spora 27
Lysimachiae Herba 27

M

Magnetitum 31
Magnoliae Flos...21
Magnoliae Officinalis Cortex 27
Maltosum 32
Malvae Semen 27
Manitis Pentadactylis Squama..30
Mantidis Ootheca...34
Margaritiferae Concha Usta 31
Massa Medica Fermentata 29
Mastodi Dentis Fossilia 30
Mastodi Ossis Fossilia 30
Maydis Stigma 28
Meliae Cortex...29
Menthae Herba 21
Mori Cortex 25
Mori Folium 21
Mori Fructus...32
Mori Ramulus...26
Morindae Officinalis Radix 32
Momordicae Fructus 25
Moslae Herba...21
Moschus 31
Moutan Cortex 23
Mume Fructus 33
Mylabris 34
Myristicae Semen 33
Myrrha...30

N

Natrii Sulfas...25
Nelumbinis Folium 24
Nelumbinis Plumula 22

Nelumbinis Rhizoma 25

Nelumbinis Rhizomatis Nodus 29

Nelumbinis Receptaculum 29

Nelumbinis Semen 33

Nelumbinis Stamen 33

Notoginseng Radix 29

Notopterygii Rhizoma seu Radix 21

O

Olibanum 30

Ophiopogonis Radix 33

Oryzae Glutinosae Radix 34

Ostreae Concha 30

P

Paeoniae Radix Alba 32

Paeoniae Radix Rubra 23,30

Panacis Quinquefolii Radix 33

Papaveris Pericarpium 33

Patriniae Herba 23

Perillae Folium 21

Perillae Fructus 25

Persicae Semen 30

Peucedani Radix 25

Pharbitidis Semen 26

Phaseoli Semen 27

Phaseoli Radiati Semen 24

Phellodendri Cortex 22

Phragmitis Rhizoma 22

Pheretima 31

Phytolaccae Radix 26

Picrorhizae Rhizoma 24

Pini Nodi Lignum 27

Piperis Fructus 28

Piperis Kadsurae Caulis 26

Piperis Longi Fructus 28

Pinelliae Rhizoma Preparatum 24

Plantaginis Semen 27

Platycladi Cacumen 29

Platycladi Semen 31

Platycodi Radix 24
Picrorhizae Radix.. 24
Pogostemonis Herba 27
Polygalae Radix 31
Polygoni Avicularis Herba...27
Polygoni Cuspidati Rhizoma 30
Polygoni Multiflori Caulis..31
Polygoni Multiflori Radix...32
Polygonati Odorati Rhizoma 33
Polygonati Rhizoma 32
Polyporus 27
Poria..27
Portulacae Herba 23
Prunellae Spica...22
Pruni Semen 26

Pseudostellariae Radix 31
Psoraleae Fructus...32
Puerariae Radix 21
Pulsatillae Radix 23
Pyritum..30

Q

Quisqualis Fructus 29

R

Radicis Lycii Chinensis Cortex.....................................23,24
Raphani Semen 29
Rehmanniae Radix 23
Rehmanniae Radix Preparata...32
Rhapontici Radix..24
Rhei Radix et Rhizoma 25
Rhinocerotis Cornu 23
Rosae Chinensis Flos 30
Rosae Laevigatae Fructus 33
Rubi Fructus..33
Rubiae Radix 29

S

Saigae Tataricae Cornu 31

Salviae Miltiorrhizae Radix...30

Sanguisorbae Radix..29

Santali Albi Lignum 28

Saposhnikoviae Radix 21

Sappan Lignum..30

Sargassii Herba 25

Sargentodoxae Caulis..23

Schisandrae Fructus 33

Schizonepetae Herba 21

Scolopendra...31

Scorpio...31

Scrophulariae Radix..23

Scutellariae Radix 22

Scutellariae Barbatae Herba...26

Setariae Fructus Germinatus 29

Sennae Folium...25

Sepiae Endoconcha 33

Sesami Semen Nigrum 33

Smilacis Glabrae Rhizoma..23

Siegesbeckiae Herba 26

Sinalpis Albae Semen 24

Sojae Semen Praeparatum...21

Sojae Semen Germinatum..21

Sophorae Flavescentis Radix 22

Sophorae Flos..29

Sophorae Fructus 29

Sophorae Tonkinensis Radix 23

Sparganii Rhizoma..30

Spatholobi Caulis 30

Spirodelae Herba 21

Stellariae Radix..23, 24

Stemonae Radix...25

Stephaniae Tetrandrae Radix 26

Sterculiae Lychnophorae Semen 25

Strychni Semen..28

Styrax..31

Sulfur...34

T

Talcum 27
Taraxaci Herba 23
Taxilli Herba 26
Terra Flava Usta 29
Testudinis Plastrum 33
Tetrapanacis Medulla...27
Tinosporae Sinensis Caulis 26
Toosendan Fructus 28
Trachelospermi Caulis 26
Trachycarpi Petiolus 29
Tribuli Fructus 31
Trichosanthis Fructus..25
Trichosanthis Pericarpium 25
Trichosanthis Radix 22
Trichosanthis Semen 25
Trigonellae Semen..32
Tritici Fructus Levis 33
Trogopteri Faeces 30
Tryonycis Carapax 33
Tsaoko Fructus 27
Typhae Pollen..29
Typhonii Rhizoma Preparatum 24

U

Uncariae Ramulus cum Uncis...31

V

Vaccariae Semen...30
Verbenae Herba...30
Veratri Nigri Radix et Rhizoma...25
Vespae Nidus..34
Violae Herba 23
Viticis Fructus..21

X

Xanthii Fructus 21

Z

Zanthoxyli Radix 26
Zanthoxyli Pericarpium 28
Zingiberis Rhizoma 28
Zingiberis Rhizoma Recens 21
Zyzyphi Spinosae Semen 31

Herb Index by Pinyin (Mandarin) Name

A

Ai Ye 29
An Xi Xiang 31

B

Ba Cou 28
Ba Dou 26
Ba Ji Tian 32
Bai Bian Dou 24
Bai Bu 25
Bai Dou Kou 27
Bai Fan 34
Bai Guo 33
Bai He 33
Bai Hua She 27
Bai Hua She She Cao 23
Bai Ji 29
Bai Ji Li 31
Bai Jiang Can 31
Bai Jiang Cao 23
Bai Jie Zi 24
Bai Lian 24
Bai Mao Gen 29
Bai Qian 24
Bai Shao 32
Bai Tou Weng 23
Bai Wei 24
Bai Xian Pi 23
Bai Zhi 21
Bai Zhu 31
Bai Zi Ren 31
Ban Bian Lian 28
Ban Lan Gen 23
Ban Mao 34
Ban Zhi Lian 26
Bei Sha Shen 33
Bi Ba 28
Bi Xie 27
Bian Xu 27
Bie Jia 33

Bing Lang..29
Bing Pian..31
Bo He..21
Bu Gu Zhi...32

C

Can Sha...26
Cang Er Zi..21
Cang Zhu...27
Cao Dou Kou..27
Cao Guo..27
Cao Wu(Zhi)...31
Ce Bai Ye...29
Cek Zoek...33
Chai Hu...21
Chan Su..34
Chang Shan...29
Chan Tui..21
Che Qian Zi..27
Chen Pi...28
Chen Xiang..28
Chi Shao..26,33
Chi Shi Zhi...33
Chi Xiao Dou...27
Chou Wu Tong..26
Chuan Bei Mu...25
Chuan Jiao...28
Chuan Lian...22
Chuan Lian Zi..28
Chuan Niu Xi...30
Chuan Shan Jia.......................................30
Chuan Shan Long.....................................26
Chuan Wu (Zhi)..31
Chuan Xiong...30
Chun Pi...33
Ci Ji Li...31
Ci Shi...31
Cong Bai..21

D

Da Dou Juan 21
Da Fu Pi 28
Da Huang 25
Da Ji (Cirsii) 29
Da Ji (Knoxiae) 26
Dai Zhe Shi 31
Dan Dou Chi 21
Dang Gui 32
Dang Shen 31
Dan Shen 30
Dan Zhu Ye 22
Da Qing Ye 23
Da Suan 29
Da Zao 32
Deng Xin Cao 27
Di Fu Zi 27
Di Gu Pi 24
Di Long 31
Ding Xiang 28
Di Yu 29
Dong Chong Xia Cao 32
Dong Gua Pi 30
Dong Gua Ren 30
Dong Gua Zi 27
Dong Kui Zi 27
Du Huo 29
Du Zhong 32

E

E Jiao 32
E Zhu 30
Er Cha 34

F

Fang Dang(dang shen) 35
Fang Feng 21
Fan Xie Ye 25
Feng Fang 34
Fo Shou 28
Fu Ling 27
Fu Long Gan 29
Fu Pen Zi 33
Fu Ping 21
Fu Xiao Mai 33
Fu Zi..(Zhi 30

G

Gan Cao 32
Gan Jiang 28
Gan Sui 26
Gao Ben 21
Gao Liang Jiang 28
Ge Gen 21
Ge Jie 32
Gou Ji 32
Gou Qi Zi 32
Gou Teng 31
Gu Ya 29
Gua Lou 25
Gua Lou Pi 25
Gua Lou Ren 25
Guan Zhong 24
Gu Sui Bu 32
Gui Ban 33
Gui Zhi 21

H

Hai Feng Teng 26
Hai Gou Shen 32
Hai Jin Sha 27

Hai Ma..32

Hai Piao Xiao...33

Hai Tong Pi..26

Hai Zao..25

Han Fang Ji..26

Han Lian Cao...33

Han Shui Shi...22

He Huan Hua..34

He Huan Pi...31

He Shou Wu..32

He Tao Ren...32

He Ye..24

He Zi..33

Hei Zhi Ma...33

Hou Po...27

Hong Hua...30

Hong Teng..23

Hu Jiao..28

Hu Tao Ren..32

Hua Shi..27

Huai Hua Mi...29

Huai Jiao..27

Huai Niu Xi..30

Hu Huang Lian..24

Hu Zhang...30

Huo Ma Ren...25

Huo Xiang..27

Hua Jiao..28

Huang Bai..22

Huang Jing...32

Huang Lian...22

Huang Qi..31

Huang Qin..22

Hu Lu Ba..32

J

Ji Nei Jin...29

Ji Xue Teng..30

Jiang Can..31

Jiang Huang...30

Jiang Xiang 30
Jie Geng 24
Jin Qian Cao 27
Jin Yin Hua 23
Jin Ying Zi 33
Jing Jie 21
Ju He 28
Ju Hong 28
Ju Hua 21
Jue Ming Zi 22

K

Ku Lian Pi 29
Ku Shen 22
Kuan Dong Hua 25
Kuan Jin Teng 26
Kun Bu 25

L

Lai Fu Zi 29
Li Lu 25
Li Zhi He 28
Lian Fang 29
Lian Qiao 23
Lian Xu 33
Lian Zi 33
Lian Zi Xin 22
Liang Mian Zhen 26
Ling Yang Jiao 31
Ling Zhi 31
Liu Huang 34
Liu Ji Nu 30
Long Dan Cao 22
Long Chi 30
Long Gu 30
Long Yan Rou 32
Lou Lu 24
Lu Dou 24
Lu Gan Shi 34
Lu Gen 22

Lu Hui..25
Lu Lu Tong...30
Lu Rong 32
Luo Han Guo..25
Luo Shi Teng..26

M

Ma Chi Xian 23
Ma Bian Cao 30
Ma Bo 23
Ma Huang 21
Ma Huang Gen...34
Ma Qian Zi 28
Man Jing Zi 21
Mang Xiao..25
Mai Men Dong..33
Mai Ya..29
Mao Dong Qing..30
Mi Meng Hua..22
Ming Dang Shen 25
Mo Han Lian...33
Mo Yao...30
Mu Dan Pi 23
Mu Gua 26
Mu Li 30
Mu Tong..27
Mu Xiang 28
Mu Zei 21

N

Nan Gua Zi...29
Nan Sha Shen..33
Niu Bang Zi 21
Niu Huang 31
Niu Xi 33
Nu Zhen Zi 33
Nuo Dao Gen 34

O

Ou Jie..29

P

Pang Da Hai...25
Pei Lan...27
Pi Pa Ye...25
Poria..30
Pu Gong Ying...23
Pu Huang...29

Q

Qi She..26
Qian Cao Gen..29
Qian Hu..25
Qian Nian Jian...26
Qian Niu Zi...26
Qian Shi...33
Qiang Huo..21
Qin Jiao...26
Qin Pi...22
Qing Dai...23
Qing Hao..24
Qing Pi...28
Qing Xiang Zi...22
Qu Mai...27
Quan Xie..31

R

Ren Dong Teng...23
Ren Shen..31
Rou Cong Rong..32
Rou Dou Kou..33
Rou Gui..28
Ru Xiang..30

S

San Leng...30
San Qi..29
Sang Bai Pi..25
Sang Ji Sheng..26
Sang Piao Xiao..34
Sang Shen..32
Sang Ye..21
Sang Zhi...26
Sha Ren..27
Sha Shen..33
Sha Yuan Zi..32
Shan Dou Gen...23
Shan Yao..32
Shan Zha..29
Shan Zhu Yu...33
Shang Lu..26
She Chuang Zi...34
She Gan...24
She Xiang...31
Shen Qu...29
Sheng Di Huang..23
Sheng Jiang...21
Sheng Ma...21
Shi Chang Pu..31
Shi Di..28
Shi Gao..22
Shi Hu..33
Shi Jue Ming...31
Shi Jun Zi...29
Shi Liu Pi...33
Shu Di Huang..32
Shui Niu Jiao...23
Sojae Semen Preparatum..21
Song Jie...27
Su He Xiang..31
Su Mu..30
Su Ya...29
Suan Zao Ren...31
Suo Yang..32

T

Tai Zi Shen...31
Tan Xiang..28
Tao Ren...30
Tian Hua Fen...22
Tian Ma..31
Tian Men Dong..33
Tian Nan Xing..24
Ting Li Zi...25
Tong Cao...27
Tu Bie Chong...30
Tu Fu Ling...23
Tu Si Zi...32

W

Wa Leng Zi..30
Wang Bu Liu Xing...30
Wei Ling Xian...26
Wu Bei Zi..33
Wu Gong...31
Wu Jia Pi...26
Wu Ling Zhi...30
Wu Mei..33
Wu Wei Zi..33
Wu Yao..28
Wu Zei Gu...33
Wu Zhu Yu...28

X

Xi Gua...22
Xi Jiao...23
Xi Xian Cao...26
Xi Xin..21
Xi Yang Shen...33
Xia Ku Cao..22
Xian He Cao..29
Xian Ling Pi...35
Xian Mao...32

Xiang Fu...28
Xiang Ru...21
Xiao Hui Xiang...28
Xiao Ji..29
Xie Bai..28
Xin Yi Hua..21
Xing Ren...25
Xu Duan..32
Xuan Fu Hua...24
Xuan Shen..23
Xue Jie...30
Xue Yu Tan...29

Y

Ya Dan Zi...23
Yan Hu Suo...30
Yin Chai Hu...23, 24
Ye Jiao Teng...31
Ye Ju Hua...23
Yi Mu Cao...30
Yi Tang...32
Yi Yi Ren...27
Yi Zhi Ren...32,33
Yin Chen Hao..27
Yin Yang Huo..32
Ying Su Ke..33
Yu Jin...30
Yu Li Ren..26
Yu Mi Xu...28
Yu Xing Cao..23
Yu Zhu..33
Yuan Hua..26
Yuan Zhi...31
Yue Ji Hua..30

Z

Zao Jia 24
Zao Jiao Ci 24
Zao Xin Tu 29
Ze Lan 30
Ze Xie 27
Zhang Nao 34
Zhe Bei Mu 25
Zhen Zhu Mu 31
Zhi Ban Xia 24
Zhi Bai Fu Zi 24
Zhi Cao Wu 28
Zhi Chuan Wu 28
Zhi Fu Zi 28
Zhi Gan Cao 35
Zhi Ke 28
Zhi Mu 22
Zhi Shi 28
Zhi Zi 22
Zhu Ru 25
Zhu Li 25
Zhu Ling 27
Zhu Sha 31
Zi Cao 23
Zi He Che 32
Zi Hua Di Ding 23
Zi Ran Tong 30
Zi Su Ye 21
Zi Su Zi 25
Zi Wan 25
Zong Lu Pi 29

A

Aa Daam Zi 23
Aa Gaau 32
Aang Suk Hok 33

B

Baa Dau 26
Baa Gik Tin 32
Baai Zoeng Cou 23
Baak Bin Dau 24
Baak Cin 24
Baak Bou 25
Baak Dau Kau 27
Baak Faa Se 27
Baak Faa Se Sit Cou 23
Baak Faan 34
Baak Fu Zi (Zai) 27
Baak Gaai Zi 24
Baak Goeng Caam 31
Baak Gwo 33
Baak Hap 33
Baak Kap 29
Baak Lim 24
Baak Maau Gan 29
Baak Mei 24
Baak Seot 31
Baak Sin Pei 23
Baak Tau Jung 23
Baak Zat Lai 31
Baak Zi 21
Baak Zoek 32
Baan Laam Gan 23
Baan Maau 34
Bak Kei(Wong Kei) 31
Bak Saa(Bak Saa Sam) 36
Ban Long 29
Bat Baat 28
Bei Gaai 27
Bin Cuk 27

Bit Gaap 33
Bing Pin 31
Bok Ho 21
Bou Gwat Zi 32
Bun Bin Lin 28
Bun Daai Hoi 25
Bun Haa (Zai) 24
Bun Zi Lin 26

C

Caai Wu 21
Caam Saa 26
Cam Hoeng 28
Can Pei 28
Cau Ng Tung 26
Ce Cin Zi 27
Cek Siu Dau 27
Cek Zeok 26
Ceon Gau 26
Ceon Pei (Fraxini) 22
Ceon Pei (Ailanthi) 33
Ci Dai 28
Ci Sek 31
Cek Sek Zi 33
Ci Zat Lai 31
Cin Nin Gin 26
Cin Wu 28
Cing Doi 23
Cing Hou 24
Cing Pei 28
Cing Soeng Zi 22
Cong Ji Zi 21
Cong Seot 27
Cou Dau Kau 27
Cou Gwo 27
Cou Wu (Zai) 30
Cung Baak 21
Cung Zit 27
Cyun Bui Mou 25
Cyun Gung 30
Cyun Hit 31
Cyun Lin 22

Cyun Lin Zi..28
Cyun Ngau Sat..30
Cyun Saan Gaap 30
Cyun Saan Lung 26
Cyun Ziu..28

D

Daai Cing Jip...23
Daai Dau Gyun 21
Daai Fuk Pei 28
Daai Gai...29
Daai Gik 26
Daai Syun 29
Daai Wong 25
Daai Zou 32
Daan Sam 30
Daam Dau Si...21
Daam Zuk Jip 22
Dang Sam Cou 27
Dei Fu Zi 27
Dei Gwat Pei 24
Dei Jyu 29
Dei Lung..31
Ding Hoeng 29
Doi Ze Sek 31
Dong Gwai 32
Dong Sam 31
Dou Zung 32
Duk Wut 26
Dung Cung Haa Cou..32
Dung Gwaa Jan 27
Dung Gwaa Pei 30
Dung Gwaa Zi 30
Dung Kwai Zi...27

F

Faa Ziu..28
Faan Se Jip..25
Fau Ping...21
Fau Siu Mak 33
Fat Sau 28

Fo Maa Jan 25
Fok Hoeng 27
Fong Dong(Dong Sam) 31
Fong Fung 21
Fu Zoeng 30
Fu Lin Pei 29
Fu Sam 22
Fu Zi (Zai) 31
Fuk Ling 27
Fuk Lung Gon 29
Fuk Pun Zi 33
Fun Dung Faa 25
Fun Gan Tang 26
Fung Fong 34

G

Gai Hyut Tang 30
Gai Noi Gam 29
Gam Cou 32
Gam Ngan Faa 23
Gam Cin Cou 27
Gam Jing Zi 33
Gam Seoi 26
Gap Gaai 32
Gat Gang 24
Gau Gei Zi 32
Gau Zek 32
Gei Zi 36
Ging Gaai 21
Goeng Caam 31
Goeng Wong 30
Goeng Wut 21
Gon Goeng 28
Gong Hoeng 30
Gou Bun 21
Gou Loeng Goeng 28
Got Gan 21
Guk Faa 21
Guk Ngaa 29
Gun Zung 24
Gwaa Lau 25
Gwaa Lau Jan 25

Gwaa Lau Pei 25
Gwai Baan 33
Gwai Zi 21
Gwat Hung 28
Gwat Seoi Bou 32
Gwat Wat 28

H

Haa Fu Cou 22
Haai Baak 28
Hang Jan 25
Hak Zi Maa 33
Hap Fun Faa 34
Hap Fun Pei 31
Hau Pok 27
Hat Tou Jan 32
Hei Cim Cou 26
Him Sat 33
Hin Ngau Zi 26
Ho Jip 24
Ho Sau Wu 32
Ho Zi 33
Hoeng Fu 28
Hoeng Jyu 21
Hoi Fung Tang 26
Hoi Gam Saa 27
Hoi Gau San 32
Hoi Maa 32
Hoi Piu Siu 33
Hoi Tung Pei 26
Hoi Zou 25
Hon Fong Gei 26
Hon Lin Cou 33
Hon Seoi Sek 22
Hung Faa 30
Hung Tang 23
Hyut Jyu Taan 29
Hyut Kit 30

J

Jam Joeng Fok 32
Jan Can Hou 27
Jan Dung Tang 23
Jan Sam 31
Je Gaau Tang 31
Je Guk Faa 23
Ji Caa 34
Ji Ji Jan 27
Ji Tong 32,33
Jik Mou Cou 30
Jik Zi Jan 32
Jin Wu Sok 30
Juk Cung Jung 32
Juk Dau Kau 33
Juk Gam 30
Juk Gwai 28
Juk Mai Seoi 28
Juk Zuk 33
Jyu Hoeng 30
Jyu Lei Jan 26
Jyu Seng Cou 23
Jyun Faa 26
Jyun Zi 31
Jyun Sam 23
Jyut Gwai Faa 30

K

Kei Se 26
Keoi Mak 27
Kwan Bou 25
Kyut Ming Zi 22

L

Lai Lou 25

Lai Zi Wat 28

Lau Gei Nou 30

Lau Lou 24

Lau Wong 34

Lin Fong 29

Lin Kiu 23

Lin Sou 33

Lin Zi 33

Lin Zi Sam 22

Ling Joeng Gok 31

Ling Zi 31

Lo Hon Gwo 25

Loi Fuk Zi 29

Loeng Min Zam 26

Lok Sek Tang 26

Lou Gam Sek 34

Lou Gan 22

Lou Lou Tung 30

Lou Wui 25

Luk Dau 24

Luk Jung 32

Lung Daam Cou 22

Lung Ci 30

Lung Gwat 30

Lung Ngaan Juk 32

M

Maa Bin Cou 30

Maa But 23

Maa Ci Jin 23

Maa Cin Zi 28

Maa Wong 21

Maa Wong Gan 34

Maan Ging Zi 21

Maau Daan Pei 23

Maau Lai 30

Mak Mun Dung..33

Mak Hon Lin..33

Mak Ngaa...29

Mat Mung Faa..22

Ming Dong Sam..25

Mong Siu...25

Mou Dung Cing..30

Muk Caak..21

Muk Gwaa...26

Muk Hoeng..28

Muk Tung...27

Mut Joek...30

N

Naam Gwaa Zi..29

Naam Saa (Naam Saa Sam) 36

Neoi Zing Zi...33

Ng Gaa Pei..26

Ng Gung..31

Ng Ling Zi..30

Ng Mei Zi...33

Ng Pui Zi...33

Ng Zyu Jyu..28

Ngaa Ling Zi..30

Ngaai Jip...29

Ngan Caai Wu...23, 24

Ngau Bong Zi..21

Ngau Sat (Waai) 33

Ngau Tang...31

Ngau Wong..31

Ngau Zit..29

Ngo Seot...30

No Dou Gan...34

O

On Sik Hoeng...31

P

Paak Zi Jan 31
Pei Paa Jip 25
Pou Gung Jing 26
Pou Wong 29
Pui Laan 27

S

Saa Jan 27
Saa Jyun Zi 32
Saa Sam 36
Saam Cat 29
Saam Ling 30
Saan Dau Gan 23
Saan Joek 32
Saan Zaa 29
Saan Zyu Jyu 33
Sai Gok 23
Sai Gwaa 22
Sai Joeng Sam 33
Sai San 21
San Ji Faa 21
San Kuk 29
Sang Dei Wong 23
Saang Goeng 21
Se Cong Zi 34
Se Gon 24
Se Hoeng 31
Sek Coeng Pou 31
Sek Gou 22
Sek Huk 33
Sek Kyut Ming 31
Sek Lau Pei 33
Seoi Ngau Gok 23
Si Gwan Zi 29
Sim Sou 34
Sim Teoi 21
Sin Cou Gan 29
Sin Hok Cou 29

Sin Ling Pei 35

Sin Maau 32

Sing Maa 21

Siu Gai 29

Siu Wui Hoeng 28

So Joeng 32

Soeng Luk 26

Soeng Saan 29

Song Baak Pei 25

Song Gei Sang 26

Song Jip 21

Song Piu Siu 34

Song Sam 32

Song Zi 26

Sou Hap Hoeng 31

Sou Muk 30

Suk Dei Wong 32

Suk Ngaa 29

Syun Fuk Faa 24

Syun Zou Jan 31

T

Taan Hoeng 28

Taai Zi Sam 31

Tin Cat 32

Tin Faa Fan 22

Tin Maa 31

Tin Mun Dung 33

Tin Naam Sing 24

Ting Lik Zi 25

Tou Bit Cung 30

Tou Fuk Ling 23

Tou Jan 30

Tou Si Zi 32

Tung Cou 27

W

Waai Faa Mai 29
Waai Gok 29
Waai Ngau Sat 30
Waat Sek 27
Wai Ling Sin 26
Wong Bat Lau Hang 30
Wong Kam 22
Wong Kei 31
Wong Lin 22
Wong Paak 22
Wong Zing 32
Wu Caak Gwat 33
Wu Joek 28
Wu Lou Baa 32
Wu Mui 33
Wu Tou Jan(Hat Tou Jan) 32
Wu Wong Lin 24
Wu Ziu 28

Z

Zaak Laan 30
Zaak Se 27
Zai Baak Fu Zi 24
Zai Bun Haa 27
Zai Cou Wu 28
Zai Cyun Wu 27
Zai Fu Zi 28
Zak Paak Jip 29
Zek Gam Cou 35
Zan Zyu Mou 31
Zi Cou 23
Zi Faa Dei Ding 23
Ji Hok 28
Ji Ho Ce 32

Zi Jin Tung 30
Zi Jyun 25
Zi Mou 22
Zi Sat... 28
Zi Sou Jip 21
Zi Sou Zi... 25
Zi Zi 22
Zit Bui Mou 25
Zoeng Nou 34
Zou Gaap 24
Zou Gok Ci 24
Zou Sam Tou 29
Zuk Jyu 25
Zuk Lik 25
Zuk Dyun... 32
Zung Leoi Pei 29
Zyu Ling 27
Zyu Saa.. 31

Formula Index by English Name

A

Abduct Phlegm Decoction.. 139
Abduct the Red Powder 69
Aconite Accessory Root Decoction.. 135
Aconite Accessory Root Infusion to Drain the Epigastrium.......................... 63
Aconite Rectify the Center Pill 75
Added Flavors Four Materials Decoction.. 92
Added Flavors Rehmannia Pills... 97
Added Flavors Two Wonders Powder 132
Agastachis Correct the Qi Powder.. 127
Aid the Living Kidney Qi Pills 102
All-Inclusive Great Tonifying Decoction 84
Amomum and Aucklandia Six Gentlemen Decoction................................... 81
Anemarrhena and Phellodendron Rehmannia Pills 97
Angelica Pubescens and Loranthus Decoction 135
Antelope Horn and Uncaria Decoction.. 123
Aucklandia and Amomum Nourish the Stomach Decoction.......................82
Armeniaca and Perilla Powder.. 124
Arrest Seizures Pill.. 143
Artemisia Annuae and Tryonicis Carapax Decoction.............................. 72
Artemisia Argyium and Cyperus Warm the Palace Decoction..................... 91
Artemisia Capillaris Decoction 128
Artemisia Five Poria Powder... 133
Ass-Hide Gelatin and Mugwort Decoction 119
Astragalus and Cinnamon Twig Five-Substance Decoction 73
Astragalus Decoction to Construct the Middle.. 76
Aucklandia and Amomum Two Aged Decoction....................................... 138
Aucklandia and Betel Nut Pill... 147
Augmented Cyperus and Perilla Leaf Powder 43
Augmented Two-Aged [Herb] Decoction 141
Augment the Primal Powder 66

B

Balmy Yang Decoction.. 78
Bamboo Leaf and Gypsum Decoction 61
Benefit the River Decoction 50
Black Rambling Powder.. 56
Bone-Setter's Purple-Gold Special Pill.. 116

Bupleurum and Cinnamon Decoction 52
Bupleurum and Four-Substance Decoction 50
Bupleurum and Kudzu Decoction to Release the Muscle Layer 41
Bupleurum and Mirabilitum Decoction 53
Bupleurum and Poria Decoction 133
Bupleurum, Citrus and Platycodon Decoction 54
Bupleurum Fall Decoction/Bupleurum Chest Bind Decoction 52
Bupleurum Leveling Decoction 51, 127
Bupleurum plus Dragon Bone and Oyster Shell Decoction 51
Bupleurum Powder to Dredge the Liver 57
Bupleurum White Tiger Decoction 60

C

Calm the Stomach and Poria Decoction 134
Cannabis Seed Pills 49
Canopy Powder 40
Capital Qi Pills 97
Change Yellow [Discharge] Decoction 111
Chinese Angelica and Peony Pills 98
Chinese Angelica and Peony Powder 90
Chinese Angelica and Rehmannia Drink 98
Chinese Angelica Six Yellows Decoction 89
Chrysanthemum and Tea Mixed Powder 120
Cimicifuga and Kudzu Decoction 42
Cinnabar Quiet the Spirit Pills 103
Cinnamon and Aconite Rectify the Center Decoction 75
Cinnamon and Poria Sweet Dew Drink 66
Cinnamon, Peony and Anemarrhena Decoction 44
Cinnamon Twig Decoction 43
Cinnamon Twig Decoction plus Dragon Bone and Oyster Shell 110
Cinnamon Twig Decoction plus Kudzu Root 43
Cinnamon Twig Decoction plus Magnolia Bark and Apricot Kernel 43
Clear Dampness and Transform Phlegm Decoction 139
Clear Dryness and Rescue the Lungs Decoction 125
Clear Epidemics and Overcome Toxicity Drink 62
Clear the Nutritive-Level Decoction 63
Clear Summerheat and Augment the Qi Decoction 67
Clear the Collaterals Drink 66
Clear the Qi and Transform Phlegm Pills 141
Clear the Stomach Powder 68
Clove and Evodia Rectify the Center Decoction 74
Cock-Waking Powder/Mint Powder 67
Cool the Bones Powder 72

Cool the Diaphragm Powder 64
Compound Major Order the Qi Decoction 47
Coptis Decoction 59
Coptis and Ass-Hide Gelatin Decoction 104
Coptis and Magnolia Bark Drink 130
Coptis Rectifying Decoction 75
Coptis Resolve Toxins Decoction 63
Coptis Warm the Gallbladder Decoction 137
Cure Discharge Pill 128
Cuscuta Seed Pill 101
Cyperus and Perilla Leaf Powder 43

D

Dang Gui Four Counterflows Decoction 79
Dang Gui Four Counterflows plus Evodia and Uncooked Ginger Decoction . 79
Disband Painful Obstruction Decoction 131
Dissolve Parasites Pill 148
Dividing and Dispersing Decoction 83
Drain the Epigastrium Decoction 71
Drain the White Powder 71
Drain the Yellow Powder 68
Drive Out Stasis Below the Diaphragm Decoction 114
Drive Out Stasis From a Painful Body Decoction 115
Drive Out Stasis From the Lower Abdomen Decoction 115
Drive Out Stasis From the Mansion of Blood Decoction 113

E

Eight Correcting Powder 129
Eight Flavors Rehmannia Pill 99
Eight Treasure Decoction 84
Eliminate Wind Drink with the Four Substances 122
Eliminate Wind Powder from Orthodox Lineage 121
Emperor of Heaven's Special Pill to Tonify the Heart 104
End Discharge Decoction 111
Engendering and Transforming Decoction 114
Ephedra Decoction 39
Ephedra, Apricot Kernel, Licorice, and Gypsum Decoction 68
Ephedra, Asarum, and Aconite Accessory Root Decoction 45
Ephedra and Notopterygium Decoction 40

Ephedra With Atractylodis added Decoction..42
Escape Restraint Pills...111
Evodia Decoction 76
Extraordinary Merit Powder 80

F

Fat Baby Pill...146
Fetus Longevity Pill..110
Five-Accumulation Powder 44
Five-Ingredient Drink to Eliminate Toxin 64,78
Five Flavors Extraordinary Merit Powder...82
Five-Peel Powder..133
Five Poria Powder..132
Fleeceflower Root and Ginseng Drink 86
Flush Phlegm Decoction 138
Flushing Away Rolling Phlegm Pill..142
Four Counterflows Decoction..77
Four Counterflows plus Ginseng Decoction..77
Four Counterflows Powder 55
Four-Fresh Pill 118
Four Gentlemen Decoction 80
Four Materials Decoction 87
Four Poria Powder 133
Four Seven Decoction 112
Four Spirits Pills...108
Four-Valiant Decoction for Well-Being..65
Four Wonders Powder 129
Fresh Ginger Drain the Heart Decoction...58
Fritillaria and Trichosanthis Powder...142

G

Gardenia and Prepared Soybean Decoction 61
Gardenia, Licorice, and Prepared Soybean Decoction....................................61
Gastrodia and Uncaria Drink...122
Generate the Pulse Powder...87
Gentiana Drain the Liver Decoction 70
Gentiana Macrophylla Support Marked Emaciation Decoction............................53
Ginger and Cinnamon Four Materials Decoction...88
Ginseng and Aconite Accessory Root Decoction 77
Ginseng and Gecko Powder 82
Ginseng and Perilla Drink 44

Ginseng Decoction to Nourish Luxuriance...85
Ginseng, Poria and Atractylodes Powder 81
Ginseng Toxin-Vanquishing Powder..44
Glehnia and Ophiopogonis Decoction 125
Golden Cabinet Kidney Qi Pills..99
Great Creation Pill...95
Great Tonify the Yin Pill 94
Ginseng White Tiger Decoction 59
Green Jade Powder/Jasper Powder 67
Gypsum Decoction...42

H

Hidden Tiger Pill..95
Honeysuckle and Forsythia Powder 41
Honeysuckle, Forsythia, and Puffball Powder 41

I

Immature Aurantium Rectify the Center Pills 75
Immortals' Formula for Sustaining Life...78
Important Formula for Painful Diarrhea...57
Improve Vision Pill With Rehmannia...93
Increase the Fluids Decoction...126
Increase Fluids and Order the Qi Decoction..46

J

Jade Candle Powder..90
Jade Fluid Decoction 126
Jade Windscreen Powder...81
Jade Woman Decoction...71

K

Kudzu Decoction.. 42
Kudzu, Scutellaria, and Coptis Decoction... 71

L

Lead to Symmetry Powder.. 121
Left Metal Pill 72
Level the Stomach Powder 127
Licorice and Ginger Decoction.. 76
Licorice Drain the Heart Decoction 58
Licorice, Wheat, and Jujube Decoction... 110
Ligusticum and Tea Mixed Powder.. 120
Lily Secure the Lungs Decoction 125
Linking Decoction.. 95
Liquid Styrax Pills... 107
Lotus and Pearl Drink 92
Lycium and Chrysanthemum Rehmannia Pills 96

M

Magnetite and Cinnabar Pill.. 103
Magnolia Bark Decoction for Warming the Middle... 112
Magnolia Flower Powder 40
Maidservant from Yue Decoction.. 68
Major Arrest Wind Pearls 123
Major Bluegreen Dragon Decoction... 42
Major Bupleurum Decoction... 54
Major Construct the Middle Decoction 76
Major Decoction [for Pathogens] Stuck in the Chest 48
Major Order the Qi Decoction 45
Melon Pedicle Powder 144
Metal and Water Six Gentlemen Decoction 138
Metal Lock Pill to Stabilize the Essence 109
Minor Bluegreen Dragon Decoction... 42
Minor Bupleurum Decoction... 50
Minor Construct the Middle Decoction 76

Minor Decoction [for Pathogens] Stuck in the Chest 140
Minor Invigorate the Collaterals Special Pill.. 121
Minor Order the Qi Decoction 45
Minor Pinellia Decoction 112
Modified Solomon's Seal Decoction.. 45
Modified Support the Center and Boost the Qi Decoction 86
Moisten the Intestines Pill from Master Shen's Book................................... 49
Mosla Powder 39
Mulberry Leaf and Apricot Kernel Decoction 124
Mume Pills 148
Mutton Stew with Tangkuei and Fresh Ginger 91
Moutan and Gardenia Rambling Powder.. 55
Mulberry Leaf and Chrysanthemum Drink 40

N

Newly Processed Orange Peel and Caulis Bambusae Decoction............... 113
Nine-Herb Decoction with Notopterygium 42
Notopterygium Decoction to Overcome Dampness..................................... 136
Nourish the Yin and Clear the Lungs Decoction 126

O

Ootheca Mantidis Powder.. 109
Ophiopogon and Schizandra Rehmannia Pills 97
Orange Peel and Caulis Bambusae Decoction... 113
Oyster Shell Powder 107

P

Peach Blossom Decoction... 108
Peony Decoction.. 69
Peony and Licorice Decoction 89
Persica and Carthamus Four Materials Decoction 87
Pill for Deafness that is Kind to the Left Kidney 98
Pinellia, Atractylodes and Gastrodia Decoction 144
Pinellia, Atractylodes and Gastrodia Decoction [Li Dong Yuan's Version]... 144
Pinellia and Magnolia Decoction... 112
Pinellia Drain the Heart Decoction 57
Pinellia Draining Six Gentlemen Decoction... 101
Polyporus Decoction 132
Poria, Cinnamon, Atractylodes and Licorice Decoction 134

Poria, Licorice, Schisandra, Ginger and Asarum Decoction 143
Powder to Take at Cock's Crow 135
Prepared Licorice Decoction 84
Preserve Vistas Pill 96
Protecting Harmony Pills 145
Pulsatilla Decoction 70
Pulsatilla, Licorice and Donkey Skin Decoction 70
Purple Snow Special Pill 105

Q

Qian's Atractylodes Powder 83
Quieting the Palace Bezoar Pills 105

R

Rambling Powder 55
Rectify the Center Pills 73
Rectify the Center and Quiet Roundworms Pills 74
Rectify the center and Transform Phlegm Pills 74
Reduce Scrofula Pill 141
Reed Decoction 71
Regulate the Center and Boost the Qi Decoction 86
Regulate the Stomach Order the Qi Decoction 46
Rehmannia Drink 101
Relax the Channels and Invigorate the Blood Decoction 117
Remove Painful Obstruction Decoction 136
Restore the Left [Kidney] Drink 94
Restore the Left [Kidney] Pill 94
Restore the Right [Kidney] Drink 100
Restore the Right [Kidney] Pill 102
Restore the Spleen Decoction 96
Restrict the Fountain Pill 109
Revive Health by Invigorating the Blood Decoction 116
Rhinoceros and Rehmannia Decoction 62
Rhubarb and Aconite Decoction 48
Rhubarb and Licorice Decoction 47
Rhubarb and Moutan Decoction 46

S

Sage-Like Healing Decoction... 88

Saposhnikovia Powder that Sagely Unblocks.............................. 43

Sargassum Decoction for the Jade Flask 142

Scallion and Prepared Soybean Decoction................................ 38

Schizonepeta and Saposhnikovia Powder to
  Overcome Pathogenic Influences 40

Scutellaria and Coptis Four Materials Decoction 89

Separate and Reduce Fullness in the Middle Pill 130

Settle the Emotions Pill.. 104

Settle the Liver and Extinguish Wind Decoction 122

Seven-Thousandths of a Tael Powder.................................... 116

Seven-Treasure Special Pill for Beautiful Whiskers.................... 100

Six Divine Pill 79

Six Flavors Rehmannia Pills 93

Six Gentlemen Decoction 80

Six-Serenity Decoction... 139

Six to One Powder 67

Small Thistle Drink 119

Soothe Depression and Clear the Liver Drink............................ 56

Sophora Flower Powder 119

Special Pill to Aid Fertility... 101

Special Pill to Restore Life 106

Stabilize Gushing Decoction 110

Stabilize the Menses Pill 119

Stephania and Astragalus Decoction................................... 134

Stephaniae, Zanthoxylum, Tingli Seed, and Rhubarb Pill............ 48

Stomach Poria Powder 128

Stop Coughing Powder 144

Strengthen the Spleen Pill 147

Sudden Smile Powder 113

Supplement the Center and Boost the Qi Decoction 86

Supplement the Liver Decoction 90

Support the Spleen and Soothe the Liver Decoction 56

Suppress Counterflow White Tiger Decoction 60

Sweet Dew Special Pill to Eliminate Toxin............................. 131

Sweet Wormwood and Scutellaria Decoction to Clear the Gallbladder 54

T

Taishan Bedrock Powder..85
Tangkuei and Six-Yellows Decoction...73
Tangkuei and Spatholobus Decoction 92
Tangkuei Decoction for Frigid Extremities 74
Tangkuei Decoction to Tonify the Blood 90
Ten Dates Decoction 48
Ten-Ingredient Warm Gallbladder Decoction..140
Ten Partially-Charred Substances Powder...118
Ten Supplements Pills 99
Three Seed Decoction 130
Three-Seed Decoction to Nourish One's Parents 143
Three-Shell Decoction to Restore the Pulse...124
Three-Substance Decoction with Magnolia Bark 47
Three-Substance Pill Prepared for Emergencies.....................................48
Three Unbinding Decoction 39
Three Wonders Powder 129
Three Yellows Four Materials Decoction 88
Three Yellows Gypsum Decoction...65
Tonify the Lungs Decoction 87
Tonify the Lungs Decoction with Ass-Hide Gelatin 96
Trauma Pill..117
Trichosanthes Fruit and Unripe Bitter Orange Decoction 140
True Man Nourish the Viscera Decoction 108
True Warrior Decoction..135
Two-Aged Decoction..136
Two Immortals Decoction 102
Two-Solstice Pill..96
Two Wonders Powder...129

U

Unaccompanied Ginseng Decoction..77
Unblock the Orifices and Invigorate the Blood Decoction.........................114
Unblock the Pulse Decoction for Frigid Extremities 77
Universal Benefit Drink to Eliminate Toxin...64
Unripe Bitter Orange and Atractylodes Pill 145
Unripe Bitter Orange Pill to Guide out Stagnation...................................146
Unripe Bitter Orange Pill to Reduce Focal Distention 148

V

Vessel and Vehicle Pill... 49

W

Warm the Gallbladder Decoction 137
Warm the Spleen Decoction 48
Warming and Clearing Drink... 65
White Penetrating Decoction 77
White Tiger Decoction... 59
White Tiger plus Atractylodis Decoction 59
White Tiger plus Cinnamon Decoction.. 59
White Tiger Order the Qi Decoction.. 60

X

Xanthium Powder.. 121

Y

Yellow Dragon Decoction.. 46
Yellow Earth Decoction... 118

Z

Zizyphus Spinosa Decoction... 103

A

Ai Fu Nuan Gong Wan 91
An Gong Niu Huang Wan 105

B

Ba Wei Di Huang Wan 99
Ba Zhen Tang 84
Ba Zheng San 129
Bai He Gu Jin Tang 125
Bai Hu Tang 59
Bai Hu Cheng Qi Tang 60
Bai Hu Jia Cang Zhu Tang 59
Bai Hu Jia Gui Zhi Tang 59
Bai Tong Tang 77
Bai Tou Weng Jia Gan Cao E Jiao Tang 70
Bai Tou Weng Tang 70
Ban Xia Bai Zhu Tian Ma Tang 144
Ban Xia Bai Zhu Tian Ma Tang (Li Dong Yuan) 182
Ban Xia Hou Po Tang 112
Ban Xia Xie Xin Tang 57
Ban Xie Liu Jun Zi Tang 101
Bao He Wan 145
Bei Mu Gua Lou San 142
Bi Yu San 67
Bu Fei E Jiao Tang 96
Bu Fei Tang 87
Bu Gan Tang 90
Bu Zhong Yi Qi Tang 86

C

Cang Er Zi San 121
Chai Ge Jie Ji Tang 41
Chai Hu Bai Hu Tang 60
Chai Hu Gui Zhi Tang 52
Cha Hu Jia Long Gu Mu Li Tang 51
Chai Hu Jia Mang Xiao Tang 53
Chai Hu Shu Gan San 57
Chai Hu Si Wu Tang 50

Chai Hu Zhi Jie Tang 54
Chai Ling Tang.. 133
Chai Ping Tang 51,127
Chai Xian Tang 52
Chuan Xiong Cha Tiao San 120
Ci Zhu Wan 103
Cong Chi Tang 38

D

Da Bu Yin Wan 94
Da Chai Hu Tang 54
Da Cheng Qi Tang 45
Da Ding Feng Zhu.. 123
Da Huang Fu Zi Tang 48
Da Huang Gan Cao Tang 47
Da Huang Mu Dan Tang 46
Da Jian Zhong Tang 76
Da Qing Long Tang.. 42
Da Xian Xiong Tang 48
Da Zao Wan... 117
Dan Zhi Xiao Yao San 55
Dang Gui Bu Xue Tang... 90
Dang Gui Di Huang Yin.. 98
Dang Gui Ji Xue Teng Tang 92
Dang Gui Liu Huang Tang 72,89
Dang Gui Shao Yao San 90
Dang Gui Sheng Jiang Yang Rou Tang................................ 91
Dang Gui Si Ni Jia Wu Zhu Yu Sheng Jiang Tang................ 79
Dang Gui Si Ni Tang 74,79
Dao Chi San... 69
Dao Tan Tang 101, 139
Di Huang Yin Zi.. 126
Di Tan Tang 138
Die Da Wan.. 117
Ding Xian Wan 143
Ding Yu Li Zhong Tang 74
Ding Zhi Wan 104
Du Huo Ji Sheng Tang... 135
Du Qi Wan 97
Du Shen Tang... 77

E

Er Chen Tang.. 136
Er Long Zuo Ci Wan 98
Er Miao San 129
Er Xian Tang 127
Er Zhi Wan 96

F

Fang Feng Tong Sheng San... 43
Fang Ji Huang Qi Tang.. 134
Fei Er Wan 146
Fen Xiao Tang 83
Fu Fang Da Cheng Qi Tang... 47
Fu Pi Shu Gan Tang 56
Fu Yuan Huo Xue Tang 116
Fu Zi Li Zhong Wan 75
Fu Zi Xie Xin Tang 63
Fu Zi Tang.. 135

G

Gan Cao Gan Jiang Tang 76
Gan Cao Xie Xin Tang 58
Gan Lu Xiao Du Dan.. 131
Gan Mai Da Zao Tang 110
Ge Gen Qin Lian Tang... 71
Ge Gen Tang 42
Ge Xia Zhu Yu Tang 114
Gu Chong Tang 110
Gu Fu Li Zhong Tang... 77
Gu Jing Wan 119
Gua Di San 145
Gua Lou Zhi Shi Tang 140
Gui Fu Li Zhong Tang 75
Gui Ling Gan Lu Yin.. 66
Gui Pi Tang 96
Gui Shao Di Huang Wan... 98
Gui Zhi Tang 43
Gui Zhi Jia Ge Gen Tang 43
Gui Zhi Jia Hou Po Xing Ren Tang 43

Gui Zhi Jia Long Gu Mu Li Tang 110
Gui Zhi Shao Yao Zhi Mu Tang 44
Gun Tan Wan 142

H

Hai Zao Yu Hu Tang 142
Hao Qin Qing Dan Tang 54
He Ren Yin 86
Hei Xiao Yao San 56
Hou Po San Wu Tang 47
Hou Po Wen Zhong Tang 112
Hu Qian Wan 95
Hua Chong Wan 148
Hua Gai San 40
Huai Hua San 119
Huang Lian E Jiao Tang 104
Huang Lian Tang 59
Huang Lian Jie Du Tang 63
Huang Lian Wen Dan Tang 137
Huang Long Tang 46
Huang Qi Gui Zhi Wu Wu Tang 73
Huang Qi Jian Zhong Tang 76
Huang Tu Tang 118
Hui Chun Dan 106
Huo Xiang Zheng Qi San 127

J

Ji Jiao Li Huang Wan 48
Ji Ming San 135
Ji Chuan Jian 50
Ji Sheng Shen Qi Wan 102
Ji Su San 67
Jia Jian Bu Zhong Yi Qi Tang 86
Jia Jian Wei Rui Tang 45
Jia Wei Er Chen Tang 141
Jia Wei Er Miao San 132
Jia Wei Liu Wei Di Huang Wan 97
Jia Wei Si Wu Tang 92
Jia Wei Xiang Su San 43

Jian Pi Wan 147
Jiang Gui Si Wu Tang 88
Jiao Ai Tang 120
Jin Gui Shen Qi Wan 99
Jin Shui Liu Jun Jian 138
Jin Suo Gu Jing Wan 109
Jing Fang Bai Du San 40
Jiu Wei Qiang Huo Tang 42
Ju Hua Cha Tiao San 120
Ju Pi Zhu Ru Tang 113
Juan Bi Tang 136

L

Li Zhong An Hui Wan 74
Li Zhong Hua Tan Wan 74
Li Zhong Wan 73
Lian Li Tang 75
Lian Po Yin 130
Lian Zhu Yin 92
Liang Ge San 64
Ling Gan Wu Wei Jiang Xin Tang 143
Ling Gui Zhu Gan Tang 134
Ling Jiao Gou Teng Tang 123
Ling Yang Gou Teng Tang 131
Liu An Jian 139
Liu Jun Zi Tang 80
Liu Shen Wan 79
Liu Wei Di Huang Wan 93
Liu Yi San 67
Long Dan Xie Gan Tang 70

M

Ma Huang Tang 39
Ma Huang Jia Zhu Tang 42
Ma Huang Qiang Huo Tang 40
Ma Huang Xi Xin Fu Zi Tang 45
Ma Xing Shi Gan Tang 68
Ma Zi Ren Wan 49
Mai Wei Di Huang Wan 97
Ming Mu Di Huang Wan 93
Mu Li San 107
Mu Xiang Bing Lang Wan 147

P

Ping Wei San 127
Pu Ji Xiao Du Yin 64

Q

Qi Bao Mei Ran Dan 100
Qi Ju Di Huang Wan 96
Qi Li San 116
Qian Zheng San 121
Qian Shi Bai Zhu San 83
Qiang Huo Sheng Shi Tang 136
Qin Jiao Fu Lei Tang 53
Qin Lian Si Wu Tang 89
Qing Gu San 72
Qing Hao Bie Jia Tang 72
Qing Luo Yin 66
Qing Qi Hua Tan Wan 141
Qing Shi Hua Tan Tang 139
Qing Shu Yi Qi Tang 67
Qing Wei San 68
Qing Wen Bai Du Yin 62
Qing Ying Tang 63
Qing Zao Jiu Fei Tang 125

R

Ren Shen Bai Du San 44
Ren Shen Bai Hu Tang 59
Ren Shen Ge Jie San 82
Ren Shen Yang Rong Tang 85
Run Chang Wan 49

S

San Ao Tang 39
San Huang Shi Gao Tang 65
San Huang Si Wu Tang 88
San Jia Fu Mai Tang 124
San Miao San 129
San Ren Tang 130
San Wu Bei Ji Wan 48
San Zi Yang Qin Tang 143
Sang Ju Yin 40
Sang Piao Xiao Tang 109
Sang Xing Tang 124
Sha Shen Mai Men Dong Tang 125
Shao Fu Zhu Yu Tang 115
Shao Yao Gan Cao Tang 89
Shao Yao Tang 69
Shen Fu Tang 77
Shen Ling Bai Zhu San 81
Shen Tong Zhu Yu Tang 115
Sheng Hua Tang 114
Sheng Jiang Xie Xin Tang 58
Sheng Ma Ge Gen Tang 47
Sheng Mai San 87
Sheng Yu Tang 88
Shen Su Yin 44
Shi Bu Wan 99
Shi Gao Tang 42
Shi Hui San 118
Shi Quan Da Bu Tang 84
Shi Wei Wen Dan Tang 140
Shi Xiao San 113
Shi Zao Tang 48
Shou Tai Wan 110
Shu Jing Huo Xue Tang 117
Shu Yu Qing Gan Tang 56
Si Jun Zi Tang 80
Si Ling San 133
Si Miao San 129
Si Miao Yong An Tang 65
Si Ni Jia Ren Shen Tang 77
Si Ni San 55

Si Ni Tang 77
Si Qi Tang 112
Si Shen Wan 108
Si Sheng Wan 118
Si Wu Tang 87
Si Wu Xiao Feng Yin 122
Su He Xiang Wan 107
Suan Zao Ren Tang 103
Suo Quan Wan 109

T

Tai Shan Pan Shi San 85
Tao Hua Tang 108
Tao Hong Si Wu Tang 87
Tian Ma Gou Teng Yin 122
Tian Wang Bu Xin Dan 104
Tiao Wei Cheng Qi Tang 46
Tiao Zhong Yi Qi Tang 86
Tong Mai Si Ni Tang 77
Tong Qiao Huo Xue Tang 114
Tong Xie Yao Fang 57
Tu Si Zi Wan 101

W

Wan Dai Tang 111
Wei Jing Tang 71
Wei Ling San 128
Wei Ling Tang 134
Wen Dan Tang 137
Wen Pi Tang 48
Wen Qing Yin 65
Wu Ji San 44
Wu Ling San 132
Wu Mei Wan 148
Wu Pi San 132
Wu Wei Xiao Du Yin 64, 78

Wu Wei Yi Gong San 82
Wu Zhu Yu Tang 76

X

Xi Jiao Di Huang Tang 62
Xian Fang Huo Ming Yin 78
Xiang Ru San 39
Xiang Sha Er Chen Tang 138
Xiang Sha Liu Jun Zi Tang 81
Xiang Sha Yang Wei Tang 82
Xiang Su San 43
Xiao Ban Xia Tang 112
Xiao Chai Hu Tang 50
Xiao Cheng Qi Tang 45
Xiao Feng San 121
Xiao Huo Luo Dan 121
Xiao Ji Yin Zi 119
Xiao Jian Zhong Tang 76
Xiao Qing Long Tang 42
Xiao Luo Wan 141
Xiao Xian Xiong Tang 140
Xiao Yao San 55
Xie Bai San 71
Xie Huang San 68
Xie Xin Tang 71
Xin Yi San 40
Xin Zhi Ju Pi Zhu Ru Tang 113
Xing Su San 124
Xuan Bi Tang 131
Xue Fu Zhu Yu Tang 113

Y

Yang He Tang 78
Yang Yin Qing Fei Tang 126
Yi Gong San 80
Yi Guan Jian 95
Yi Huang Tang 111
Yi Yuan San 66
Yin Chen Hao Tang 128

Yin Chen Wu Ling San.. 133
Yin Qiao San.. 41
Yin Qiao Ma Bo San 41
You Gui Wan.. 102
You Gui Yin.. 100
Yu Dai Wan.. 128
Yu Nu Jian 71
Yu Ping Feng San.. 81
Yu Ye Tang 158
Yu Zhu San 90
Yue Bi Tang 68
Yue Zhu Wan 111

Z

Zan Yu Dan.. 101
Zeng Ye Cheng Qi Tang 46
Zeng Ye Tang 126
Zhen Gan Xi Feng Tang 122
Zhen Ni Bai Hu Tang 60
Zhen Ren Yang Zang Tang 108
Zhen Wu Tang 170
Zheng Gu Zi Jin Dan 116
Zhi Bai Di Huang Wan 97
Zhi Gan Cao Tang 84
Zhi Shi Dao Zhi Wan 146
Zhi Shi Li Zhong Wan 75
Zhi Shi Xiao Pi Wan 148
Zhi Sou San 182
Zhi Zhu Wan 145
Zhi Zi Chi Tang 61
Zhi Zi Gan Cao Chi Tang 61
Zhong Man Fen Xiao Wan 130
Zhou Che Wan 49
Zhu Jing Wan.. 96
Zhu Ling Tang.. 132
Zhu Sha An Shen Wan 103
Zhu Ye Shi Gao Tang 61
Zi Xue Dan 105
Zuo Gui Wan.. 94
Zuo Gui Yin.. 94
Zuo Jin Wan.. 72

B

Baak Fu Gaa Cong Seot Tong...59
Baak Fu Gaa Gwai Zi Tong 59
Baak Fu Sing Hei Tong...60
Baak Fu Tong 59
Baak Hap Gu Gam Tong 125
Baak Tau Jung Gaa Gam Cou Aa Gaau Tong 70
Baak Tau Jung Tong...70
Baak Tung Tong 77
Baat Jing Saan...129
Baat Mei Dei Wong Jyun 99
Baat Zan Tong 84
Bik Juk Saan 67
Bou Fai Aa Gaau Tong 96
Bou Fai Tong 87
Bou Gon Tong...90
Bou Wo Jyun 145
Bou Zung Jik Hei Tong 86
Bui Mou Gwaa Lau Saan 142
Bun Haa Baak Seot Tin Maa Tong 144
Bun Haa Baak Seot Tin Maa Tong (Li Dong Yuan) 144
Bun Haa Hau Pok Tong 112
Bun Haa Se Sam Tong 57
Bun Se Luk Gwan Zi Tong 101

C

Caai Got Gaai Gei Tong 41
Caai Haam Tong...52
Caai Ling Tong...133
Caai Ping Tong 51, 127
Caai Wu Baak Fu Tong...60
Caai Wu Gaa Lung Gwat Maau Lai Tong 51
Caai Wu Gaa Mong Siu Tong 53
Caai Wu Gwai Zi Tong 52
Caai Wu Sei Mat Tong 50
Caai Wu So Gon Saan 57
Caai Wu Zi Gat Tong 54
Cat Bou Mei Jim Daan 100
Cat Lei Saan 116
Ceon Kau Fu Leoi Tong 53
Ci Zyu Jyun...103

Cing Cou Gau Fai Tong 125
Cing Hei Faa Taam Jyun 141
Cing Sap Faa Taam Tong 139
Cin Si Baak Seot Saan 83
Cing Hou Bit Gaap Tong 72
Cing Gwat Saan 72
Cing Jing Tong 63
Cing Lok Jam 66
Cing Syu Jik Hei Tong 67
Cing Wai Saan 68
Cing Wan Baai Duk Jam 61
Cong Ji Zi Saan 121
Cong Si Tong 38
Cyun Gung Caa Tiu Saan 120

D

Daai Bou Jam Jyun 94
Daai Caai Wu Tong 54
Daai Cing Lung Tong 42
Daai Ding Fung Jyu 123
Daai Gin Zung Tong 76
Daai Haam Hung Tong 48
Daai Sing Hei Tong 45
Daai Wong Fu Zi Tong 48
Daai Wong Gam Cou Tong 47
Daai Wong Maau Daan Tong 46
Daai Zou Jyun 95
Daan Zi Siu Jiu Saan 55
Dei Wong Jam Zi 101
Dik Taam Tong 138
Ding Haan Jyun 143
Ding Jyu Lei Zung Tong 74
Ding Zi Jyun 104
Dit Da Jyun 117
Dong Gwai Bou Hyut Tong 90
Dong Gwai Dei Wong Jam 98
Dong Gwai Gai Hyut Tang Tong 92
Dong Gwai Luk Wong Tong 73,89
Dong Gwai Sang Goeng Joeng Juk Tong 91
Dong Gwai Sei Jik Gaa Ng Zyu Jyu Sang Goeng Tong 79
Dong Gwai Sei Jik Tong 74,79
Dong Gwai Zoek Joek Saan 90
Dou Cek Saan 69
Dou Hei Jyun 118

Dou Taam Tong 139
Duk San Tong 77
Duk Wut Gei Sang Tong 135

F

Faa Cung Jyun 148
Fan Siu Tong 83
Fei Ji Jyun 146
Fok Hoeng Zing Hei Saan 127
Fong Fung Tung Sing Saan 43
Fong Gei Wong Kei Tong 134
Fu Cim Jyun 95
Fu Pei Syu Gon Tong 56
Fu Zi Lei Zung Jyun 75
Fu Zi Se Sam Tong 63
Fu Zi Tong 135
Fuk Fong Daai Sing Hei Tong 47
Fuk Jyun Wut Hyut Tong 116

G

Gaa Gaam Bou Zung Jik Hei Tong 86
Gaa Gaam Wai Jeoi Tong 45
Gaa Mei Hoeng Sou Saan 43
Gaa Mei Ji Can Tong 141
Gaa Mei Ji Miu Saan 132
Gaa Mei Luk Mei Dei Wong Jyun 97
Gaa Mei Sei Mat Tong 92
Gaak Haa Zuk Jyu Tong 114
Gaau Ngaai Tong 120
Gai Ming Saan 135
Gai Sou Saan 67
Gam Cou Gon Goeng Tong 76
Gam Cou Se Sam Tong 58
Gam Gwai San Hei Jyun 99
Gam Lou Siu Duk Daan 131
Gam Mak Daai Zou Tong 110
Gam Seoi Luk Gwan Zin 138
Gam So Gu Zing Jyun 109
Gau Mei Goeng Wut Tong 42
Gei Guk Dei Wong Jyun 96

Gei Ziu Lik Wong Jyun 48
Gin Pei Jyun 147
Ging Fong Baai Duk Saan 40
Goeng Gwai Sei Mat Tong 88
Goeng Wut Sing Sap Tong 136
Got Gan Kam Lin Tong 71
Got Gan Tong 42
Gu Cung Tong 110
Gu Ging Jyun 119
Guk Faa Caa Tiu Saan 120
Gwaa Dai Saan 145
Gwaa Lau Zi Sat Tong 140
Gwai Fu Lei Zung Tong 75
Gwai Ling Gam Lou Jam 66
Gwai Pei Tong 96
Gwai Zi Gaa Got Gan Tong 43
Gwai Zi Gaa Hau Pok Hang Jan Tong 43
Gwai Zi Zoek Joek Zi Mou Tong 44
Gwai Zi Gaa Lung Gwat Maau Lai Tong 110
Gwai Zi Tong 43
Gwai Zoek Dei Wong Jyun 98
Gwan Taam Jyun 142
Gwat Pei Zuk Jyu Tong 113
Gyun Bei Tong 136

H

Hak Siu Jiu Saan 56
Hang Sou Saan 124
Hau Pok Saam Mat Tong 47
Hau Pok Wan Zung Tong 112
Hin Zing Saan 121
Ho Jan Jam 86
Hoeng Jyu Saan 39
Hoeng Saa Ji Can Tong 138
Hoeng Saa Joeng Wai Tong 82
Hoeng Saa Luk Gwan Zi Tong 81
Hoeng Sou Saan 43
Hoi Zou Juk Wu Tong 142
Hou Kam Cing Daam Tong 54
Hyut Fu Zuk Jyu Tong 113

J

Jan Can Hou Tong 128
Jan Can Ng Ling Saan 133
Jan Sam Baai Duk Saan 44
Jan Sam Baak Fu Tong 59
Jan Sam Gap Gaai Saan 82
Jan Sam Joeng Wing Tong 85
Jat Gun Zin 95
Jau Gwai Jam 100
Jau Gwai Jyun 102
Jeon Coeng Jyun 49
Ji Can Tong 171
Ji Gung Saan 80
Ji Lung Zo Ci Jyun 98
Ji Miu Saan 129
Ji Sin Tong 102
Ji Zi Jyun 96
Jik Jyun Saan 66
Jik Wong Tong 111
Joeng Jam Cing Fai Tong 126
Joeng Wo Tang 78
Juk Jik Tong 126
Juk Neoi Zin 71
Juk Ping Fung Saan 81
Juk Zuk Saan 90
Jyu Daai Jyun 128
Jyun Daai Tong 111
Jyut Guk Jyun 111
Jyut Pei Tong 68

K

Kam Lin Sei Mat Tong 89

L

Lei Zung Faa Taam Jyun 74
Lei Zung Jyun 73
Lei Zung On Wui Jyun 74
Lin Lei Tong 75

Lin Pok Jam 130
Lin Zyu Jam 92
Ling Gam Ng Mei Goeng San Tong 143
Ling Gok Ngau Tang Tong 123
Ling Gwai Seot Gam Tong 134
Loeng Gaak Saan 64
Luk Gwan Zi Tong 80
Luk Jat Saan 67
Luk Mei Dei Wong Jyun 93
Luk On Zin 139
Luk San Jyun 79
Lung Daam Se Gon Tong 70

M

Maa Hang Sek Gam Tong 68
Maa Wong Gaa Seot Tong 42
Maa Wong Goeng Wut Tong 40
Maa Wong Sai San Fu Zi Tong 45
Maa Wong Tong 39
Maa Zi Jan Jyun 49
Maau Lai Saan 107
Mak Mei Dei Wong Jyun 97
Ming Muk Dei Wong Jyun 93
Muk Hoeng Ban Long Jyun.. 147

N

Ng Ling Saan 132
Ng Mei Ji Gung Saan.. 82
Ng Mei Siu Duk Jam 64,78
Ng Pei Saan.. 133
Ng Zik Saan 44
Ng Zyu Jyu Tong.. 76
Ngaai Fu Nyun Gung Jyun.. 91
Ngan Kiu Maa But Saan 41
Ngan Kiu Saan.. 41

O

On Gung Ngau Wong Jyun.. 105

P

Ping Wai Saan 127
Pou Zai Siu Duk Jam 64

S

Saa Sam Mak Mun Dung Tong 125
Saam Aau Tong 39
Saam Gaap Fuk Mak Tong 124
Saam Jan Tong 130
Saam Mat Bei Gap Jyun 48
Saam Miu Saan 129
Saam Wong Sek Gou Tong 65
Saam Wong Sei Mat Tong 88
Saam Zi Joeng Can Tong 143
Sai Gok Dei Wong Tong 62
Sam Fu Tong 77
Sam Sou Jam 44
San Ji Saan 40
San Ling Baak Seot Saan 81
San Tung Zuk Jyu Tong 115
San Zai Gwat Pei Zuk Jyu Tong 113
Sang Faa Tong 114
Sang Goeng Se Sam Tong 58
Sang Mak Saan 87
Sap Bou Jyun 99
Sap Cyun Daai Bou Tong 84
Sap Fui Saan 118
Sap Mei Wan Daam Tong 140
Sap Zou Tong 48
Sat Siu Saan 113
Sau Toi Jyun 110
Se Baak Saan 71
Se Sam Tong 71
Se Wong Saan 68
Sei Cat Tong 112
Sei Gwan Zi Tong 80
Sei Jik Gaa Jan Sam Tong 77
Sei Jik Saan 55
Sei Jik Tong 77
Sei Ling Saan 133

Sei Mat Siu Fung Jam... 122
Sei Mat Tong.. 87
Sei Miu Jung On Tong 65
Sei Miu Saan... 129
Sei San Jyun.. 108
Sei Sang Jyun.. 118
Sek Gou Tong.. 42
Sin Fong Wut Ming Jam.. 78
Sing Jyu Tong.. 88
Sing Maa Got Gan Tang 42
Siu Bun Haa Tong.. 112
Siu Caai Wu Tong 50
Siu Cing Lung Tong 42
Siu Fuk Zuk Jyu Tong 115
Siu Fung Saan 121
Siu Gai Jam Zi 119
Siu Gin Zung Tong 76
Siu Haam Hung Tong 140
Siu Jiu Saan.. 55
Siu Lo Jyun 141
Siu Sing Hei Tong 45
Siu Wut Lok Daan 121
So Jyu Cing Gon Jam 56
Song Guk Jam 40
Song Hang Tong 124
Song Piu Siu Saan 109
Sou Hap Hoeng Jyun... 107
Suk Cyun Jyun 109
Syu Ging Wut Hyut Tong 117
Syun Bei Tong 131
Syun Zou Jan Tong.. 103

T

Taai Saan Pun Sek Saan...85
Tin Maa Ngau Tang Jam 122
Tin Wong Bou Sam Tong.. 104
Tiu Wai Sing Hei Tong 46
Tiu Zung Jik Hei Tong 86
Tou Faa Tong 108
Tou Hung Sei Mat Tong 87
Tou Si Zi Jyun 101
Tung Hiu Wut Hyut Tong 114

Tung Mak Sei Jik Tong 77
Tung Se Jiu Fong 57

W

Waa Goi Saan 40
Waai Faa Saan 119
Wai Ging Tong 71
Wai Ling Saan 128
Wai Ling Tong 134
Wan Cing Jam 65
Wan Daam Tong 137
Wan Pei Tong 48
Wong Kei Gin Zung Tong 76
Wong Lin Aa Gaau Tong 104
Wong Kei Gwai Zi Ng Mat Tong 73
Wong Lin Gaai Duk Tong 63
Wong Lin Tong 59
Wong Lin Wan Daam Tong 137
Wong Lung Tong 46
Wong Tou Tong 118
Wu Mui Jyun 148
Wui Ceon Daan 106

Z

Zaan Juk Daan 101
Zai Cyun Zin 50
Zai Sang San Hei Jyun 102
Zan Gon Sik Fung Tong 122
Zan Jan Joeng Zong Tong 108
Zan Jik Baak Fu Tong 60
Zan Mou Tong 135
Zang Jik Sing Hei Tong 46
Zang Jik Tong 126
Zau Ce Jyun 49
Zek Gam Cou Tong 84
Zi Paak Dei Wong Jyun 97
Zi Sat Dou Zai Jyun 146
Zi Sat Lei Zung Jyun 75
Zi Sat Siu Pei Jyun 148

Zi Sau Saan...145
Zi Seot Jyun 145
Zi Syut Daan 105
Zi Zi Gam Cou Si Tong 61
Zi Zi Si Tong.. 61
Zing Gwat Zi Gam Daan 116
Zo Gam Jyun 72
Zo Gwai Jam...94
Zo Gwai Jyun 94
Zoek Joek Gam Cou Tong 89
Zoek Joek Tong 69
Zuk Jip Sek Gou Tong 61
Zung Mun Fan Siu Jyun 130
Zyu Ging Jyun 96
Zyu Ling Tong 132
Zyu Saa On San Jyun 103

Bibliography

Chen, J., Chen, T. (2009) Chinese Herbal Formulas and Applications, City of Industry, CA Art of Medicine Press

Finney, D., Flaws, B. (1996) A Handbook of TCM Patterns & Their Treatments 2nd Ed., Boulder, CO Blue Poppy Press

Flaws, B. (1994) 70 Essential Chinese Herbal Formulas, Boulder, CO Blue Poppy Press

Flaws, B. (1999) 260 Essential Chinese Medicinals, Boulder, CO Blue Poppy Press

Lau, S., (1977) A Practical Cantonese-English Dictionary, Hong Kong The Government Printer

Scheid, V., Bensky, D., Ellis, A., Barolet, R. (2009) Chinese Herbal Medicine Formulas & Strategies, Seattle, WA Eastland Press

Electronic Sources:
Key Systems-GMBH mdbg.net CC-CEDICT

Love, M. (2000-2017) Pleco Chinese Dictionary for iOS (Version 3.2.15) [Mobile Application Software] Retrieved from iTunes/apple.com
Dictionaries included in the application bundle:
CCCanto © 2015-2017 Pleco Inc. Portions adapted from CC-CEDICT from mdbg.net

DeFrancis, J. (2003-2016), ABC Chinese-English Comprehensive Dictionary, University of Hawai'i Press

Guangzhouhua Fangyan Cidian ©2010 Commercial Press

Hanwang Handwriting Recognizer ©2003-2012 Hanwang Technology, Co. Ltd.

Pleco Basic Chinese-English Dictionary based on A Chinese-English Dictionary, ©1995 Foreign Language Teaching & Research Press, © 2009-2013 Pleco Software Incorporated

Practical Dictionary of Chinese Medicine E-C (Pleco Revision I) ©1998-2012 Paradigm Publications

Practical Dictionary of Chinese Medicine C-E (Pleco Revision I) ©1998-2012 Paradigm Publications

CPSIA information can be obtained
at www.ICGtesting.com
Printed in the USA
BVHW010224300321
603700BV00015B/400